AMERICA AND THE HOLY LAND

Earlier volumes in the With Eyes Toward Zion series

With Eyes Toward Zion I. Scholars Colloquium on America–Holy Land Studies, 1977

With Eyes Toward Zion II. Themes and Sources in the Archives of the United States, Great Britain, Turkey, and Israel, 1986

With Eyes Toward Zion III. Western Societies and the Holy Land, 1991

AMERICA AND THE HOLY LAND

WITH EYES TOWARD ZION—IV

Moshe Davis

Westport, Connecticut
London

Library of Congress Cataloging-in-Publication Data

Davis, Moshe.
   America and the Holy Land / Moshe
   Davis.
         p.   cm.—(With eyes toward Zion, ISSN 1079–0381; IV)
      Includes bibliographical references and index.
   ISBN 0–275–94621–5
      1. Palestine in Judaism.   2. Palestine in Christianity.
   3. Judaism—United States—History—19th century.   4. Names,
   Geographical—United States.   I. Title.   II. Series.
   BM729.P3D34   1995
   296.3—dc20   94–28005

British Library Cataloguing in Publication Data is available.

Library of Congress Catalog Card Number: 94–28005
ISBN: 0–275–94621–5
ISSN: 1079–0381

First published in 1995

Praeger Publishers, 88 Post Road West, Westport, CT 06881
An imprint of Greenwood Publishing Group, Inc.

Printed in the United States of America

The paper used in this book complies with the
Permanent Paper Standard issued by the National
Information Standards Organization (Z39.48–1984).

10 9 8 7 6 5 4 3 2 1

FOR
LOTTIE
ALWAYS

THE AMERICA–HOLY LAND PROJECT
Avraham Harman Institute of Contemporary Jewry,
The Hebrew University of Jerusalem
and
The International Center for University Teaching of
Jewish Civilization

The Avraham Harman Institute of Contemporary Jewry
Haim Avni, Head
Avraham Bar-Gil, Administrative Director

The International Center for University Teaching of
Jewish Civilization
Nehemia Levtzion, Academic Chairman
Priscilla Fishman, Director of Publications

Contents

Acknowledgments

Our gratitude goes to the Jacob Blaustein Fund for American Studies, whose grants make possible ongoing research in America–Holy Land Studies; to Irving Neuman for his profound interest in all that pertains to creative scholarship; to the Lucius N. Littauer Foundation and its President, William Lee Frost, for their support in the publication of this volume; to Yohai Goell, perceptive research associate, for his textual acumen; to Rosemary E. Krensky and Elsie O. Sang for their abiding devotion; to Sharon Jacobs for her assistance in the preparation of the manuscript; to Shulamit Nardi for her critical advice and judgment; to Lottie K. Davis, editorial coordinator, *With Eyes Toward Zion* series.

Introduction: America–Holy Land Studies as a Field of Scholarly Inquiry

The study of the continuing America–Holy Land relationship has implications for American and Jewish history that extend beyond the historical narrative and interpretation.

The Holy Land has constituted an important element in the American experience. This factor contributes to a better comprehension of the harmonious blending within American Jewry of America as its native land and Eretz Israel as the center of its tradition and of the Jewish People. There are, of course, some similarities between American Jewry's ties to Eretz Israel and the American Irish involvement in Ireland or the active role played by Central European immigrants in America in establishing new states in Central Europe after World War I. But the devotion of American Jews, as of American Christians, to the Holy Land extends into the spiritual realm, and the Holy Land, in turn, penetrates American homes, patterns of faith, and education.

The challenge of exploring this largely untilled research field captured my heart and mind in the early years of the newly established State of Israel. My work had previously focused on American Jewish religious history. But Israel's young, dynamic democracy was symbolic of bridging the Orient and the Occident, antiquity and modernity, spiritual truth and technological progress. Furthermore, international recognition of the State of Israel's nationhood, in which the American government played so great a part, called for proper explication of the enduring relationship between these two cultures.

These thoughts possessed me as I pursued my studies of the past and contemporary condition of the American Jewish community. But my ardor was tempered by the host of research problems that I would have to confront. Conceptually: How to weave the variant strands together and yet remain within the contours of my specialization in the American Jewish experience? Intrinsically: How to denote the unique interchange between American Jewry on behalf of Eretz Israel and the American government, the American churches, and the broad cultural components of American life and institutions?

Good fortune, sheer *mazal*, came my way in the person of Robert Theodore Handy, a young church historian, new to the nondenominational, primarily Protestant Union Theological Seminary, located across the street from the Jewish Theological Seminary in Manhattan, where I taught and served as Provost.

Our very first meeting in 1952 set the foundation for a lifelong partnership in the research, publication, and teaching on the America–Holy Land nexus. We were brothers in initiating a subfield in American Jewish and Christian history. I invited Robert Handy to lecture on the topic "Zion in American Christian Movements" at the newly founded Seminary Israel Institute. As he later attested, the subject was a new avenue for him, so he began by digging into the meaning of the word "Zion" in Protestant hymns, magazine articles, and book titles; in the names of a number of Christian denominations and churches; and in the origins of certain place-names in the United States. Professor Handy became increasingly convinced that the America–Holy Land subject was important for both Christian scholarship and historical scholarship in general. Participating in a scholars' colloquium in New York almost two decades later, Handy elaborated on the remarkable encounter of past and present history inherent in the subject—the very insight that had caught my own imagination—while emphasizing the special character of the historic Christian attitude.

> We now have three and a half centuries of history of American Christian interest in the Holy Land. It runs in many dimensions and shows many patterns. Much Christian thought about the Holy Land rises out of Christian interest in biblical materials, out of the study of the Bible. And therefore, for much of the Christian world, the primary focus of interest in the Holy Land is the Holy Land of ancient times, not the modern land at all. There have been Christian scholars and Christian pilgrims in the Holy Land who have been very little aware of contemporary life in Israel. Their minds and thoughts

were back centuries ago. Nevertheless, this provides indirectly a fund of feelings, of ideas, of concepts, which do bear upon the attitude of Christians today. Many of these arise out of the long past, which is "remembered" in the many parts of the Christian world today through emphasis on the Bible.[1]

While the Jewish and Christian components are essential to the total comprehension of America–Holy Land Studies, other dimensions, both cultural and political, require careful study. In broadly cultural terms, there are many Americans who, although they express interest in the historic Holy Land, do not identify themselves either as Jews or as Christians. For them, this region is one of the wellsprings of Western civilization, a fountainhead of our culture. Need I cite the biblical imagery so deeply embedded in American literature, thought, and art?

America's political interest in the Holy Land dates back to the early decades of the nineteenth century, from the term of President John Adams. One finds in it a characteristic American mixture of humanitarian zeal, Christian devotion, and practical concerns. As in the case of Lieutenant W. F. Lynch's expedition to the Jordan River and the Dead Sea, the lines of demarcation were not always clear. Americans generally expressed a wide range of views on domestic and international issues. Political attitudes on the Middle East in general and the Holy Land in particular were no exception. Many American national figures did not confine themselves to encouraging statements but actually advocated and devised pragmatic schemes that could have long-term implications for the region. In this regard, the Herbert Hoover population transfer plan and Walter Clay Low-dermilk's Jordan Valley Authority are striking illustrations.

Writing these lines at the beginning of 1994 in the matrix of the current Middle East negotiations, I cannot dismiss the import of the exchange between Felix Frankfurter and Prince Faisal after World War I when, in view of the deepening conflict of interests between Arabs and Jews, it became clear to prescient leaders that a satisfactory solution to the political problem in the Holy Land would require the intercession of the United States. Nevertheless, it was apparent to many that the ultimate resolution could be achieved only by the two parties residing in the Holy Land and neighboring countries. Hence the quest for Arab–Jewish coexistence.

The correspondence between Felix Frankfurter and Prince Faisal, which emerged from the prince's conversations with Dr. Chaim Weizmann in Arabia and in Europe, was a remarkable attempt to foster that goal. Both Frankfurter and Faisal recognized the need for "a reformed and revived Near East." As Faisal wrote in Paris on March 3, 1919, "We Arabs, especially the educated among us, look with the deepest sympathy on the Zionist Movement. . . ."

Replying that very day to "His Royal Highness," Felix Frankfurter wrote:

> For both the Arab and the Jewish peoples there are difficulties ahead—diffi-
> culties that challenge the united statesmanship of Arab and Jewish leaders.
> For it is no easy task to rebuild two great civilizations that have been suffering
> oppression and misrule for centuries. We each have our difficulties; we shall
> work out as friends, friends who are animated by similar purposes, seeking
> a free and full development for the two neighboring peoples. The Arabs and
> Jews are neighbors in territory; we cannot but live side by side as friends.[2]

To enhance our knowledge and perception of the political issues, in the mid-sixties, Handy and I became associated with Selig Adler, then Professor of History at the University of Buffalo, who had written extensively on United States policy in the Woodrow Wilson, Franklin Roosevelt, and Harry Truman eras.

We drew up an overall research plan for America–Holy Land Studies, emphasizing the following areas:

Diplomatic Policy: political interest; consular protection; economic missions;

Christian Devotion: The Holy Land in the historical Christian tradition;
   Zion in American Christian movements;

Cultural Aspects: The Holy Land in thought, language, literature and art;
   pilgrimage and travel;

Jewish Attachment: The Holy Land in Jewish tradition; Eretz Israel in Jewish communal life.

With this conceptual construct, we were better prepared for the formidable spadework ahead. The principal sources for the study of America and the Holy Land are to be found in the United States, Israel, and several other countries, such as England and Turkey. We faced a range of archives, from relatively well-organized institutional depositories to private family collections, and often found ourselves shaking the dust from many neglected, if not forgotten, files. In some instances, almost as in a jigsaw puzzle, fragments of correspondence in one collection correlated with the material found in another.

In addition, we needed to ferret out, sort, and describe a vast body of documentary materials—correspondence, manuscripts, periodicals, rare books and pamphlets, records, and so forth—before we could undertake major interpretative monographs. We came to realize that we could achieve scholarly progress only through organization on an intercontinental basis. This became possible when the American Jewish Historical Society in Waltham, Massachusetts, and the Hebrew University's Institute of Contemporary Jewry in Jerusalem conjoined to sponsor the program.

Institutional sponsorship, of and by itself, does not explain the progression of colloquia, pedagogic literature, and publications that enriched the field. Robert Handy gave a comprehensive evaluation of our enterprise in volume 3 of this series, in the chapter "The America–Holy Land Project: A Personal Statement." I can add that our emphasis has always been to attract a variety of scholars to the field, as well as to expand and deepen the work beyond the historical discipline, along the lines proposed by Deborah Dash Moore in her constructive analysis in that same volume, "Studying America and the Holy Land: Prospects, Pitfalls and Perspectives."

Publication and international distribution of the 72–volume Reprint Series of America–Holy Land Sources, thematic bibliographies, and the four-volume *Guide* to archival sources motivated ranking scholars to pursue the subject in their independent research. The list of works produced thus far within the purview of the project reflects the original conceptual framework, and the books cited make this clear.

Diplomatic Policy

Naomi W. Cohen, *The Year After the Riots: American Responses to the Palestine Crisis of 1929–30* (Detroit, 1988).

Vivian D. Lipman, *Americans and the Holy Land Through British Eyes, 1820–1917: A Documentary History* (London, 1989).

Ruth Kark, *American Consuls in the Holy Land 1832–1914* (Jerusalem & Detroit, 1994).

Christian Devotion

Robert T. Handy, ed., *The Holy Land in American Protestant Life 1800–1948: A Documentary History* (New York, 1981).

Yaakov Ariel, *On Behalf of Israel: American Fundamentalist Attitudes Toward Jews, Judaism and Zionism, 1865–1945* (Brooklyn, 1991).

Gershon Greenberg, *The Holy Land in American Religious Thought, 1620–1948: The Symbiosis of American Religious Approaches to Scripture's Sacred Territory* (Lanham, Md., 1994).

Cultural Aspects

David Klatzker, "American Christian Travelers to the Holy Land, 1821–1939" (Ph.D. diss., Temple University, 1987).

Lester I. Vogel, *To See a Promised Land: Americans and the Holy Land in the Nineteenth Century* (University Park, Penn., 1993).

Jewish Attachment

Arthur A. Goren, ed., *Dissenter in Zion: From the Writings of Judah L. Magnes* (Cambridge, Mass., 1982).

Menahem Kaufman, *An Ambiguous Partnership: Non-Zionists and Zionists in America 1939–1948* (Jerusalem and Detroit, 1991).

Michael Brown, *Israel's American Connection* (in preparation).

Joseph B. Glass, "From New to Old Zion: North American Jewish Aliyah and Settlement in Eretz–Israel, 1917–1939" (Ph.D. diss., Hebrew University of Jerusalem, in preparation).

Beyond these full-length volumes, there is a treasure trove of studies in learned journals and periodical literature, primarily in the United States and Israel, often resulting from masters degree dissertations and seminar papers prepared for Holy Land courses in various universities. In many cases, these themes relate to subjects that are fertile fields for continuing research. Indeed, a third generation of scholars in America–Holy Land Studies has come of age.

In this volume, I have attempted to bring together some of my own studies, with the hope that others will carry forward where I have need to pause. The papers selected exemplify areas that await further research. References cited throughout these chapters are themselves guides for further investigation. In Part I, I introduced the concept of American spiritual history as illustrated by Jewish and Christian distinctiveness. In Part II, I chose to examine leading Jewish figures of the nineteenth century.

Part III illuminates the interconnection of Americans and the Holy Land through the constellation of place-names. Maps in that section have been specially prepared for this volume. It is my intention in the annotated bibliography—Part IV—of selected primary source volumes to present a comprehensive overview of the field in its totality.

In reworking these chapters, I have considered the criticism of reviewers and colleagues, eliminated known errors, and introduced archival and primary documentation that surfaced subsequent to their first publication. The scholarly community can now determine whether they should be enlarged into fuller monographs.

The writings of Ecclesiastes teach: "A season is set for everything, a time for every experience under heaven." As the coming generation of students and scholars embark on their own creative works in the field of America–Holy Land Studies, for me this is the time for ingathering.

NOTES

1. Proceedings of the Colloquium were first published in *American Jewish Historical Quarterly (AJHQ)* 62, no. 1 (September 1972).

2. Central Zionist Archives, Jerusalem, A264, folders 9 and 10.

PART I
ZION IN AMERICA'S FAITH

Chapter 1

The Holy Land in American
Spiritual History

The opportunity offered to all religious and ethnic groups to become an organic part of American society, despite some serious lapses, is an impressive phenomenon in history. Most significant has been the encouragement given such communities, in the spirit of American voluntarism, to develop their distinctive values and to contribute those values to the total complex of American civilization. This is a unique quality of the American experience. It is at the core of the spiritual history of America, as valuable for an understanding of American democracy as the political, economic, or cultural dimensions.

The concept "spiritual," as I understand it, is not a synonym for "religious"; it encompasses the spectrum of religious, cultural, and ethnic history—the accumulated moral, ethical, and creative divisions made by individuals and groups. In this sense, the America–Holy Land theme is integral to America's spiritual history.

The broad concept of Holy Land or Zion or Eretz Israel (Land of Israel) has been a pervasive theme in American thought and action since the very beginnings of European settlement on the Western continent. This conception has appeared in many variations: From the earliest formulations in Colonial times of the Puritan aspiration to a biblical commonwealth, where America itself was considered to be the embodiment of Zion; pilgrimages by Americans to the Holy Land; and in mid-twentieth century, Restoration under Jewish sovereignty in which the United States plays a strategic role.

Devotion to Zion has been shared by Americans of diverse backgrounds and cultural orientations. Attachment to the Holy Land extends into American homes, patterns of faith, and education, illuminating the interplay of ideas among different religions and cultures. Here many varied elements meet, sometimes antithetically, but most often cooperatively. To delineate the historical and contemporary impress of the Holy Land Idea on the American spirit, and more particularly on its Hebraic matrix, we select four elements: Biblical Heritage; Hebrew Language; The Holy Land as Zion, Land of Israel; and Jewish Restoration.

BIBLICAL HERITAGE

In the American tradition, the Bible is the source of the common faith, a cohesive force in national aspirations. When the Congress, under the Articles of Confederation, voted in favor of appropriating funds to import twenty thousand copies of the Bible, its members voted, quite literally, to supply a household need. As the most widely read book in America during the Colonial era and the nineteenth century, the Bible was the unimpeachable source for both supporting and conflicting opinions in the struggle for political independence and in the antebellum period. In trying as well as in glorious times of American history, prophets and idolaters, kings and commoners who lived centuries ago in ancient Israel rose to play contemporary roles.

Moreover, as Samuel H. Levine points out, running through the literature "is the meta-physical transference of Holy Land specifics to New World identities."[1] The Fathers of the Republic, for example, did not cite Holy Scriptures in the past tense, but as living, contemporary reality. Their political condition was described as "Egyptian slavery": King George III was Pharaoh; the Atlantic Ocean nothing other than the Red Sea; and Washington and Adams—Moses and Joshua. What could have been a more appropriate seal for the underlying purpose of the Revolution, according to a committee composed of Franklin, Adams, and Jefferson, than the portrayal of the Israelites' exodus from Egypt? In the words of Thomas Jefferson: "Pharaoh sitting in an open chariot, a crown on his head and a sword in his hand passing thro' the divided waters of the Red Sea in pursuit of the Israelites: rays from a pillar of fire in the cloud, expressive of the divine presence, and command, reaching to Moses who stands on the shore and, extending his hand over the sea, causes it to overwhelm Pharaoh." The inscription—a motto by Benjamin Franklin—read: "Rebellion to Tyrants is Obedience to God."[2]

Puritan and Pilgrim identification with biblical thought permeated their political system and gave impetus to a distinctive principle of that system; namely, covenant theology. As Richard B. Morris points out, "This covenant theology (see Genesis 9:8–9, 17:2–4; Exodus 34:10, 28; Psalm 106; Jeremiah 31:31) . . . was the keystone to the democratic control of church government. . . . It is government based upon consent of the people, although the Puritan leaders maintained that it must be a government in accord with God's will."[3]

How this ancient civil polity was interpreted in the calls for revolutionary separatism is exemplified in one of the typical "election sermons"—a morality preachment delivered by Samuel Langdon, president of Harvard College, in the Massachusetts Bay Colony, on 13 May 1775:

> The Jewish Government, according to the original constitution which was divinely established, if considered merely in a civil view, was a perfect republic. . . . Every nation, when able and agreed, has a right to set up over themselves any form of government which to them may appear most conducive to their common welfare. The civil polity of Israel is doubtless an excellent general model; allowing for some peculiarities, at least some principal laws and orders of it may be copied to great advantage in more modern establishments.[4]

The Bible was more than a predominating influence on free American institutions. It influenced the individual lives of new Americans, immigrants who came to settle in their "Promised Land." Underlying the events that comprise the history of the United States are the individual sagas of men and women who, each in his or her own way, sought the purpose of their life, the meaning of human existence. To a great extent, this search was centered in the family circle, as its members drew together to study the Bible. Some of the most remarkable treasures may be found in the large family Bibles, in which the records of births, marriages, and deaths were inscribed and which were handed down from parent to child. In these family Bibles we discover the spiritual folklore of America.

Another manifestation of spiritual folklore is the map of America itself. If one's child could be called by a biblical name, why not one's home, one's town and city?[5] Thus began to appear along America's expanding frontier hundreds of place-names of biblical origin.[6] Numerous places carry such names as Eden, Rehoboth, Sharon, Bethel, Canaan, Hebron, Mamre, Mt. Moriah, Mt. Tabor, Pisgah, Shiloh, Sinai, and Tekoa. Indeed, viewing the "biblical" map of America, one senses how founders with an intimate knowledge of scriptural sources instituted a spiritual folklore. Some locations are mentioned only once in the Bible: Elim, Nebraska (Exodus 15:27);

Ai, Ohio (Joshua 8:18); Shushan, New York (Book of Esther); Elijah's Zarephath in New Jersey (I Kings 17:8). A Californian in search of gold named his settlement Havilah (Genesis 2:11).

Zion as a place-name reflected the organic relationship between the United States and the Land of Israel. At least fifteen locations are called Zion in almost as many states (Arkansas, Illinois, Iowa, Kentucky, Maryland, Minnesota, Nebraska, New Jersey, North Dakota, Pennsylvania, South Carolina, Utah, and Virginia).

A much-favored biblical name dotting the map is Salem. There are no fewer than twenty-seven towns, cities, and counties called Salem, and New Jersey has both a city and a county by that name. Thus, the founders of these settlements symbolically extended their own "feast of peace" offerings (see Genesis 14:18) to neighboring inhabitants. As is well known, one of America's earliest settlements was Salem, Massachusetts. In 1626–1628, when the Pilgrims received corn from the Indians, they immediately associated the event with the patriarch Abraham and Melchizedek, king of Salem.

Of historical interest is the fact that this particular place-name symbolizes the movement termed "progressive pioneering"—the transmission of a familial belief from generation to generation. For example, Aaron Street the elder migrated from Salem, New Jersey, to Ohio, where he founded a town by the name of Salem. Together with his son, he moved to Indiana and there founded another town named Salem. The third lap of the journey was by the son to Iowa, where he plotted the Salem in Henry County.[7]

As biblical ideas and images pervaded early American consciousness, the Bible became *The Book* of common knowledge. From it children were taught reading; and as they grew and matured, the indelible pages of the Scriptures, their first reader, served as their guide and sometimes even as a determining factor in their vocational choice. One of the most remarkable testimonies of the direct connection between childhood biblical training and vocational purpose is that of the nineteenth-century archaeologist Edward Robinson, whose name today is so closely related to current excavations near the Western Wall. Robinson's Arch is one of the wonders of scholarly ingenuity evidenced for all who come to the reconstructed Temple Mount. In his three-volume *Biblical Researches in Palestine, Mount Sinai and Arabia Petraea*, Robinson writes that his scientific motivation issued from biblical fervor:

> As in the case of most of my countrymen, especially in New England, the scenes of the Bible had made a deep impression upon my mind from the earliest childhood; and afterwards in riper years this feeling had grown into a strong desire to visit in person the places so remarkable in the history of the human race. Indeed in no country of the world, perhaps, is such a feeling

more widely diffused than in New England; in no country are the Scriptures better known, or more highly prized. From his earliest years the child is there accustomed not only to read the Bible for himself; but he also reads or listens to it in the morning and evening devotions of the family, in the daily village-school, in the Sunday-school and Bible-class, and in the weekly ministrations of the sanctuary. Hence, as he grows up, the names of Sinai, Jerusalem, Bethlehem, the Promised Land, become associated with his earliest recollections and holiest feelings. . . . With all this, in my own case, there had subsequently become connected a scientific motive. . . .[8]

A similar tone was struck by Dean Lawrence Jones of Howard University in 1976 in an address on "The Black View of the Holy Land."

It is still the case in the Bible Belt that the Bible holds a unique place in the life of the people. I can remember as a child growing up that we could not even write on the Bible. When I went to the Seminary and some of my professors told me, "Just write in the margin," that was a real traumatic experience for me to take a pencil and write in the Bible. My father always said that if a Bible wore out you didn't destroy it or throw it in the trash; you burned it up. It was sacred—the book itself was invested with a certain sacredness.[9]

Thus, Americans expressed themselves in personal memory and around the family hearth.[10] In ordeal and triumph, whether in Abraham Lincoln's characterization of the Bible as "the best gift God has given to man" or in Woodrow Wilson's insight that it is the "Magna Charta of the human soul," the biblical heritage became indissoluble from the American tradition.

HEBREW LANGUAGE

From the very beginning of indigenous American culture, Hebrew was not just another "foreign" language documented in theological and literary writings—and molded into the seals of such major universities as Columbia, Dartmouth, and Yale. Hebrew was the Holy Tongue, *leshon hakodesh*, bearer of eternal values, which brought Zion close to the basic elements of American civilization.

A quite remarkable example is the list of topics for Master of Arts subjects relating to the Scriptures presented at Harvard between 1655 and 1791. Some of the subjects are intriguing. For example: "Is the Hebrew language the oldest of all?"; "Was the confusion of tongues at Babel only a diversity of opinions?" Jonathan Trumbull, later governor of Connecticut, delivered a thesis in 1730 on the question, "Are there in the Sacred Scriptures real contradictions which cannot in any way be explained?"[11]

The story that Hebrew was proposed as the official language of the newly independent United States is an intriguing legend, which H. L. Mencken deflated in characteristic fashion. The legend originated in deep-seated anti-English feeling, which prompted a suggestion to adopt a language other than English as the official language of the United States. Actually, the traveler the Marquis de Chastellux made the suggestion. Greek, too, was considered, but rejected. As Charles Astor Bristed, grandson of John Jacob Astor, wrote in his essay "The English Language in America": ". . . it would be more convenient for us to keep the language as it is, and make the English speak Greek." Beyond these rationales and jesting, it is particularly interesting that the suggested substitute languages related to the two cultures underlying the Anglo-Saxon civilization—the Hellenic and the Hebraic.[12]

The continuing bond between Americanism and Hebraism—first established by the Puritans, who saw themselves as the renewers of the Bible in their generation—has undergone several transformations. From the Colonial period until the beginning of the nineteenth century, the study of Hebrew was set in a strictly theological framework. Throughout the nineteenth century and until the turn of the twentieth, Hebrew was relegated to the realm of philology and was taught in the departments of Semitics that existed in a few universities, far from the mainstream of contemporary thought. In our time, essentially because of its renaissance in Eretz Israel and the existence of a Jewish community there for whom Hebrew is the vernacular, the study of Hebrew has flourished, becoming a branch of general culture without in any way curtailing its role in the two previous areas of theology and Semitics.

This Bible–Hebrew–Holy Land nexus is quaintly expressed in Governor William Bradford's *History of Plimoth Plantation*, which includes portions of his Hebrew handwriting.

> Though I am growne aged, yet I have had a longing desire to see with my own eyes, something of that most ancient language, and holy tongue, in which the law and Oracles of God were write; and in which God and angels spake to the holy patriarchs of old time; and what names were given to things from creation. And though I cannot attaine to much herein, yet I am refreshed to have seen some glimpse hereof (as Moyses saw the land of Canan a farr of). My aime and desire is, to see how the words and phrases lye in the holy texte; and to discerne somewhat of the same for my owne contente.[13]

Puritan doctrine flowed easily into higher education. Samuel Johnson, the first president of King's College—now Columbia University—himself a Hebrew scholar, concluded that the Hebrew language "is essential to a gentleman's education"; hence all teachers in his institution were to possess a knowledge of Hebrew.[14] The Reverend Ezra Stiles, who served as minister in Newport, Rhode Island, entertained a rewarding friendship with the messenger from "Hebron, near Jerusalem," Raphael Haim Isaac Carigal. When Carigal was invited by the congregation to preach at the synagogue on the Festival of Shavuot, Stiles came to hear him and noted in his diary a rather extensive summary of the sermon delivered in Spanish, interspersed with Hebrew, including a colorful description of Carigal's dress and mien. The English version was the first Jewish sermon published in North America.[15] After becoming president of Yale, Stiles made Hebrew a required part of the curriculum, claiming that he would be ashamed if any graduate should be entirely ignorant of the holy language when he ascended to heaven.[16]

Stiles's emphatic concern that his family and students should acquire a Hebraic education pervaded his thoughts even as revolutionary events raged about him. After giving a disturbing account of the Battle of Bunker Hill to Raphael Haim Isaac Carigal, who was in Barbados in July 1775, he adds:

> My son Ezra is gone to the University in Connecticutt to study Wisdom among the Sons of the prophets in the *bet midrash* [school]: May the Mantle of Elijah, the *ruach elohim* [God's spirit] defend & rest upon him. My son Isaac daily reads to me the grand Shema *shma yisrael* to *u-v'sh'arecha* ["Hear, O Israel": Deuteronomy 6:49]—Molly & the rest of the Children often inquire affectionately after Hocham R. Carigal. I shd take it as a favor if you will write Ezra a short letter in Hebrew: for tho' he cannot answer it as yet in Hebrew, it may excite his Ambition & engage him more attentively to study that most excellent & devine Language. For the same purpose & to teach & p[er]fect me in the epistolary stile, I should be glad if you would write some of your Letters to me in Hebrew. May I hope for one in Answer to my long Hebrew Letter of 1773.[17]

Conceived as both language and bearer of a specific religious complex, the significance of Hebrew was enhanced in the consciousness of wider American circles. The account of Joseph Smith, founder of the Mormon Church, explains the reason and manner of his devotion to Hebrew, shedding light on a little-known aspect of American cultural and religious life.

The key to Smith's account is in a document that I found in the Mormon archives at Salt Lake City. Dated 30 March 1836, and signed by Joshua Seixas, it attests that Joseph Smith successfully completed a course of Hebrew under Seixas's guidance. Some years before, Smith had been in the process of recording his own version of the Bible because, according to the Book of Mormon, "many plain and precious things" had been removed from the Bible by the Gentiles. From time to time, according to Smith, several of these passages were revealed to him and written down by him. In 1830 he was instructed to stop his notation until he moved to Ohio. There Smith and his followers built a temple in the city of Kirtland.[18] They felt they needed to know Hebrew in order to fully understand the new revelations, especially to comprehend the differences between the Hebrew Scriptures and Smith's version. Special courses were organized and Joshua Seixas was engaged to teach them Hebrew.

Seixas, the son of Gershom Mendes Seixas of Shearith Israel in New York, was a Hebraist and teacher of Hebrew at several institutions of higher learning throughout the country, including Andover and Western Reserve. In 1833 he published *A Manual Hebrew Grammar for the Use of Beginners*. At the time he met Smith he was an instructor of Hebrew at Oberlin College.[19]

From selected entries in Joseph Smith's diary, we can follow some of the progress made by the founder of the church and his "school of prophets" in Seixas's Hebrew course.

> Tuesday, [January] 26. Mr Seixas arrived from Hudson, to teach the Hebrew language, and I attended upon organizing of the class, for the purpose of receiving lectures upon Hebrew grammar. His hours of instruction are from ten to eleven, a.m.; and from two to three, p.m. His instruction pleased me much. I think he will be a help to the class in learning Hebrew.
>
> Thursday, [February] 4. Attended school, and assisted in forming a class of twenty-two members to read at three o'clock, p.m. The other twenty-three read at eleven o'clock. The first class recited at a quarter before two, p.m. We have a great want of books, but are determined to do the best we can. May the Lord help us to obtain this language, that we may read the Scriptures in the language in which they were given.
>
> Wednesday, 17. Attended the school and read and translated with my class as usual. My soul delights in reading the word of the Lord in the original, and I am determined to pursue the study of the languages [sic], until I shall become master of them, if I am permitted to live long enough. At any rate, so long as I do live, I am determined to make this my object; and with the blessing of God, I shall succeed to my satisfaction. . . .[20]

Smith's certificate was awarded to him by his teacher at the end of the month.[21] It read as follows:

> Mr Joseph Smith Junr. has attended a full course of Hebrew lessons under my tuition; & has been indefatigable in acquiring the principles of the sacred language of the Old Testament Scriptures in their original tongue. He has so far accomplished a knowledge of it, that he is able to translate to my entire satisfaction; & by prosecuting the study he will be able to become a [sic]

proficient in Hebrew. I take this opportunity of thanking him for his industry, & his marked kindness towards me.

J. Seixas

Kirtland Ohio March 30th 1836.

This document and its background help to explain much of the Mormon experience in Kirtland, Ohio, at a crucial moment in the evolution of its theology and program. Beyond that, some of the implications of the later relationship between Mormons and Jews become logical. Essentially, it was through this kind of experience that the inseparable bond of Mormon, Hebrew, Bible, and Holy Land was consecrated.[22]

The trend away from the strictly theological study of the Hebrew language toward its philological conception began early in the nineteenth century; it was reflected in the beginnings of Hebrew grammar and didactic textbook writing.[23] Hebrew was taught as a classical language in several secular colleges established in the course of the century, as well as in those affiliated divinity schools where biblical subjects remained dominant. By 1917 the number of higher institutions that included Hebrew in their curriculum reached fifty-five, according to the *American Jewish Year Book (AJYB)*.[24]

While intellectual curiosity about the Hebrew language tapered off in the nineteenth century, its subsequent resurgence in this century is nothing less than phenomenal. Quite apart from its renaissance in Jewish culture, classical and modern Hebrew is now taught in more than four hundred and fifty institutions of higher learning in the United States—colleges, universities, and Christian institutions and seminaries.[25] In 1940, only nine institutions taught modern Hebrew whereas sixty-eight had classical, or biblical, Hebrew in their curriculum. What is striking about this comparative statistic is that the trend shows continuing increase. Writing in a secular, cultural vein, but yet reminiscent in spirit of Ezra Stiles's reflections, Edmund Wilson explained why he considered the study of Hebrew sources indispensable to any "ideal University."[26] In an autobiographical piece, Wilson tells us how he himself first came to study Hebrew.

I discovered a few years ago, in going through the attic of my mother's house, an old Hebrew Bible that had belonged to my grandfather, a Presbyterian minister, as well as a Hebrew dictionary and a Hebrew grammar. I had always had a certain curiosity about Hebrew, and I was perhaps piqued a little at the thought that my grandfather could read something that I couldn't, so, finding myself one autumn in Princeton, with the prospect of spending the winter, I enrolled in a Hebrew course at the Theological Seminary, from which my grandfather had graduated in 1846. I have thus acquired a smattering that has enabled me to work through Genesis, with constant reference to the English translation and the notes of the Westminster commentaries, and this first acquaintance with the Hebrew text has, in several ways, been to me a revelation. In the first place, the study of a Semitic language gives one insights into a whole point of view, a system of mental habits, that differs radically from those of the West.[27]

Alfred Kazin adds a poignant note to Wilson's love for the Hebrew language, perhaps influenced by Grandfather Thaddeus's old Presbyterianism. "One of his favorite maxims," Kazin writes, "in his lonely Wellfleet winters was *Hazak Hazak Venithazek* . . . 'Be Strong, Be Strong, and Let Us Strengthen One Another!' In Hebrew letters, this is engraved on his tombstone in the Wellfleet cemetery."[28]

What has given rise to this vital interest in Hebrew as language and culture? Certainly the rootedness of the American spirit in Hebraism is a pervasive influence. The indigenous quality of Jewish life in America, with its multifaceted communal and educational enterprise, is a correlative factor. However, the most salient force is the rapid emergence of the *Yishuv* in Eretz Israel as the contemporary embodiment of ancient Hebrew civilization—a phenomenon that has fired the imagination of the cultural and intellectual world. The fact that out of Zion have come forth literary figures, scholars, scientists, and artists has impelled an attitude of respect and appreciation for the language in which they live and create.

HOLY LAND AS ZION

The personal attitude of Americans to the Holy Land may be examined mainly in two historical categories, both of which go back to the early days of the American nation: literary records, essentially pilgrimage literature; and actual settlement by individuals and groups.

The many sources of pilgrimage literature constitute a fruitful and largely untapped mine in the history of the American individual's involvement in the Holy Land.[29] Written by scholar or novelist, missionary or tourist, who were for the most part Christian pilgrims inspired by religious doctrine or by stories heard at their mother's knee about Zion and Jerusalem, this literature takes on a variety of forms. From it emerge not only the meditations and feelings of those who journeyed to the Holy Land and beheld it, but also its reflection of the yearnings and dreams of those who never so much as came near it.[30]

"Pilgrimage," to introduce the reader to his volume, wrote the Reverend Stephen Olin, then president of Wesleyan University, "is little less than to be naturalized in the Holy Land. . . . It is a commentary on the Bible. . . ."[31]

The real Holy Land seen by most nineteenth-century travelers largely dispelled the vision with which they had come. They were rudely shaken by the discrepancy between their expectation and the reality they encountered. "Renowned Jerusalem itself, the stateliest name in history, has lost all its ancient grandeur and is become a pauper village. . . ." "Palestine sits in sackcloth and ashes." These are not quotations from the book of Lamentations. These are the words of Mark Twain in *The Innocents Abroad*, a book recording his travels in Europe and the Holy Land in 1867 and subtitled *The New Pilgrim's Progress*. Mark Twain's humor vanished rather rapidly as he conveyed his shocked reactions to the scenes he witnessed.[32]

It took Herman Melville to draw the transcending conclusion. Melville went to the Holy Land in 1857 and set down his experiences in *Clarel*, a long philosophical poem.[33] For Melville, as Howard Mumford Jones pointed out, the Holy Land was, "in its ruined state, an outward and visible vision of the loss of religions among modern men and, to some degree, the ruin of the world."[34] Melville kept a special "Jerusalem" diary in which we read:

Whitish Mildew pervading whole tracts of landscape—bleached—leprosy—encrustation of curses—old cheese—bones of rocks—crunched, knawed & mumbled—mere refuse & rubbish of creation—like that lying outside of Jaffa Gate—all Judea seems to have been accumulations of this rubbish—You see the anatomy—compares with ordinary regions as skeleton with living & rosy man. So rubbishy, that no chiffonier could find any things all over it. No moss as in other ruins no grace of decay—no ivy—the unleavened nakedness of desolation—whitish [ashes]—lime kilns—black goats.[35]

Such was the land most travelers saw, wasted for centuries. But the dream persisted. Fortunately, many were able to see beyond the barren hillsides and dismal valleys.[36] American Christian devotion to the Holy Land embraced a wide spectrum of religious trends in the United States. Individuals viewed the land not only through their own eyes but also through the prism of the religious tradition in which they were born and raised. In one acute passage, Mark Twain remarked:

I am sure, from the tenor of books I have read, that many who have visited this land in years gone by, were Presbyterians, and came seeking evidences in support of their particular creed; they found a Presbyterian Palestine, and they had already made up their minds to find no other, though possibly they did not know it, being blinded by their zeal. Others were Baptists, seeking Baptist evidences and a Baptist Palestine. Others were Catholics, Methodists, Episcopalians, seeking evidences endorsing their several creeds, and a Catholic, a Methodist, an Episcopalian Palestine. Honest as these men's intentions may have been, they were full of partialities and prejudices, they entered the country with their verdicts already prepared, and they could no more write dispassionately and impartially about it than they could about their own wives and children. Our pilgrims have brought *their* verdict with them.[37]

More than a century later we find a lyrical account of the influence of Christian upbringing, as expressed by Ralph McGill, then editor of the influential *Atlanta Constitution*. In his book *Israel Revisited*, he describes the strong impact of the Presbyterian tradition:

As a boy, I came up in the country and in the Presbyterian faith, and if the hot breath of Calvin has not always been strong upon my neck, it is no fault of my family. I grew up knowing the old hymns in which Jordan's "Stormy banks," Galilee, and "Jerusalem the Golden" were sung mightily on the Sabbath and at Prayer Meetings. As a boy I used to dream of some day seeing the golden domes of Jerusalem and the blue reaches of the Sea of Galilee.

My grandmother, who was a "Blue Stocking" Presbyterian, was responsible for this. She yearned all her years to see the Holy Land. In her last years, she would walk out on the front porch of our farm house in East Tennessee, which looked across a meadow and a bottom field where Indian corn grew every year, to the Tennessee River and say, reflectively, "Son, we've all got one more river to cross . . . the river of Jordan." I did not know, being then but a young boy immensely fond of his grandmother, that she was speaking symbolically. I used to ponder on it and wonder why all of us Presbyterians someday would have to cross over Jordan. At any rate, the pull of the ancient land there on the Mediterranean was planted in me as a child.[38]

This attachment to the Holy Land was confined for the most part to prayer and to home training. While some few American groups and individuals did attempt to settle in the Holy Land in the nineteenth century, most of those ventures were abortive. Yet as the incipient movements of scientific study, travel, and settlement coalesced, a new totality emerged, namely, to cite the title of Yehoshua Ben-Arieh's seminal work, *The Rediscovery of the Holy Land in the Nineteenth Century*.

Exploring the Holy Land was unlike the penetration of Africa or the discovery of other unknown regions. Here, even the unknown was somehow familiar. The Bible, Josephus, the writings of the church fathers, Crusader chronicles—all seemed to come alive out of the dusty ruins and the forsaken landscape. To this day, archaeological discoveries in Israel have this familiar quality about them. The same spirit permeated even the study of the physical characteristics and the natural history of Palestine.[39]

History and geography began to meet again. In his comprehensive study of the physical geography of the Holy Land, published in 1841, John Kitto succinctly established that relationship between land and people.

> But even considered in itself, Palestine is a country, small though it be, well worthy of attention, and in some respects as peculiar as the people whose history is inseparably connected with it. It does not, like most other small countries, constantly remind you that it is physically but part of a larger country, from which it is but conventionally separated; but it is a *complete country*—a compact, distinct, and well-proportioned territory. It offers, as it were, an epitome of all the physical features by which different countries are distinguished, and which very few possess in combination.[40]

Yehoshua Ben-Arieh develops this theme in his perceptive study "The Geographical Exploration of the Holy Land." He paraphrases Kitto's definition of the Holy Land as "a country of concentrated history" combining "two main factors which determine the landscape form of a settled country: natural conditions and man's activities."[41] Applying Kitto's conclusion to later nineteenth-century and early twentieth-century developments, Ben-Arieh puts his finger on the phenomenon that heightened "the process of rediscovery" of the Holy Land, thus differentiating it from other Oriental countries: "the renewed settlement of the Jewish people in its historic homeland." "It appears," he concludes, "that historical coincidence was primarily responsible for the particular circumstances which brought together the 'rediscovery' of the land and the 'rediscovery' of the people who wished to return to this land."[42]

Seen in such a light, while the specific efforts at personal settlement may largely have been failures, they assume a collective pioneer importance beyond the interest they contain in themselves. In 1852 the American "consul" at Jerusalem, Warder Cresson, who subsequently converted to Judaism and adopted the Hebrew name Michael Boaz Israel, tried to establish an agricultural colony in Emek Rephaim near Jerusalem.[43] Another colony, "Mount Hope," was started by Clorinda Minor on land now situated in the Tel Aviv–Jaffa area;[44] and in 1866 George Jones Adams, accompanied by 150 colonists from Maine, came to settle in Jaffa.[45] In the latter part of the nineteenth century and in the first decades of the twentieth, while the early Jewish colonies were taking root, some fresh attempts at American Christian settlement were made. The history of the American Colony in Jerusalem was set down by Bertha Spafford Vester, who was brought to the land as a child of three, in her book called *Our Jerusalem*.[46]

Jewish colonization was also sporadic until the final decades of the century, when immigration to and settlement in the Holy Land gained impetus from the plight of the Jews in eastern Europe. Of course, American consuls, under the power of their capitulatory rights, played a crucial role in the Holy Land itself in granting protection to stateless Jews who fled from persecution in the lands of their birth (particularly Russia) and who had to face degradation by the Muslim populace and Ottoman functionaries.[47]

The Articles of Incorporation of *Shelom Yerushalayim* (Peace of Jerusalem) aptly sum up this period. While it deals with an early attempt to establish an American *Kollel* (community) in Jerusalem in 1879, its contents relate to that period in Holy Land history when not only American Jews but Jews from other lands who had never been granted citizenship and hence were totally disenfranchised acquired legal status from American consuls. In this case, it was to Consul J. G. Willson that the newly formed American community turned with a request "to protect it and to bring it under the shelter of his kindness."[48]

Programs for American Jewish settlement in the Holy Land were part of the *Hibbat Zion* (Love of Zion) movement in the last decades of the nineteenth century and then of the Zionist movement. Jewish immigration to Eretz Israel from the United States during that period involved a small segment of the American Jewish community, but its flow was constant. An early corporate, American Jewish entity—which still exists in Jerusalem today—was established in 1896 and was called "The American Congregation, The Pride of Jerusalem, or in Hebrew, *Kollel America Tifereth Yerushalayim.*"[49]

Other sporadic efforts resulted in a society called *Shavei Zion* (Returners to Zion), which counted Adam Rosenberg, Joseph Isaac Bluestone, and Alexander Harkavy among its founders.[50] Early in the twentieth century, a group of students from the Jewish Agricultural College at Woodbine, New Jersey, *HaIkkar Hatzair* (the Young Farmer), started a settlement program that later developed through the initiative of Eliezer Jaffe, one of its founders, into the first cooperative, small-holder's settlement—*Nahalal*, in the Valley of Jezreel. American Jewish settlement in Eretz Israel was also promoted by the creation of *Achooza* land-purchasing companies and the American Zion Commonwealth. Their main purpose was to prepare homesteads in Eretz Israel in anticipation of the members' future settlement.[51] Following the Balfour Declaration, there was a surge among American Jews to settle in Eretz Israel. Idealists such as Judah L. Magnes, Jessie Sampter, Henrietta Szold, and Alexander Dushkin looked forward to exemplifying in their lifestyle and deed those values they espoused in the United States and sought to realize them in the burgeoning young *Yishuv*.[52]

Judah Magnes, the first president of the Hebrew University, was widely respected as one of the most earnest spirits concerned with preserving Judaism in the United States. Arguing against the antinationalism that held sway in his circles, he maintained that contact with the living Jewish People—its Torah, language, custom, ceremony, and observances—was the certain way to bring American Jews out of their spiritual wasteland. For him, as he said on the eve of his departure for Eretz Israel in 1922, the Holy Land was "part and parcel of my whole Jewish makeup." In a trenchant essay, written in 1930, he stated:

> Three great things this poor little land has already given Israel in two generations. Hebrew has become a living possession and has thus restored to us and our children the sources of our history and our mind, and has thus given us the medium again for classic, permanent Jewish expression. The second great thing is the return of Jews to the soil, not only for the sake of a living from the soil but also for the sake of their love for this particular soil and its indissoluble connection with the body of the Jewish people. Third, the brave attempt on the part of the city-bred, school-bred young Jews—moderns of the modern—to work out in life, in the cities and on the land, a synthesis between the radicalism of their social outlook and their ancestral Judaism. It is problems of the same nature that a whole world in travail is laboring to solve; and among Jewry no more splendid attempt at a synthesis has been made than here, in everyday life and not in theory alone.[53]

In our own era, the old-new religious spirit was expressed by Walter Clay Lowdermilk, land conservationist par excellence. In his vision, the Holy Land could indeed be again "a land of brooks of water, of fountains and depths springing forth in valleys and hills" (Deuteronomy 8:7).

Speaking from Jerusalem in 1939, Lowdermilk formulated an "Eleventh Commandment," which he dedicated to the Jewish colonies whose "good stewardship in redeeming the damaged Holy Land was for me a source of great inspiration."

> Thou shalt inherit the Holy Earth as a faithful steward, conserving its resources and productivity from generation to generation. Thou shalt safeguard thy fields from soil erosion, thy living waters from drying up, thy forests from desolation, and protect thy hills from overgrazing by the herds, that thy descendants may have abundance forever.[54]

JEWISH RESTORATION

"For I really wish the Jews again in Judea an independent nation." This key sentence in John Adams's letter of 1819 to Mordecai Manuel Noah is probably the first declaration by an American statesman in favor of a sovereign Jewish state in Eretz Israel. It is true that in the long line of declarations over the years, we come across many that reflect age-old attitudes of the Christian Church toward the Jews. In 1788, for example, a reader of the *Hartford Courant* vigorously protested against a resolution submitted to the Constitutional Convention (especially paragraph 24), which provided that the president of the United States was to be commander-in-chief of the armed forces. The reader was fearful that "should he [the president] hereafter be a Jew, our dear posterity may be ordered to rebuild Jerusalem."[55] Notwithstanding the eccentricity of this fear, we cannot ignore its implication, namely, the reader's conviction that Jerusalem might in effect be rebuilt and the Jewish People restored to its land. In fact, while Adams himself clearly expressed his favorable attitude to Jewish Restoration, the last sentence of his letter shows just as clearly that this positive attitude is firmly rooted in Christian belief.

M. M. Noah Esq.

March 15th, 1819

Dear Sir,

I have to thank you for another valuable publication your travels in "Europe & Africa" which though I cannot see well enough to read. I can hear as well ever & accordingly have heard read two thirds of it & shall in course hear all the rest. It is a magazine of ancient & modern learning of judicious observations & ingenious reflections. I have been so pleased with it that I wish you had continued your travels—into Syria, Judea & Jerusalem. I should attend more to your remarks upon those interesting countries than to those of any traveller I have yet read. If I were to let my imagination loose I should wish you had been a member of Napoleons [sic] Institute at Cairo nay farther I could find it in my heart to wish that you had been at the head of a hundred thousand Israelites indeed as well disciplined as a French Army—& marching with them into Judea & making a conquest of that country & restoring your nation to the dominion of it. For I really wish the Jews again in Judea an independent nation. For I believe the most enlightened men of it have participated in the ameliorations of the philosophy of the age, once restored to an independent government & no longer persecuted they would soon wear away some of the asperities & peculiarities of their character & possibly in time become liberal Unitarian christians for your Jehovah is our Jehovah & your God of Abraham Isaac & Jacob is our God. I am Sir with respect & esteem your obliged humble servant

John Adams[56]

These citations are adduced to demonstrate the highly complex nature of the American attitude to Jewish Restoration and the admixture of conflicting and often paradoxical positions.[57]

In Protestantism, which of course is the main source for American Christian interest in the Holy Land before the present century, we must be particularly careful not to take for granted any consistency between church tenets and specific church action; or between an individual's avowed affiliation to a particular church group and the political and cultural activities in which he is engaged in a private capacity. Moreover, in any attempt to delineate the character of American Christian relations to the Holy Land, the Catholic position should also be taken into full account, particularly during those decades of its growth and influence, which brought about a major revision in the religious posture of the country.[58] Thus, while the bulk of American Christians may have been denominationally neutral on any one issue concerning Holy Land Restoration, action on an individual basis has been often positive and constructive; and such action generally derived from the individual's Christian faith. In other words, while Christian denominations as such did not organize themselves on behalf of—or, for that matter, against—restoration of Eretz Israel to Jewish sovereignty (with a few exceptions on both sides of the issue), individual Christians did join with one another along transdenominational lines in favor of Jewish statehood.[59]

America's Jews were naturally not free from the impact of these prevailing norms and modes. They determined to design their Jewish Restoration goals in the American pattern. Like Americans in general, they did not evolve a unified response; rather, the response consisted of differing approaches, some of which clashed or overlapped. Until the establishment of the State of Israel, disagreement most often centered on the political aspiration of Zionism. There was agreement in the areas of practical aid to the *Yishuv* in Eretz Israel, in effect adopting Restoration as a reality. In time, the preponderant elements of organized American Jewry agreed to a formulation that recognized the validity of Zionism in terms of the American ideal and global concerns. On this basis it was possible for the American Jewish community to awaken public opinion in favor of Eretz Israel on many crucial issues.

The historian benefits from the gift of hindsight. He is mindful of the changing manifestations of Jewish Restoration within the multiple-organized American community. At the same time, he perceives contemporary American commitment as rooted in the beginnings of the American nation. It then becomes relatively more simple to trace the historical line of America's evolving polity on behalf of Jewish sovereignty in the Holy Land.

Whether by oration, prayer, or report by Catholic, Mormon, Jew, or Protestant, as we shall see in the following nineteenth-century illustrative sequence, the argument for Jewish Restoration was set forth as if with one mind: The decline of the Turkish Empire is imminent; the Jews, though now dispersed, will return to the Land; blessed will be that nation—hopefully America—which will induce Holy Land regeneration. Inevitably, the image of the biblical Cyrus rises as the symbol of inspired statesmanship.

A sincere introduction to this emergent formulation in the context of an American domestic issue came from Thomas Kennedy, a young Catholic who militated for equality for the Jews of Maryland. Kennedy had never seen a Jew. In his presentation in favor of the "Jew Bill" (1818), he declared:

> But if we are Christians in deed and in truth, we must believe that the Jewish nation will again be restored to the favor and protection of God. The story of that wonderful people, from the days of Abraham unto the present time, is full of interest and instruction; their first emigration into Egypt; their leaving that country for the land of Canaan; their passage through the Red Sea; their journey in the wilderness; their settlement in Canaan; their captivity in Babylon; their restoration and final dispersion, afford a theme that never has been, never can be exhausted. They were once the peculiar people; though scattered and dispersed in every country and in every clime, their future state will no doubt be more glorious than ever. . . . And he who led their fathers through the deserts, has promised to lead them again to their native land. He who raised up and called Cyrus by name, can, by the same power and with the same ease, raise up a deliverer to his once favored nation; and it is probable that the time is not far distant when this great event shall take place. Who that has ever contemplated the rise and progress of the Russian empire, and noticed the decline and fall of that of Turkey, but will agree that wondrous changes will ere long take place in that part of the world; and when the crescent shall submit to the eagle, may we not hope that the banners of the children of Israel shall again be unfurled on the walls of Jerusalem on the Holy Hill of Zion?[60]

Twenty-three years later, this time in the Holy Land itself, the Restoration theme was carried forward by Elder Orson Hyde, delegated to perform the first formal act of the Mormon Church: to travel to the Mount of Olives in Jerusalem to pray for the land's reclamation by the Jews. Hyde, who had been a fellow student of Joseph Smith in Joshua Seixas's Hebrew course, arrived in Jerusalem in October 1841 and offered the Church's prayer, which was incorporated into the Mormon prayer book, forming a cornerstone in the Church's faith:

> Thou O Lord, did once move upon the heart of Cyrus to show favor unto Jerusalem and her children. Do thou also be pleased to inspire the hearts of kings and the powers of the earth to look with a friendly eye towards this

place, and with a desire to see Thy righteous purposes executed in relation thereto. Let them know that it is Thy good pleasure to restore the kingdom unto Israel—raise up Jerusalem as its capital, and continue her people a distinct nation and government, with David Thy servant, even a descendant from the loins of ancient David to be their king.

Let that nation or that people who shall take an active part in the behalf of Abraham's children; and in the raising up of Jerusalem, find favor in Thy sight. Let not their enemies prevail against them, neither let pestilence or famine overcome them, but let the glory of Israel overshadow them, and the power of the Highest protect them; while that nation or kingdom that will not serve Thee in this glorious work must perish according to Thy word—"Yea, those nations shall be utterly wasted.". . .[61]

In that very same spirit and instruction, Brigham Young and David H. Wells wrote on 15 October 1872 to the president of the Mormon Church, George A. Smith, on the eve of his extensive tour through Europe and Asia Minor, including—of course—the Holy Land. "When you go to the Land of Palestine, we wish you to dedicate and consecrate that land to the Lord, that it may be blessed with fruitfulness, preparatory to the return of the Jews in fulfillment of prophecy, and the accomplishment of the purposes of our Heavenly Father."[62] However, as Raphael Mahler observed, "The Messianic belief amongst American Jews was quite distinct from the Messianic searchings in Christian circles. It had become deeply embedded in their consciousness in its political aspects of rebuilding the Jewish state in Palestine." Mahler aptly illustrates this view by citing, among others, the sermons preached between 1799 and 1807 by Gershom Mendes Seixas, the spiritual leader of the Shearith Israel Congregation in New York, in which Seixas stated his belief in the eventual return of the Jews to the Land of Israel.[63]

One of the most imposing forerunners of Zionism in America was Mordecai Manuel Noah. Active on many fronts in American political life, Noah had suffered a stunning defeat in his attempt to found, in 1825, a city of refuge for the Jews on Grand Island near Buffalo, New York, naming it Ararat after the precedent of his biblical namesake. But this "Messiah: American Style," to borrow the title of Harry Sackler's drama, had learned an important lesson from the failure of his grandiose scheme.[64] He came to understand, as Herzl would almost half a century later, that no other place but Eretz Israel would do as the Jewish homeland. Only there could the Jews gather once again to fulfill the ancient prophecy of Return. This lesson was the most significant and enduring outcome of Noah's Ararat scheme.

What interests us particularly is not only Noah's "Zionist" outlook but the way he presented it before his American compatriots—as an American citizen who considered political restoration a means to rescue those Jews who were oppressed in other lands, he found it natural to direct his arguments to the conscience of the American nation. The approach of Noah and of those who were to follow him throughout the nineteenth century and well into the twentieth presupposed that helping the Jews in Eretz Israel not only conformed to the spirit of America but enhanced it. America, Noah stated, was "the only country which has given civil and religious rights to the Jews equal with other sects. . . ." Consequently, an even greater responsibility devolved upon it.

> Where can we plead the cause of independence for the children of Israel with greater confidence than in the cradle of American liberty? . . . Let me therefore impress upon your minds the important fact, that the liberty and independence of the Jewish nation may grow out of a simple effort which this nation may make in their behalf. That effort is to procure for them a permission to purchase and hold land in security and peace; their titles and possessions confirmed, their fields and flocks undisturbed. They want only *Protection*, and the work is accomplished.[65]

The composite Jewish Restoration portrait assumes an unexpected gradation in the prescient and ofttimes poetic report of W. F. Lynch, naval commander of the United States expedition to the River Jordan. From the book written by Lieutenant Lynch, as well as from records preserved at the National Archives, we learn of America's interest that the Holy Land be settled by a stable population amicably disposed toward the United States. On Friday, 31 March 1848, when the American sailors pitched their tents outside the confines of Haifa, Lynch noted:

> For the first time, perhaps, without the consular precincts, the American flag has been raised in Palestine. May it be the harbinger of regeneration to a now hapless people! . . . It needs but the destruction of that power which, for so many centuries, has rested like an incubus upon the eastern world, to ensure the restoration of the Jews to Palestine. The increase of toleration; the assimilation of creeds; the unanimity with which all works of charity are undertaken, prove, to the observing mind, that, ere long, with every other vestige of bigotry, the prejudices against this unhappy race will be obliterated by a noble and a God-like sympathy. . . . The fulfillment of the prophecy with regard to the Egyptians ensures the accomplishment of the numerous ones which predict the restoration of the tribes. . . .[66]

Within several decades, the vision of Restoration was darkened by the Russian pogroms of the 1880s. Yet it was the violence of the pogroms that gave rise in America, as elsewhere in the Jewish world, to the urgency of a Zionist solution to the Jewish plight. Without entering into the broad ramifications of the historical developments, suffice it to note Emma Lazarus's plea, which clarified the American Zionist position. Lazarus felt the pain and anguish of her fellow Jews in Russia, and she realized, much before others did in America and Europe, that Eretz Israel was the only possible destination for the Russian refugees. She, who composed the inscription on the Statue of Liberty that called America the haven for the oppressed of the world, also knew that Eretz Israel was the haven for the Jewish People.[67]

In 1882, the very year of the great pogroms and flight of the Jews, Samuel Sullivan Cox, member of the House of Representatives, wrote a "contemporary" editorial in his *Orient Sunbeams, or From the Porte to the Pyramids, By Way of Palestine*. Walking among the "Patriarchs in Israel" at the then "Wailing Wall," overlooking their old and worn volumes, Cox grasped the ultimate truth: Jerusalem and the Jew belong to one another.

> in the full blaze of history, one cannot help but feel that this is especially the city of the Jews. Christians may fight for and hold its holy places: Moslems may guard from all other eyes the tombs of David and Solomon,: the site of the temple on Mount Moriah may be decorated by the mosques of Omar and Aksa; but if ever there was a material object on earth closely allied with a people, it is this city of Jerusalem with the Jews. In all their desolation and wandering, was there ever a race so sensitive as to the city of its heart and devotion? All the resources, native and acquired, of this rare race, including its love of music and domestic devotion, have been called in to summarize and aggrandize the soreness of its weeping and the tearfulness of its anguish over the fate of Jerusalem and the restlessness of its exiles.[68]

It is of the essence of historical research to relate beginnings to ends, to discern permanent trends through the study of origins. In this chapter we have concentrated on one—albeit singular—dimension of the total continuing relationship between America and the Holy Land. Oral testimony, which encases the thesis and written documentation, was given by Harry S Truman.

In November 1953, the former president visited the Jewish Theological Seminary with his friend Eddie Jacobson. In the course of their conversation with Professors Louis Finkelstein and Alexander Marx, Eddie Jacobson, pointing at HST, proclaimed, "This is the man who helped create the State of Israel." Truman called out: "What do you mean 'helped create'? I am Cyrus, I am Cyrus!"[69]

NOTES

1. Samuel H. Levine, "Palestine in the Literature of the United States to 1867," *Early History of Zionism in America*, ed. Isidore S. Meyer (New York: American Jewish Historical Society and Theodor Herzl Foundation, 1958), 23.

2. *The Papers of Thomas Jefferson* I, ed. Julian P. Boyd (Princeton: Princeton University Press, 1950), 494–95, 677–79. For drawing of the seal by Benjamin J. Lossing, see Oscar S. Straus, *The Origin of Republican Form of Government in the United States of America*, 2d rev. ed. (New York and London: G. P. Putnam's Sons, 1901), frontispiece. Compare Isidore S. Meyer, "The Book of Esther: American Midrash," *Hebrew Studies* 17 (1976): 49–68. See especially the "Sermon" (pp. 56–58), originally published on the first page of the *New York Journal or General Advertiser*, 1 September 1774, as moral support of the first Continental Congress, in which King George III is Ahasuerus and Lord North is Haman. Benjamin Franklin was a master of biblical paraphrase, often based on his imitations of a Bible text. Notable is his "Parable Against Persecution," inspired by scriptural language relating to the patriarch Abraham, reflective of Franklin's tolerance of his fellow men. See Arthur A. Chiel, "Benjamin Franklin, His Genesis Text," *Judaism* 25, no. 3 (Summer 1976): 353–56.

3. Richard B. Morris, "Civil Liberties and the Jewish Tradition in Early America," *Publications of the American Jewish Historical Society (PAJHS)* 46, no. 1 (September 1956): 22. Compare II Maccabees 2:27. See also Daniel J. Boorstin, "Pilgrim Fathers to Founding Fathers" (from Reith Lectures, 1975), *The Listener* 20 (November 1975): 667–70.

4. *The Pulpit of the American Revolution*, ed. J. W. Thornton, 239–40, quoted by Truman Nelson, "The Puritans of Massachusetts: From Egypt to the Promised Land," *Judaism* 16, no. 2 (Spring 1967): 206.

5. Not all children were called by such patronymics as Abraham, Isaac, Jacob, and Israel. Even remote names, such as Nebuchadnezzar, were used. Family pets, too, were called by biblical appellations. Compare Stanley D. Brunn and James O. Wheeler, "Notes on the Geography of Religious Town Names in the U.S.," *Names* 14, no. 4 (December 1966): 197–202. In this connection it is interesting to note the comment in the Talmud on the biblical text "Sidonians call Hermon Sirion, and the Amorites call it Senir" (Deuteronomy 3:9): "Senir and Sirion are mountains in the land of Israel; this verse, however, teaches us that every one of the nations of the world went and built for itself a large city naming it after a mountain of the land of Israel, thus teaching you that even the mountains of the land of Israel are dear to the nations of the world." Babylonian Talmud, *Hullin* 60b (London: Soncino Press, 1948).

6. Lottie and Moshe Davis, *Land of Our Fathers: Guide to Map of Biblical Names in America* (New York: Associated American Artists, 1954).

7. Jerusalem as a name appears less frequently, perhaps out of awe of the Holy City. Yet there is a Jerusalem in four states. An illustrative anecdote of grass-roots, immigrant amalgam in America was related about a mining town in

Nevada. An Irishman and a Jew were two principal mine owners. As a delicate compliment to these leading citizens, the other miners left it to them to give the new camp a name. The Irishman stood out for a name taken from Gael, while the Jew wanted one that would be suggestive of Israel. After pressure from the impatient miners, the pair came to a compromise: "Tipperusalem." In 1875, New Jerusalem was founded in California. The selection of the title was made by Jewish settlers, according to one researcher, "[surely] because of the meaning this [Jerusalem] had for these pioneers in their own tradition. . . ." See L. and M. Davis, (see note 6 above).

8. Edward Robinson, *Biblical Researches in Palestine, Mount Sinai and Arabia Petraea* I (Boston: Crocker & Brewster, 1841), 46. Henry White Warren (1831–1912), a Methodist Episcopal clergyman, in his *Sights and Insights, or Knowledge by Travel* (New York: Nelson & Phillips, 1874), opened a chapter typically titled "Familiar Palestine" with the following lines:

> This is the first country where I have felt at home. Yet I have been in no country that is so unlike my own. Somehow this seems as if I had lived here long ago in my half-forgotten youth, or possibly in some antenatal condition, dimly remembered. As I try to clear away the mists, bring forward the distant, and make present what seems prehistoric, I find myself at my mother's side and my early childhood renewed. Now I see why this strange country seems so natural. Its customs, sights, sounds, and localities were those I lived among in that early time, as shown to me by pictures, explained by word, and funded as a part of my undying property (p. 246).

9. Transcript at the Oral History Division, Institute of Contemporary Jewry, Hebrew University of Jerusalem, dated 12 December 1976, p. 6. See also Jones's "Afro-Americans and the Holy Land," *With Eyes Toward Zion* I, ed. Moshe Davis (New York: Arno Press, 1977), 57–62, especially his statement on p. 58: "It was via the Bible and the church that Blacks first encountered the 'Holy Land.'"

10. Alexis de Tocqueville, *Democracy in America* 2 (New York: Vintage Books, 1954), 152:

> On his return home he (the American) does not turn to the ledgers of his business, but he opens the book of Holy Scripture; there he meets with sublime and affecting descriptions of the greatness and goodness of the Creator, of the infinite magnificence of the handiwork of God, and of the lofty destinies of man, his duties, and his immortal privileges.

11. Compare *Proceedings of the Massachusetts Historical Society* 18 (1880–1881), 140–42; see also, Shalom Goldman, "Biblical Hebrew in Colonial America: The Case of Dartmouth," *American Jewish History* 79 (1989–1990): 173–80.

12. For the scholarly unraveling of this legend, see H. L. Mencken, *The American Language*, Supplement I (New York: Knopf, 1945), 136–38; see also, Marquis de Chastellux, *Travels in North America in the Years 1780, 1781 and 1782* 2 (Chapel Hill: University of North Carolina Press, 1963), 498; *Quarterly Review* (January 1814): 528; A. W. Read, "The Philological Society of New York, 1788," *American Speech* 9, no. 2 (April 1934): 131.

13. In his introduction, Bradford stresses the value of knowing the Bible in the original. See Isidore S. Meyer, *The Hebrew Exercises of Governor William Bradford* (Plymouth, Mass.: Pilgrim Society, 1973). For a comprehensive study of Hebrew in Colonial America, see Eisig Silberschlag, "Origin and Primacy of Hebrew Studies in America," *Hagut Ivrit Be'Amerika* 1 (Tel Aviv: Brit Ivrit Olamit, 1972, Hebrew), 15-41. See also, D. De Sola Pool, "Hebrew Learning Among the Puritans of New England Prior to 1700," *PAJHS* 20 (1911): 31–83.

14. S. E. Morison, *The Puritan Pronaos* (New York: New York University Press, 1936), 41–42; Isidore S. Meyer, "Doctor Samuel Johnson's Grammar and Hebrew Psalter," *Essays on Jewish Life and Thought; Presented in Honor of Salo Wittmayer Baron* (New York: Columbia University Press, 1959), 359–74; William J. Leonard, "The Study of Hebrew in American Protestant Institutions of Higher Learning," *Hebrew Studies* 17 (1976): 138–43.

15. It was published under the title *A Sermon Preached at the Synagogue, in Newport, Rhode Island, Called "The Salvation of Israel," on the Day of Pentecost, or Feast of Weeks, the 6th Day of the Month of Sivan, the Year of the Creation, 5533: or, May 28, 1773, Being the Anniversary of Giving the Law at Mount Sinai: by the Venerable Hocham, the Learned Rabbi Haijm Isaac Karigal, of the City of Hebron, near Jerusalem, in the Holy Land.* For the text of the sermon, with a foreword by Stanley F. Chyet, see *Rabbi Carigal Preaches in Newport* (Cincinnati: American Jewish Archives, 1966). See also, George Alexander Kohut, "Early Jewish Literature in America," *PAJHS* 3 (1895): 123–25; Max Kohler, "The Jews in Newport," *PAJHS* 6 (1898): 78–79.

16. One of Stiles's students recorded this. See *Memoirs, Auto-biography and Correspondence of Jeremiah Mason* (1873; reprint, Kansas City, Mo.: Lawyers International Publishing, 1917), 11:

> During our Senior year the President took the whole charge of our instruction. Ethics constituted our chief class study, and Locke's treatise our only text-book. Some attention was paid to a general review of our previous college studies and the President insisted that the whole class should undertake the study of Hebrew. We learned the alphabet, and worried through two or three Psalms, after a fashion; with most of us it was mere pretense. The President had the reputation of being very learned in Hebrew, as well as several other Eastern dialects. For the Hebrew he professed a high veneration. He said one of the Psalms he tried to teach us would be the first we should hear sung in heaven, and that he should be ashamed that any one of his pupils should be entirely ignorant of that holy language.

For Stiles's own version of the teaching of Hebrew at Yale, see *The Literary Diary* 3, ed. F. B. Dexter (New York: Scribners, 1901), 397:

> From my first accession to the Presidency 1777–1790 I have obliged all the Freshmen to study Hebrew. This has proved very disagreeable to a number of students. This year I have determined to instruct only those who offer themselves voluntarily, and that at subsecivis horis only without omitting any of the three daily classical Recitations to their Tutor. Accordingly of 39 Fresh 22 have asked for Instruction in Heb.

and these Accordingly I teach at iv. P.M. Mondays, Wednesdays, Fridays. I have besides several of the other classes at other times.

See also, W. Willner, "Ezra Stiles and the Jews," *PAJHS* 8 (1900): 119–26; Morris Jastrow Jr., "References to Jews in the Diary of Ezra Stiles," *PAJHS* 10 (1902): 5-36; George Alexander Kohut, *Ezra Stiles and the Jews; Selected Passages from his Literary Diary Concerning Jews and Judaism* (New York: Philip Cowen, 1902).

17. *The Event Is with the Lord*, edited with an introduction by Stanley F. Chyet (Cincinnati: American Jewish Archives, 1976). The story of their friendship is told by Lee M. Friedman, *Rabbi Haim Isaac Carigal: His Newport Sermon and His Yale Portrait* (Boston: privately printed, 1940).

18. From details furnished in a letter dated 17 May 1965, from Lauritz G. Petersen of the office of the Church Historian, the Church of Jesus Christ of Latter-Day Saints, Salt Lake City. For an enlightening study of Mormon-Jewish relations, see Rudolf Glanz, *Jew and Mormon: Historic Group Relations and Religious Outlook* (New York: privately printed, 1963).

19. Seixas's biography is somewhat obscure. For his relations with the Mormons, see Leroi C. Snow, "Who was Professor Joshua Seixas?" *The Improvement Era* (February 1936), 67–71.

20. *History of the Church of Jesus Christ of Latter-Day Saints* 2 (Salt Lake City: Deseret News, 1948), 385ff.

21. LDS Church Archives. Used by Permission.

22. Compare Harris Lenowitz, "Hebrew, The Mormons and Utah," *Iggeret: A Newsletter of the National Association of Professors of Hebrew in American Institutions of Higher Learning* 46 (Spring 1988): 2–3.

23. William Chomsky, "Hebrew Grammar and Textbook Writing in Early Nineteenth-Century America," *Essays in American Jewish History* (Cincinnati: American Jewish Archives, 1958), 123–45. See also, William J. Leonard, "The Study of Hebrew in American Protestant Institutions of Higher Learning," *Hebrew Studies* 17 (1976): 138–43. An early example of Jewish encouragement to spread the knowledge of the Hebrew language in American universities is recorded by Bertram Wallace Korn, *The Early Jews of New Orleans* (Waltham, Mass.: American Jewish Historical Society, 1969), 249.

24. "American Colleges in Which Hebrew Is Taught," *AJYB* (1917–1918), 406. See also, Abraham I. Katsh, *Hebrew Language, Literature and Culture in American Institutions of Higher Learning* (New York: Payne Educational Sociology Foundation, 1950); David Mirsky, "Hebrew in the United States: 1900–1920," *Herzl Year Book* 5 (1963): 83–111. Note Mirsky's citation (p. 85) of Henry Hyvernat, "Hebrew in Our Seminaries," *Catholic University Bulletin* 14 (1898): 384.

25. Council on the Teaching of Hebrew, *Bulletin* 8, updated (1991). For earlier studies, see David Rudavsky, "Hebraic and Judaic Studies in American Higher Education," *Bulletin of the Council of the Study of Religion* 6, no. 2 (April 1975): 4; Abraham I. Katsh (see note 24 above); *Hebrew in Colleges and Universities*, ed.

Judah Lapson (New York: Hebrew Culture Service Committee for American High Schools and Colleges, 1958); Arnold J. Band, "Jewish Studies in American Liberal-Arts Colleges and Universities," *AJYB* 67 (1966): 3–30.

26. Edmund Wilson, "The Need for Judaic Studies," *A Piece of My Mind: Reflections at Sixty* (Garden City, N.Y.: Doubleday, 1958), 146–53.

27. Edmund Wilson, "On First Reading Genesis," *Red, Black, Blond and Olive* (New York: Oxford University Press, 1956), 387.

28. Alfred Kazin, *New York Jew* (New York: Alfred A. Knopf, 1978), 290. See the review of Wilson's *Letters on Religion and Politics 1912–1917*, by Harry Levin, *The New York Review* (27 October 1977).

29. For a bibliography of representative writings by Americans who visited or worked in the Middle East prior to 1850, see David H. Finnie, *Pioneers East: The Early American Experience in the Middle East* (Cambridge, Mass.: Harvard University Press, 1967), 287–94. For the second half of the nineteenth century, see Yohai Goell and Martha B. Katz-Hyman, "Americans in the Holy Land, 1850–1900: A Select Bibliography," *With Eyes Toward Zion* I, ed. M. Davis (see note 9 above), 100–25.

30. Jesse Lyman Hurlbut, *Traveling in the Holy Land Through the Stereoscope* (New York: Underwood & Underwood, 1900), 12–13. For examples of travel literature by black Americans, who were essentially ministers, see David F. Dorr, *A Colored Man Round the World* (Cleveland: Author, 1858); Daniel P. Seaton, *The Land of Promise* (Philadelphia: Publishing House of the A.M.E. Church, 1895); and Charles T. Walker, *A Colored Man Abroad: What He Saw and Heard in the Holy Land* (Augusta, Ga.: John M. Weigle, 1892). See also, the chapter "Black Travelers" in David Klatzker, "American Christian Travelers to the Holy Land, 1821–1939" (Ph.D. diss., Temple University, 1987), 208–22.

31. Stephen Olin, *Travels in Egypt, Arabia Petraea, and the Holy Land* I (New York: Harper & Bros., 1843), ix–x. See also, David Millard, *A Journal of Travels in Egypt, Arabia Petraea, and the Holy Land* (New York: Lamport, Blakeman & Law, 1853), v–vi; Henry C. Potter, *The Gates of the East: A Winter in Egypt and Syria* (New York: E. P. Dutton, 1877), 247–53.

32. Mark Twain, *The Innocents Abroad* (Hartford: American Publishing, 1869), 2 vols. The voyage to the Holy Land is described in vol. 2, beginning with chap. 14. See Franklin Walker, *Irreverent Pilgrims: Melville, Browne and Mark Twain in the Holy Land* (Seattle: University of Washington Press, 1974), ch. 7–8; see also, Reingard Nethersole, "Mark Twain in the Holy Land," *The Holy Land in History and Thought*, ed. Moshe Sharon (Leiden, The Netherlands: E. J. Brill, 1988), 96–104, especially the comparison of Twain's subtitle, *The New Pilgrim's Progress*, to John Bunyan's *The Pilgrim's Progress* of 1678, p. 98.

33. Herman Melville, *Clarel: A Poem and Pilgrimage in the Holy Land*, ed. Walter E. Bezanson (New York: Hendricks House, 1960); see F. Walker (see note 32 above), ch. 5–6.

34. Howard Mumford Jones, "The Land of Israel in the Anglo-Saxon Tradition," *Israel: Its Role in Civilization*, ed. Moshe Davis (New York: Harper &

Bros., 1956), 248. For a penetrating analysis of Melville's understanding of the Jewish relationship to the Holy Land, see Miriam Baker and Ruth Miller, "'New Canaan's Promised Shores': The Idea of Jerusalem in American Literature, 1630–1894" (in Hebrew), *Keshet* 18, no. 4 (Summer 1976), especially pp. 128–32. See also, Louise Abbie Mayo, "Herman Melville, the Jew and Judaism," *American Jewish Archives* 28, no. 2 (November 1976): 172–79, and Milton R. Konvitz, "Herman Melville in the Holy Land," *Midstream* 25, no. 10 (December 1979): 50–56.

35. Herman Melville, *Journal of a Visit to Europe and the Levant, October 11, 1856 May 5, 1857*, ed. Howard C. Horsford (Princeton: Princeton University Press, 1955), 137–38.

36. Compare the vision of Melville's contemporary, J. T. Barclay, *The City of the Great King: Jerusalem As It Was, As It Is and As It Is to Be* (Philadelphia: James Challen, 1857), 12–13.

37.   Mark Twain (see note 32 above), vol. 2, p. 243.

38. Ralph McGill, *Israel Revisited* (Atlanta: Tupper & Love, 1950), 1–2.

39. Yehoshua Ben-Arieh, *The Rediscovery of the Holy Land in the Nineteenth Century* (Jerusalem and Detroit: Magnes Press and Wayne State University Press, 1979), 12.

40. John Kitto, *Palestine: The Physical Geography and Natural History of the Holy Land* (London: Charles Knight, 1841), xxix. On this, compare Allan Nevins:

> Any Gentile visitor to Israel is struck by the fact, never clearly realized by the mere reading of books, that Biblical history is local history writ large; for Palestine is smaller than many an American county, and the immortal place names, from Beer-sheba up to Nazareth, Tiberias, and Safed, are the names of villages sprinkled over that tiny map as villages besprinkle Putnam County and Dutchess County.

"The Essence of Biography: Character Study," *The Writing of American Jewish History*, ed. Moshe Davis and Isidore S. Meyer (New York: American Jewish Historical Society, 1957), 439.

41. Yehoshua Ben-Arieh, "The Geographical Exploration of the Holy Land," *Palestine Exploration Quarterly (PEQ)* 104 (1972): 81–92. A thorough summary of American scientific exploration of the Holy Land is found in Philip J. King, "The American Archaeological Heritage in the Near East," *Bulletin of the American Schools of Oriental Research (Bulletin ASOR)* 217 (February 1975): 55–65.

42. Yehoshua Ben-Arieh (see note 41 above): 91–92. Compare the thesis of W. D. Davies in his *The Territorial Dimension of Judaism* (Berkeley: University of California Press, 1982), especially the "Epilogue."

43. On Cresson, see Abraham J. Karp, "The Zionism of Warder Cresson," *Early History of Zionism in America*, ed. I. S. Meyer (see note 1 above), 1–20; Frank Fox, "Quaker, Shaker, Rabbi—Warder Cresson: The Story of a Philadelphia Mystic," *Pennsylvania Magazine of History and Biography* 95 (1971): 147–94; Arthur A. Chiel, "An Inquisition of Lunacy," *Liberty* 75, no. 6 (November–December 1980): 16–20. It is interesting to note that the nineteenth-

century English writer W. M. Thackeray, in his *Eastern Sketches—A Journey from Cornhill to Cairo* (Boston: Estes & Lauriat, 1888), refers to Warder Cresson, although not by name.

> The kind, worthy, simple man took me to his temporary consulate-house at the American Missionary Establishment; and, under pretence of treating me to white wine, expounded his ideas; talked of futurity as he would about an article in *The Times*; and had no more doubt of seeing a divine Kingdom established in Jerusalem than you that there will be a levee next spring at St. James's. (p. 408).

44. Clorinda Minor's work is recorded in her diary and letters, in accounts by travelers, and in several studies. See J. E. Hanauer, "Notes on the History of Modern Colonisation in Palestine," *Quarterly Statement of the Palestine Exploration Fund* (1900): 128–32; N. M. Gelber, "A Pre-Zionist Plan for Colonizing Palestine: The Proposal of a Non-Jewish German-American in 1852," *Historia Judaica* I (1939): 82–85; Mrs. Minor was in contact with Isaac Leeser, who published one of her letters in *The Occident* 12 (1854): 200–206. See Leeser's announcement of her death, ibid. 13 (1856): 603.

45. On the Adams Colony: Peter Amann, "Prophet in Zion: The Saga of George J. Adams," *New England Quarterly* 7 (1964): 477–500; Shlomo Eidelberg, "The Adams Colony in Jaffa 1866–1868," *Midstream* 3 (Summer 1957): 52–61, based upon the Hebrew press of the period; Reed M. Holmes, *The Forerunners* (Independence, Mo.: Herald Publishing, 1981). For contemporary accounts by two American travelers, see Robert Morris, *Freemasonry in the Holy Land* (New York: Masonic Publishing, 1872), 265–69; John Franklin Swift, *Going to Jericho: Or Sketches of Travel in Spain and the East* (New York: A. Roman, 1868), 190–204. The Manuscript Department of the Jewish National and University Library in Jerusalem holds archival material relating to the Adams Colony (Ms. Var. 849), consisting of correspondence with senators from Maine and the Department of State, who investigated the colonists' plight.

46. Bertha Spafford Vester, *Our Jerusalem: An American Family in the Holy City, 1881–1949* (Garden City, N.Y.: Doubleday, 1950).

47. See David Landes, "Palestine Before the Zionists," *Commentary* 61, no. 2 (February 1976): 47–56; and the discussion in letters to the editor, ibid. (May 1976): 18–22; Frank E. Manuel, *The Realities of American-Palestine Relations* (Washington, D.C.: Public Affairs Press, 1949), 35–44.

48. The original document, dated 22 Adar 5639 (17 March 1879), is in the National Archives of the United States, Records of Foreign Service Posts of the Department of State—R. G. 84 Jerusalem, and was published in facsimile in *Guide for America–Holy Land Studies: Specimen Pages* (Jerusalem: Institute of Contemporary Jewry, Hebrew University of Jerusalem, 1973). A free translation from the Hebrew, by Nathan M. Kaganoff, is deposited at the Archives. For the background and the outcome of this attempt, see F. E. Manuel (see note 47 above), 34–35.

49. For the constitution of the American "community," see J. D. Eisenstein, *Constitution of the American Organization* (New York: 1898). A full description

of its early days, including a list of members, is found in Simcha Fishbane, "The Founding of Kollel America Tifereth Yerushalayim," *American Jewish Historical Quarterly (AJHQ)* 64 (1974–1975): 120–36.

50. Israel Klausner, "Adam Rosenberg: One of the Earliest American Zionists," *Herzl Year Book* I (1958), 232–87; Hyman B. Grinstein, "The Memoirs and Scrapbooks of the Late Dr. Isaac Bluestone of New York City," *PAJHS* 35 (1939): 53–64.

51. The full story of *HaIkkar Hatzair*, whose members sought to contribute to the regeneration of the Holy Land through introduction of American agricultural methods, is amply described in Margalit Shilo, "The Beginning of the Concept of the *Moshav* 'HaIkkar Hatzair,' an American Group in the Second Aliyah," *Cathedra* 25 (September 1982, Hebrew): 79–98. For brief treatments, see Joseph Brandes, *Immigrants to Freedom: Jewish Communities in Rural New Jersey since 1882* (Philadelphia: University of Pennsylvania Press, 1971), 245, 337–38; Alex Bein, *The Return to the Soil: A History of Jewish Settlement in Israel* (Jerusalem: Youth and Hechalutz Dept., Zionist Organization, 1952), 88–91, 223–27. For a study of one of these settlements, see Nili Fox, "Balfouriya: An American Zionist Failure or Secret Success," *American Jewish History (AJH)* 78 (1988–1989): 497–512. A succinct document describing Poriya is found in the intelligence report submitted to the U.S. High Commission in Constantinople by Lieutenant Commander James G. Ware USN to Rear Admiral M. L. Bristol USN under date of 17 May 1922 (National Archives and Records Services, RG-38).

52. Compare Felix Frankfurter, "The Palestine Situation Restated," *Foreign Affairs* (April 1931), esp. p. 412.

53. Judah L. Magnes, *Like All Nations?* (Jerusalem: Author, 1930), 26.

54. Walter Clay Lowdermilk, *Palestine Land of Promise* (New York: Harper & Bros.; London: V. Gollanz, 1944), frontispiece. Compare the chapter "American Christian Devotees in the Holy Land." This vision was not foreseen by earlier Holy Land protagonists such as Edward Robinson who wrote in 1852: "It is hardly necessary to remark, that the idea of speedily converting the Jews, living as strangers in Palestine, into an agricultural people, is altogether visionary." Edward Robinson, E. Smith, and Others, *Later Biblical Researches in Palestine and in the Adjacent Regions: A Journal of Travels in the Year 1852* (Boston: Crocker and Brewster, 1857), 274. As the decades passed, this view was slowly altered. See, for example, James Parton, in 1870: ". . . but there is reason to believe that the people who once made their land a proverb for its abundant harvests, are about to recover their skill in the cultivation of the soil." James Parton, "Our Israelitish Brethren," *Atlantic Monthly* 26 (October 1870): 387–88.

55. *Hartford Courant*, 28 January 1788, p. 3. See also, "Restoration of the Jews," *National Magazine* 4 (1854): 521–24, in which the concluding thought is: "We may regard their future conversion as *certain*—their future *return*, if not certain, at least *highly* probable. They are a monumental people." (Emphasis in the original.)

56. The original letter is in the Adams Papers, Massachusetts Historical Society, and is reprinted by permission of the Adams Memorial Trust. Mordecai Manuel Noah quotes part of the letter in the preface to his *Discourse on the Restoration of the Jews* (New York: Harper & Bros., 1854), vii. The book referred to by Adams is Noah's *Travels in England, France, Spain and the Barbary States in the Years 1813–14 and '15* (New York: Kirk, 1819). For an analysis of Adams's interest in Judaism and the Jews, see Isidore S. Meyer, "John Adams Writes a Letter," *PAJHS* 37 (1947): 185–201.

57. For a comprehensive overview of American attitudes, see Milton Plesur, "The American Press and Jewish Restoration during the Nineteenth Century," *Early History of Zionism in America*, ed. I. S. Meyer (see note 1 above), 55–76. One specific example, of which there are literally hundreds in local history annals, is described in Lloyd P. Gartner, *History of the Jews of Cleveland* (Cleveland: Western Reserve Historical Society, 1978), 6–7.

58. See Esther Feldbaum, "On the Eve of a Jewish State: American Catholic Responses," *AJHQ* 64 (1974–1975): 99–119.

59. See Robert T. Handy, "Studies in the Interrelationships Between America and the Holy Land: A Fruitful Field for Interdisciplinary and Interfaith Cooperation," *Journal of Church and State* 13 (1971): 290–93, 298–300.

60. *Votes and Proceedings of the House of Delegates of Maryland, 1818 Session* (Annapolis: John Green, 1819), 26; E. Milton Altfeld, *The Jew's Struggle for Religious and Civil Liberty in Maryland* (Baltimore: M. Curlander, 1924), 22. For background on the "Jew Bill," see Edward Eitches, "Maryland's 'Jew Bill,'" *AJHQ* 60 (1970–71): 258–79; *The Jews of the United States 1790–1840: A Documentary History* 1, ed. Joseph L. Blau and Salo W. Baron (New York: Columbia University Press, 1963), 33–49. See also, Theodore R. McKeldin, "History of the Jews in Maryland," an address delivered at a meeting of the *Beth Tfiloh* Brotherhood in Baltimore on 31 January 1954, and read into the *Congressional Record: Proceedings and Debates of the 83rd Congress, Second Session* by Sen. Herbert H. Lehman, 11 February 1954.

61. *History of the Church of Jesus Christ of Latter-Day Saints* 4, 2nd. rev. ed. (Salt Lake City: Deseret News, 1957), 456–59. See also, Marvin Sidney Hill, "An Historical Study of the Life of Orson Hyde, Early Mormon Missionary and Apostle, from 1805–1852" (Typescript, 1955), pp. 43–65, 113–18.

62. *Correspondence of Palestine Tourists, Comprising a Series of Letters by George A. Smith, Lorenzo Snow, Paul A. Schettler, and Eliza R. Snow of Utah. Mostly Written while Traveling in Europe, Asia and Africa in the Years 1872 and 1873* (Salt Lake City: Deseret News Steam Print, 1875), 1–2. For extensive analysis of the Mormon Church's attitude to the Jewish people and Zionism, see Karl E. Ettinger and Abraham G. Duker, "A Christian Zionist Centenary," *New Palestine* 32, no. 2 (17 October 1941): 15–16; Eldin Ricks, "Zionism and the Mormon Church," *Herzl Year Book* 5 (1963), 147–74; LeGrand Richards, *The Mormons and the Jewish People* (Salt Lake City: Church of Jesus Christ of Latter-Day Saints, n. d.).

63. Raphael Mahler, *A History of Modern Jewry, 1780–1815* (London: Vallentine Mitchell, 1971), 13–14.

64. Louis Ruchames, "Mordechai Manuel Noah and Early American Zionism," *AJHQ* 64 (1974–1975): 195–223; Bernard D. Weinryb, "Noah's Ararat Jewish State in Its Historical Setting," *PAJHS* 43 (1953–1954): 170–91; Selig Adler and Thomas E. Connolly, *From Ararat to Suburbia* (Philadelphia: Jewish Publication Society of America, 1960), 5–9.

65. M. M. Noah, *Discourse...* (see note 56 above), 10, 51.

66. William Francis Lynch, *Narrative of the United States' Expedition to the River Jordan and the Dead Sea* (Philadelphia: Lea & Blanchard, 1849). For a discussion of the Lynch expedition, see D. H. Finnie (see note 29 above), 262–70; and for a characterization of Lynch, see especially 269–70.

67. Emma Lazarus, *An Epistle to the Hebrews* (New York: Cowen, 1900), especially 73–74, 77.

68. Samuel S. Cox, *Orient Sunbeams, or From the Porte to the Pyramids, By Way of Palestine* (New York: G. P. Putnam's Sons, 1882), 295–96.

69. Confirmed in a letter to the author, 30 April 1969.

Chapter 2

Jewish Distinctiveness Within the American Tradition: The Eretz Israel Dimension

THE JEWISH COMMUNITY OF AMERICA

My conceptual framework for the study of Jewish life and institutions within American society consists of three elements: socioeconomic integration; religio-cultural identity; world Jewish involvement.

While the triad must be seen as a whole, it is the third element that marks a basic difference between the Jewish community and most other religious and ethnocultural groups of European origin. The Jews strove to preserve and practice their religio-cultural tradition as they maintained and fostered mutual responsibilities with Jewish communities throughout the world. The Jews identified their individual future and the future of their children with that of America, but they also saw themselves as part of *Kelal Yisrael*, thus collectively sharing in the destiny of the Jewish People.

It is suggested that a more accurate characterization of the Jewish entity is the "Jewish Community of America" rather than, for example, "American Jewry" or "Jewish Americans."[1] In the culturally pluralistic society of America, the Jews as individuals are part of the whole; distinctiveness resides in their group culture as *they* express it and as it is perceived. However, the Jewish experience in America cannot be written exclusively, or even essentially, in the context of American society. Obviously, this contextual perspective is indispensable, but it is inadequate, as contemporary Jewish history demonstrates conclusively.[2]

By mid-twentieth century, the climacterics of world Jewish history—the destruction of European Jewry and the rise of the State of Israel—transformed the Jewish Community of America. Seemingly, all of Jewish history—exile, martyrdom, and redemption—were compressed into two decades. Subsequently, the Jewish Community of America became not only the largest in the world, but also the Diaspora's most vital center. While overwhelmingly involved in ensuring world Jewish survival, the creative capacity of American Jewry burgeoned as never before.

Thus, the fuller construct of the Jewish Community of America should relate its creative impulse to the continuum of the Jewish tradition and culture in time; and in the contemporary era, to the worldwide People and its heartland in Eretz Israel—the biblical term for the Land of Israel. Time and space are to be understood in global perspective.

What are the historiographical implications of this view? Essentially, it offers a deeper understanding of the American heritage. The study of Jews and Judaism in America casts special light on the shaping of the American spirit and purpose. To cite Daniel Boorstin:

> Apologists of Judaism in recent years, in a frenetic search for identities, have dulled their vision of what is distinctive in either the Jewish or the American experience . . . those who would equate "Judaism" with "Americanism," by the very terms of their argument may well prevent the discovery of any fruitful relation between cultures. . . . To overlook the distinctions in favor of the supposed similarities or identities of the Jewish and American historical experiences is to destroy the peculiar qualifications of Jews as pupils, critics, and mentors.[3]

Global perspective also has implications for world Jewish history. The growth and development of the Jewish Community of America illustrate in great measure the centrifugal and centripetal forces transcending boundaries of space and time that affect most Jewish communities in the contemporary world. In terms of "the contemporary relevance of history"—to borrow the concept from Salo W. Baron—has there been any more striking example of the dedication of the Jews in America to world Jewish communities than their persistent concern for the welfare of Russian Jewry? That concern and, indeed, dedication pervaded the Jewish Community of America, from the pogroms of the 1880s until the cataclysmic events in the end years of this century.[4] In that sense—over and above its own absolute identification with the American idea and future—the unique posture of the Jewish Community of America emerges precisely in its collective commitment and responsibility to the Jewish People wherever they may dwell.

THE ERETZ ISRAEL DIMENSION

To exemplify this duality in the American and Jewish experience, I choose the Eretz Israel dimension. Indeed, world Jewish involvement can also be viewed through the pervasive commitment of American Jews to East European Jewry. But, I suggest, in the greater part of the twentieth century this basic aspect of Jewish life in America is more dynamically illuminated in the Eretz Israel relationship, that is, in the harmonization within the Jews of America between America as their native land and Eretz Israel as the center of their tradition and of the Jewish People.

As we have emphasized in the central thesis of this volume, the significance of Eretz Israel in American Jewish life is both of a substantive and historiographical character. Substantively, the Holy Land, Zion, or Eretz Israel is part of the spiritual history of America. It is organic to American Christianity and thus serves as an important factor in the interplay of ideas among the religious faiths in America.

As regards American Jewish history, it should be emphasized that the Jewish tradition and the Jews have exerted a qualitative influence on America much greater than numbers would indicate. From the early decades of the nineteenth century, Jewish activity on behalf of Eretz Israel, precisely because it was cast in an indigenous American Jewish idiom, has had a deep impact on the American community generally, stimulating it on behalf of Zion.

From the methodological viewpoint, within the broad field of cross-cultural and pluralistic exchange in the Unites States, the America–Eretz Israel theme represents a meeting point of Jewish and American history. Though the two elements are separately discernible, they intertwine, mutually illuminating each other. While such confluence is not exclusive to the American scene, particularly in post-emancipation Jewish history, it is a pervasive factor in the United States. Other examples of American and Jewish history confluence come to mind: the Jewish labor movement in America, particularly in the early twentieth century; the large number of Jewish writers and Jewish themes in American literature since the mid-1900s; and certainly the similarities in problems of ethnic assimilation and maintenance of identity. The Zion theme reveals this integrality in conspicuous form. Here many diverse elements meet, sometimes antithetically, but most often cooperatively.

JEWISH INNER AND OUTER ORIENTATIONS

The attempt to comprehend the contiguities between the American nation and the subcultures within it has been dealt with amply in relevant sociological and historical literature. In my formulation, I rely considerably upon Erik Erikson's conception of "joint historical actualities" wherein, as he put it, "the alternative to an exclusive totalism is a wholeness of a more inclusive identity."[5]

The Holy Land–Zion–Israel theme in America is a striking example of this concept of "joint historical actualities," or what I prefer to call "common parlance." Early American historical sources, Christian and Jewish, reveal almost identical language, symbols, and manner of discourse regarding Jewish Restoration in the Holy Land.[6] A textual comparison of John McDonald's *Isaiah's Message to the American Nation* (1814) with Mordecai M. Noah's *Discourse on the Restoration of the Jews* (1845), as well as with Orson Hyde's first Mormon prayer on the Mount of Olives (1841), reflects such common parlance.[7] In this literature, the young American nation is admonished to help bring about the Restoration of the Jews, as part of its responsibilities to itself and to the world. "Land of the overshadowing wings" (Isaiah 18:11) is interpreted to be the United States of America, and the symbolism employed for this mission is Cyrus (=American eagle) as described in 46:11.[8]

We cite Mordecai Manuel Noah not only because of his historical precedence, but essentially to underscore in this context what many have overlooked. Noah's pre-Zionism called for an *asylum* for the Jews in the State of New York so that "our people may so familiarize themselves with the science of government and the lights of learning and civilization as may qualify them for that great and final *restoration* to their ancient heritage, which the times so powerfully indicated."[9] (Italics: M.D.) Jonathan Sarna, in his *Jacksonian Jew*, delineating "the two worlds of Mordecai Noah," emphasizes the key point, namely, that "Noah did not see Ararat as a surrogate Jerusalem."[10]

Thus, he spoke to his fellow-Jews in American terms: America as Land of Promise, though not the Promised Land.

> But will they go, I am asked, when the day of redemption arrives? All will go who feel the oppressor's yoke. *We* may repose where we are free and happy, but those who, bowed to the earth by oppression, would gladly exchange a condition of vassalage for the hope of freedom; that hope the Jews never can surrender; they cannot stand up against the prediction of our prophets, against the promises of God; they cease to be a nation, a people, a sect, when they do so.[11]

This *inner* and *outer* orientation was possible precisely because America recognized religio-cultural diversity as compatible with its ideas of civil unity. It was Thomas Jefferson who stated that the maxim of civil government is "reversed in that of religion, where its true form is 'divided we stand, united we fall.'"[12] In this spirit the organized Jewish community succeeded in developing a state of cohesiveness within America and virtually total involvement with World Jewry, which characterize it today.

Except for some prescient minds, several decades elapsed during the nineteenth century before awareness of the opportunities inherent in a pluralistic America found clear and explicit expression in norms and modes of Jewish public life in which world Jewish ties were also legitimated. Americanization would not mean immigrant assimilation or gross acculturation; it would mean Jewish *distinctiveness* in the American amalgam. And the character of that distinctiveness had to be consistent with American culture, Jewish historical continuity, and continuing world Jewish commitment. During the nineteenth and twentieth centuries, varied Jewish subgroups in quest of their continuing interdependence with the Jewish People incorporated the Holy Land, Zion, or Eretz Israel dimension into their respective conceptions of an indigenous Jewish Community existence in America, each in a manner compatible with its own ideology and program.

Thus, the Jewish belief in Zion Restored—later, political Zionism—could prosper on American soil, firmly supported by people of various faiths and orientations. In the twentieth century, Horace Kallen succinctly formulated the Americanism underlying his Zionist faith. "My Zionism, based as it was on the American idea (of equality for all), confirmed my right to be different, which had been promised by the Declaration of Independence. It was the working out of that faith in action."[13]

It is not my intention either to trace how the Eretz Israel component came to be incorporated within selected subgroups or to compare contemporary evolutions. Representative documents, composed at crucial points in the history of the respective subgroups, serve as supportive evidence and amplification of my central thesis. The citations are from the historical record of the Jewish religious groups (Orthodox, Conservative, Reform, Reconstructionist) and political Zionism. In their composite, these subgroups encompassed the great majority of identified Jews in America.

ERETZ ISRAEL FORMULATIONS IN AMERICAN CONTEXT

Orthodox Judaism

Forerunner of the twentieth-century "native" American Orthodox movement was the Orthodox Jewish Congregational Union of America. Established in June 1898, its general purpose was to "promote the religious interests of the Jews in America and to further the welfare of the Orthodox Congregations in America."[14] The need to define Zionism was one of the four specific aims described in the convening proclamation. Issued in Hebrew and English, the proclamation called for: definition of the permanent principles of the conference; Sabbath observance; Zionism; strengthening the Orthodox congregational union. The text in the Hebrew version's description of "Zionism" is virtually a definition: *"Hibbat Zion ve-yishuv Eretz Yisrael"* (Love of Zion and settlement of the Holy Land).

In the principles adopted by the founding convention, the "endeavor to advance the interests of Judaism in America" was interpreted to include: convening a Jewish Synod; affirmation of belief in the Divine revelation of the Bible; adherence to the acknowledged codes of the Rabbis and the thirteen principles of Maimonides; belief in the coming of a personal Messiah.

On relations with the Jewish People, I cite the text in full:

> We protest against the idea that we are merely a religious sect, and maintain that we are a nation, though temporarily without a national home, and
>
> Furthermore, that the restoration to Zion is the legitimate aspiration of scattered Israel, in no way conflicting with our loyalty to the land in which we dwell or may dwell at any time.[15]

Conservative Judaism

The dynamic constants of "historical and traditional Judaism" as developed by Solomon Schechter and the Jewish Theological Seminary faculty at the beginning of the twentieth century were Scholarship, Torah and *Mitzvot*, Zionism-Hebraism, and the "American center." In contrast to the Seminary board, the faculty consisted of declared Zionists and, in some cases, active participants in the Zionist movement. However, while the Zionism of the Conservative movement stressed the national factor in Jewish history, it did not relegate a secondary position to the religious character of that history. Nor did the architects of the Conservative movement in American Judaism (for example, Louis Ginzberg and Israel Friedlaender) ignore the danger, as they saw it, of an exclusive, nationalist, Zionist viewpoint developing a philosophy negating the Diaspora. This point of view expressed itself in the formula "Diaspora plus Eretz Israel": On the one hand, Jewish resettlement in the Holy Land and, on the other, the building of a vital center of Judaism in America.

Schechter's American formulation of Zionism became the hallmark of the Conservative group's ardent relationship to Eretz Israel reborn. Calling it "the Declaration of Jewish Independence from all kinds of slavery, whether material or spiritual," Schechter wrote in his famous "Zionism: A Statement":

> Zionism is an ideal, and as such is indefinable. It is thus subject to various interpretations and susceptive of different aspects. It may appear to one as the rebirth of a national Jewish consciousness, to another as a religious revival, whilst to a third it may present itself as a path leading to the goal of Jewish culture; and to a fourth it may take the form of the last and only solution of the Jewish problem. By reason of this variety of aspects, Zionism has been able to unite on its platform the most heterogeneous elements; representing Jews of all countries and exhibiting almost all the different types of culture and thought as only a really great and universal movement could command.
>
> Zionism declares boldly to the world that Judaism means to preserve its life by *not* losing its life. It shall be a true and healthy life, with a policy of its own, a religion wholly its own, invigorated by sacred memories and sacred environments, and proving a tower of strength and of unity not only for the remnant gathered within the borders of the Holy Land, but also for those who shall, by choice or necessity, prefer what now constitutes the Galuth.[16]

Reform Judaism

The forum and tribunal for the developing Reform movement of Judaism were the annual conventions of the Central Conference of American Rabbis. The annals of those conventions clearly reflect how Reform began to "re-form" itself from the second decade of the twentieth century onward. Many changes that surfaced in that decade were clearly stimulated by the Zionists within the Reform movement who had been actively dissenting from the majority view since the late nineteenth century.[17] Fifty-two years after a basic anti-Zionist statement was formulated in what is known as the Pittsburgh Platform, the Columbus Platform of 1937 was a historical watershed in Reform Judaism. Actually, the crucial step in the movement's Eretz Israel posture had been taken in 1935 when the classic anti-Zionist formula was discarded and a neutral clause was adopted in its stead:

> Whereas, at certain foregoing conventions of the Central Conference of American Rabbis, resolutions have been adopted in opposition to Zionism. . . .
>
> Be it resolved, that the Central Conference of American Rabbis takes no official stand on the subject of Zionism. . . .[18]

The new set of "Guiding Principles of Reform Judaism" was organized under three main divisions—Judaism and its foundations; ethics; religious practice. The passage relating to Eretz Israel was subsumed under another heading of Israel (as People).

> *Israel.* Judaism is the soul of which Israel is the body. Living in all parts of the world, Israel has been held together by the ties of a common history, and above all, by the heritage of faith. . . .
>
> In all lands where our people live, they assume and seek to share loyally the full duties and responsibilities of citizenship and to create seats of Jewish knowledge and religion. In the rehabilitation of Palestine, the land hallowed by memories and hopes, we behold the promise of renewed life for many of our brethren. We affirm the obligation of all Jewry to aid in its upbuilding as a Jewish homeland by endeavoring to make it not only a haven of refuge for the oppressed but also a center of Jewish culture and spiritual life.
>
> Throughout the ages it has been Israel's mission to witness to the Divine in the face of every form of paganism and materialism. We regard it as our historic task to cooperate with all men in the establishment of the kingdom of God, of universal brotherhood, justice, truth and peace on earth. This is our Messianic goal.[19]

While "Zionism" as a concept or movement does not appear in the document, the ideas of "The Jewish People" and "Jewish Community" are introduced. The Columbus declaration, as we now know, was the beginning of Reform Judaism's redefinition of its basic tenets.

Reconstructionism

Mordecai M. Kaplan, founder of the Reconstructionist movement (1935), created the term "living in two civilizations" as the keystone of his Jewish social ideology. Kaplan's basic concern was to provide the Jews in the American diaspora with the means to contend constructively with their problems of Jewish identity as Americans and Jews. In his classic *Judaism as a Civilization*, he expounded his views on the need for "conscious Jewish renascence." Kaplan also introduced the term Jewish "peoplehood" in his translation of *Am Israel* at a time when others were defining the Jews as a "race," or "religion," or "nationality." In the early days of the movement, Reconstructionism was a transmovement school of thought; only later did it become a fourth religious movement in American Judaism. But its banner remained, to use another of Kaplan's formulations, "the corporate reality of the Jewish People." The Reconstructionist program was graphically represented in a seal on the cover of the *Reconstructionist* magazine, with its legend inscribed in English and in Hebrew.

The form is that of a wheel. The hub of the wheel is Palestine, the center of Jewish civilization from which all the dynamic forces of Judaism radiate. Religion, culture and ethics are the spokes by which the vital influence of Palestine affects and stimulates Jewish life everywhere and enables it to make its contribution to the civilization of mankind. The wheel has an inner and an outer rim. The inner rim represents the Jewish community that even in the dispersion, maintains its contact with the Jewish civilization rooted in Palestine, by the spiritual bonds of religion, ethics and culture. The outer rim is the general community, for us the community of America, with which the Jewish civilization as lived by the Jewish community maintains contact at every point. The seal thus symbolizes the whole philosophy of the Reconstructionist movement.[20]

Political Zionism

The Kishinev pogroms of 1903 and 1905 had shaken American Jewry out of its isolation. A national Committee for the Relief of Sufferers from Russian Massacres was soon organized. In November 1906, the American Jewish Committee was founded "to prevent the infraction of the civil and religious rights of Jews, in any part of the world. . . ." The horror of the "City of Slaughter," as Hayyim Nahman Bialik called it, gave tragic credence to the Zionist analysis of European Jewry's plight. Emil G. Hirsch, fervent antinationalist, cried out under the stress and agony of the pogroms, "I am now a Zionist."

But what did it mean to be a Zionist in America? This was the question that agitated the minds not only of the Zionist leadership, but also of those Jews who were concerned for their brethren overseas yet would not associate themselves with the world Zionist credo. The dread specter of "double loyalty" rose early in the minds of those whose chief ideology was "Americanization," as they understood it.

The leaders of the Federation of American Zionists—Richard Gottheil, Cyrus Sulzberger, Harry Friedenwald, Jacob de Haas—could not wish away what was seen as the potential conflict between Zionism and American patriotism. They faced the issue squarely and formulated a response that was later to become part of the official lexicon of Zionist ideology in America. I have impressive documentation—although not conclusive evidence—that this "American" Zionist response not only evolved with the direct assistance of Theodor Herzl, Max Nordau, and Israel Zangwill, but was substantively formulated by Herzl himself.[21]

In brief, this response opens with Richard Gottheil's request of Herzl "to think out a precise form" to meet the "one great question that is uppermost in the minds of all Americans whom we approach . . . how to square Zionism with the duties and obligations of a patriotic American citizen of the strenuous stamp of Theodore Roosevelt."

Herzl's response, "Zionism and Patriotism," was printed posthumously in *The Maccabaean* with an editorial introduction: "The following note for the first time made public was written by the late leader in answer to a question propounded to him on this side of the Atlantic." What is remarkable about Herzl's manner of presentation is the combination of ideas in his argument.

> Participation in the Zionist movement means nothing which is not in the clearest and highest form in unison with the patriotism of a true American. He who labors for the creation of a home for the Jews in Palestine, a home assured by the public law and recognized by all the nations of the earth, will perform his duties as an American citizen with pleasure. . . .
>
> On the contrary the Jews, even those not American citizens, will ever thankfully recall the noble spirit America has always manifested towards them, and but lately in the splendid intervention of President [Theodore] Roosevelt to further the cause of the Russian Jews. And neither the American nor the non-American Jews will ever forget that the United States was an asylum for the persecuted. . . .
>
> The aid offered by Zionism is the diversion of the stream of persecuted immigrants. The American Jews are convinced that the Government can only decide with a heavy heart to regulate the movement of unfortunate people. Zionism is the only humane and at the same the only practical end. . . .
>
> . . . the American Jews aid their beloved fatherland when they aid an unhappy people from whom they spring. That is not disloyalty, in no way, but a double measure of loyalty.[22]

Does one not hear an echo of Herzl in the addresses of Brandeis, of which we here cite a brief passage?

> Let no American imagine that Zionism is inconsistent with Patriotism. Multiple loyalties are objectionable only if they are inconsistent. A man is a better citizen of the United States for being also a loyal citizen of his state, and of his city; for being loyal to his family, and to his profession or trade; for being loyal to his college or his lodge. Every Irish American who contributed towards advancing home rule was a better man and a better American for the sacrifice he made. Every American Jew who aids in advancing the Jewish settlement in Palestine, though he feels that neither he nor his descendants will ever live there, will likewise be a better man and a better American for doing so. . . .
>
> Indeed, loyalty to America demands rather that each American Jew become a Zionist. For only through the ennobling effect of its [Zionism's] strivings

can we develop the best that is in us and give to this country the full benefit of our great inheritance.[23]

It is remarkable that for all of Brandeis's ardent advocacy of Zionism, his fundamental involvement in American democracy and aspirations was not impugned. One of the most majestic descriptions of Brandeis was that of Dean Acheson:

> The Justice was an arresting figure; his head of Lincolnian cast and grandeur, the same boldness and ruggedness of features, the same untamed hair, the eyes of infinite depth under bushy eyebrows, which in moments of emotion seemed to jut out. As he grew older, he carried a prophetic, if not intimidating aura. It was not in jest that later law clerks referred to him as Isaiah.[24]

A CONCLUDING NOTE

While we scanned in the selected sections a wide spectrum of the Jewish Community of America, obviously there are other important subgroups that I have not dealt with in this chapter. For example, the non-Zionists, who opposed the movement for the State though not the upbuilding of Eretz Israel as the Holy Land of the Jewish People; the secular-cultural elements, social and fraternal orders; the variety of communal associations; "other Jews," that is, the mass of self-identified but not necessarily affiliated Jews; and, finally, that highly individualist nongroup that Saul Bellow classifies as "Americans who are also Jews."

Nevertheless, I submit, my central thesis can be demonstrated in these areas as well, and even fortified if developments *after* the State of Israel's establishment are taken into account.

What emerges from the historical analysis is the remarkable correlation between involvement in the Jewish People as a whole and commitment to Eretz Israel as its dynamic center. Equally clear is the almost total agreement within the Jewish Community of America that its responsibility for the welfare of the Jewish People and the State of Israel can best be realized through the spiritual as well as physical home created by the Jewish Community in America.

The Balfour Declaration and its impact gave American Jewry a "glow," an élan vital. To American Jewry, which was then—in the 1920s and 1930s—at an institutional low, it gave the possibility for the first time to identify with world Jewry, for spiritual if not political union. The Balfour Declaration had the power of a dream to be realized—the establishment of a Jewish National Home under the aegis of Britain, America's political ally. Hence the question of dual loyalty was not even envisaged.[25]

As regards the direct America–Eretz Israel relationship, a process of accommodation—not compromise—continues both in theory and practice between the classic versions of Zionism that arose in European Jewry and the Eretz Israel orientations as they have evolved within the Jewish Community of America. The protagonists of Israeli Zionism have come to recognize—without necessarily accepting—the American Jewish perception of Eretz Israel as compatible with a creative Jewish Community in the United States. The Jewish Community of America, in turn, has adopted the centrality of the State of Israel for the future of world Jewish existence.

APPENDIX 2A: COMMON PARLANCE

"The Restoration of the Jews Aided by the American Nation"

John McDonald
A New Translation of Isaiah,
Chapter XVIII (1814).

"God calls aloud on the American nation—her situation and national characteristics described—sheltered under the outspread wings of her own eagle—placed beyond the rivers of Cush at that time the western boundary of Jewish Geographical knowledge—sending ambassadors by sea and in vessels of reeds on the face of her own waters. . . .

The American nation, uniting with the friends of Christ of all nations, in presenting the Jews wonderfully changed, as an oblation to God of the first fruits of men, in Mount Zion." (p. 7)

Mordecai M. Noah
Discourse on the Restoration of the Jews (1845) [The title page of the text available to me in Jerusalem of Noah's *Discourse* is a facsimile of the title page of the address as first published, printed with a map of the Land of Israel and the imprint in Hebrew of the verse in Isaiah: Ch. 40:1 *Nahamu Nahamu Ami* (Comfort, O comfort My people, says your God).]

"If I am right in this interpretation, and that this is the land which is beyond the rivers of Ethiopia, what a glorious privilege is reserved for the free people of the United States: the only country which has given civil and religious rights to the Jews equal with all other sects; the only country which has not persecuted them, selected and pointedly distinguished in prophecy as *the* nation which, at a proper time, shall present to the Lord his chosen and trodden-down people, and pave the way for their restoration to Zion. . . ." (pp. 49–50)

"I propose, therefore, for all Christian societies who take an interest in the fate of Israel, to assist in their restoration by aiding to colonize the Jews in Judea. . . ." (p. 37)

The Cyrus Image

John McDonald
A New Translation of Isaiah

"That our application of this epithet to the American nation, is in strict analogy to other predictions of the same prophet already accomplished, will appear from his celebrated description of Cyrus, Chp. xlvi. 10,11. God had appointed him by prophecy as the scourge of Babylon and the deliverer of the captive Jews. . . . It may with confidence be asked, can the *over-shadowing wing*, when applied to America, be less intelligible than *eagle*, when applied to Cyrus?" (p. 10)

Thomas Kennedy
His presentation in favor of the "Jew Bill," in Maryland in 1818. *Votes and Proceedings of the House of Delegates of Maryland, 1818 Session* (1819).

"But if we are Christians indeed and in truth, we must believe that the Jewish nation will again be restored to the favor and protection of God. . . . He who raised up and called Cyrus by name, can, by the same power and with the same ease, raise up a deliverer to his once favored nation; and it is probable that the time is not far distant when this great event shall take place." (p. 26)

Orson Hyde
Prayer on the Mount of Olives (First formal act of the Mormon Church in 1841). *History of the Church of Jesus Christ of Latter-Day Saints* 4.

"Thou, O Lord, did once move upon the heart of Cyrus to show favor unto Jerusalem and her children. Do Thou now also be pleased to inspire the hearts of kings and the powers of the earth to look with a friendly eye towards this place. . . . Let them know that it is Thy good pleasure to restore the kingdom unto Israel—raise up Jerusalem as its capital, and constitute her people a distinct nation and government. . . ." (p. 457)

APPENDIX 2B: ZIONISM AND AMERICAN PATRIOTISM

The Problem:

From a letter: Richard Gottheil to Theodor Herzl, 30 November 1903 (Herzl File, Central Zionist Archives HV III/289)

There is something in which we need your help, though I know your time is even more occupied than mine is. With the help of (Cyrus) Sulzberger and Herbert Friedenwald we are starting in to gain the class of men here that we need. We had a meeting with one of them for three hours yesterday and I think we have won him over. There are one or two questions at which he still balks. But it has become apparent to us that for use here we must draw up a leaflet of some three or four pages stating in a succinct form the aims and purposes of our movement. The one great question that is uppermost in the minds of all Americans whom we approach and which will be the one most hotly contested is the patriotic question—how to square Zionism with the duties and obligations of a patriotic American citizen of the strenuous stamp of Theodore Roosevelt. It may seem curious to you; but this is the chief difficulty that we have to meet, and we have to formulate our answer to it in this leaflet as succinctly as we know how. Our conference yesterday desired me to communicate with you in order to get from you as good a working of our answer to this question as is possible. I would therefore ask you to give me sufficient of your time to think out a precise form in which we may meet this objection. If we can do this, I feel that half our battle is won. It will then be our purpose to get expressions of opinion on the basis of this statement, from Theodore Roosevelt, ex-President Cleveland and others of a like stamp. With greetings from hours to house, I am, as ever,

Most faithfully yours,
Richard Gottheil

From the Responses Of:

Theodor Herzl—"Zionism and Patriotism" (Maccabaean 9 [November 1905])

Participation in the Zionist movement means nothing which is not in the clearest and highest form in unison with the patriotism of a true American. He who labors for the creation of a home for the Jews in Palestine, a home assured by the public law and recognized by all the nations of the earth, will perform his duties as an American citizen with pleasure. . . .

. . . the Jews, even those not American citizens, will ever thankfully recall the noble spirit America has always manifested towards them and but lately in the splendid intervention of President Roosevelt to further the cause of the Russian Jews. And neither the American nor the non-American Jews will ever forget that the United States was an asylum for the persecuted. . . .

. . . the American Jews aid their beloved fatherland when they aid an unhappy people from whom they spring. That is not disloyalty, in no way, but a double measure of loyalty. (p. 243)

Israel Zangwill—"Zionism and Loyalty" (Maccabaean 6 [March 1904])

Zionism appeals to the American Jew not only as a Jew, but also as an American. It calls upon him, in one sense, no more than it calls upon his fellow citizens of all other creeds, to help wind up one of the oldest tragedies of history: a tragedy which is not even remote, but which comes knocking at his own gates in the shape of the alien immigration problem. The foremost of modern peoples is asked to help the most ancient of peoples to a resting-place in its ancient land. The mere fact that an American is a Jew is not reason for his ceasing to be an American, with all the care for the highest and broadest ideals that the name should imply. If, therefore, a non-Jewish American might well find it within his duty to help Zionism; the mere assistance in providing a home for the outraged masses of Russia and Roumania can surely not call into question the patriotism of a Jewish American. On the contrary, the better the man the better the patriot. (p. 133)

Louis D. Brandeis—"The Jewish Problem—How To Solve It" (Maccabaean 26 [June 1915])

. . . And we Jews, by our own acts, give a like definition to the term Jew. When men and women of Jewish blood suffer—because of that fact—and even if they suffer from quite different causes, our sympathy and our help goes out to them instinctively in whatever country they may live and without inquiring into the shades of their belief or unbelief.

Let no American imagine that Zionism is inconsistent with Patriotism. Multiple loyalties are objectionable only if they are inconsistent. A man is a better citizen of the United States for being also a loyal citizen of his state, and of his city; for being loyal to his family, and to his profession or trade; for being loyal to his college or his lodge. Every Irish American who contributed towards advancing home rule was a better man and a better American for the sacrifice he made. Every American Jew who aids in advancing the Jewish settlement in Palestine, though he feels that neither he nor his descendants will ever live there, will likewise be a better man and a better American for doing so. (pp. 105–10)

NOTES

1. For approaches to the study of the Jewish Community of America relating to this view, see Salo W. Baron, "American Jewish Communal Pioneering," *Steeled by Adversity* (Philadelphia: Jewish Publication Society, 1971), 127–46; Daniel J. Elazar, *People and Polity: The Organizational Dynamics of World Jewry* (Detroit: Wayne State University Press, 1989), Preface; Henry L. Feingold, *Zion in America: The Jewish Experience from Colonial Times to the Present* (New York: Hippocrene Books, 1974), Preface; Arthur Hertzberg, *The Jews of the United States*, ed. Priscilla Fishman (Jerusalem: Keter Publishing House, 1974), vii–xvii; Oscar S. Janowsky, ed., *The American Jew: A Reappraisal* (Philadelphia: Jewish Publication Society, 1964), vii–viii, 385–99; Jonathan D. Sarna, ed., *The American Jewish Experience* (New York: Holmes & Meier, 1986), xiii–xix; Marshall Sklare, ed., *The Jewish Community in America* (New York: Behrman House, 1974), 9–16.

For other formulations, see "Jewry . . . as equivalent to Judaism," Joseph L. Blau, *Judaism in America: From Curiosity to Third Faith* (Chicago: University of Chicago Press, 1976), 13–15; "Mutual enrichment and absorption inherent in the confrontation between minority and majority," Naomi W. Cohen, *Not Free to Desist: A History of the American Jewish Committee 1906–1966* (Philadelphia: Jewish Publication Society, 1972), 560; "The interplay of living cultures," Lucy S. Dawidowicz, *On Equal Terms: Jews in America 1881–1981* (New York: Holt, Rinehart & Winston, 1982), 162–64; "A Part and Apart," Arnold M. Eisen, *The Chosen People in America* (Bloomington: Indiana University Press, 1983), 3–22, 173–82; "Part of an evolving religious civilization that has persisted for millennia," Henry L. Feingold, "Series Editor's Foreword," *The Jewish People in America* 1 (Baltimore: Johns Hopkins University Press, 1992), xii; "The Jewish community as a definable entity rather than as a gathering of institutions," Lloyd P. Gartner, *History of the Jews of Cleveland* (Cleveland: Western Reserve Historical Society, 1978), xii; "Judaism is tied up organically with a specific people, indeed, a nation," Nathan Glazer, *American Judaism*, 2d ed. (Chicago: University of Chicago Press, 1972), 3; "Jewish continuity in America in a transformed community," Calvin Goldscheider, *Jewish Continuity and Change: Emerging Patterns in America* (Bloomington: Indiana University Press, 1986), xiv; "Consensual identity," Arthur Aryeh Goren, "Strategies of Survival: American Jews and the Uses of Pluralism," *The American Experience in Historical Perspective*, ed. Shlomo Slonim (Ramat Gan, Israel: Turtledove Publishing, 1976), 117; "Community of fate," Ben Halpern, *The American Jew: A Zionist Analysis* (New York: Theodor Herzl Foundation, 1956), 66; ". . . the Jews . . . voluntary communities of free men, governing themselves in accord with their own interests," Oscar Handlin, *Adventure in Freedom: Three Hundred Years of Jewish Life in America* (New York: McGraw-Hill, 1954), 260; "Dual-image identity," Abraham J. Karp, *Haven and Home (New York: Schocken, 1985), 370–71; "The intertwining relationship of Judaism and the American ideal," Milton R. Konvitz, Judaism and the Ameri-*

can Idea (Ithaca: Cornell Press, 1978), Preface; "The Jewish community . . . [as] conscious about the incompatibility of integration and survival," Charles S. Liebman, *The Ambivalent American Jew: Politics, Religion, and Family in American Jewish Life* (Philadelphia: Jewish Publication Society, 1973), viii; "The Jews constitute a people . . . a tightly knit fellowship," Jacob R. Marcus, *The Colonial American Jew 1492–1776* I (Detroit: Wayne State University Press, 1970), xxiii; "Ethnic individuality," C. Bezalel Sherman, *The Jew Within American Society: A Study in Ethnic Individuality (Detroit: Wayne State University Press, 1961), v–ix; "The sense of community concerning the formation of Jewish identity,"* The *Future of the Jewish Community in America,* ed. David Sidorsky (New York: Basic Books, 1973), 20; "A certain—singular—people," Charles E. Silberman, *A Certain People: American Jews and Their Lives Today* (New York: Summit Books, 1985), 21–27; "Religio-ethnic character of American Jewry," Chaim I. Waxman, *America's Jews in Transition* (Philadelphia: Temple University Press, 1983), xxiv.

2. See, for example, Gerson D. Cohen, "From *Altneuland* to *Altneuvolk*: Toward an Agenda for Interaction Between Israel and American Jewry," *World Jewry and the State of Israel,* ed. Moshe Davis (New York: Arno Press, 1977), 237–57; Steven M. Cohen, *American Modernity and Jewish Identity* (New York: Tavistock, 1983), 154–70; Eli Ginsberg, *Agenda for American Jews,* 4th printing, with new Foreword (New York: King's Crown Press, 1964), Foreword and chapter VI: "Israel"; Arthur Hertzberg, *The Jews in America: Four Centuries of an Uneasy Encounter—A History* (New York: Simon & Schuster, 1990), especially the Introduction—"Who Are the Jews in America?"

3. Daniel J. Boorstin, "A Dialogue of Two Histories," *Commentary* 8 (1949): 316–31. Compare Jacob R. Marcus, *Early American Jewry* I (Philadelphia: Jewish Publication Society, 1951), vii–xi; Will Herberg, *Protestant-Catholic Jew: An Essay in American Religious Sociology* (New York: Doubleday, 1955), 49–54. See also, Allan Nevins, "The Essence of Biography: Character Study," *The Writing of American Jewish History,* ed. Moshe Davis and Isidore S. Meyer (New York: American Jewish Historical Society, 1957), 435.

4. See D. Sidorsky (see note 1 above), pp. 20–21.

5. Erik H. Erikson, "The Concept of Identity in Race Relations: Notes and Queries," *The Negro American,* ed. Talcott Parsons and Kenneth B. Clark (Boston: Houghton Mifflin, 1966), 247.

6. See Appendix 2A.

7. John McDonald, *A New Translation of Isaiah, Chapter XVIII, With Notes Critical and Explanatory, A Remarkable Prophecy, Respecting the Restoration of the Jews, Aided by the American Nation* (Albany: E. & E. Hosford, 1814); for the activities of Reverend McDonald in Albany, see *Collections on the History of Albany, from its Discovery to the Present Time, with Notices of Its Public Institutions and Biographical Sketches of Citizens Deceased* I (Albany: J. Munsell, 1865), 419–30; Mordecai M. Noah, *Discourse on the Restoration of the Jews* (New York: Harper & Bros., 1845), in facsimile: *Beginnings: Early American*

Judaica, ed. Abraham J. Karp (Philadelphia: Jewish Publication Society, 1975). See also, Max J. Kohler, "Some Early American Zionist Projects," *PAJHS* 8 (1900): 75–118, especially 89–90. For the prayer by Orson Hyde, see *History of the Church of Jesus Christ of Latter-Day Saints* 4, 2d rev. ed. (Salt Lake City: Deseret News, 1949), 456–59.

8. For oral documentation on this theme, see Eliahu Elath, *Harry S Truman— The Man and Statesman*, First Annual Harry S Truman Lecture (Jerusalem: Harry S Truman Research Institute, Hebrew University, 1977), 48–49; *America and the Holy Land: A Colloquium* (Jerusalem: Institute of Contemporary Jewry, Hebrew University, 1972), 43.

9. "Noah's Proclamation to the Jews, 1825," *The Jews of the United States 1790–1840* 3, ed. Joseph L. Blau and Salo W. Baron (New York: Columbia University Press, 1963), 894–95.

10. Jonathan D. Sarna, *Jacksonian Jew* (New York: Holmes & Meier Publishers, 1981), 68.

11. M. M. Noah, *Discourse* . . . (see note 7 above), p. 50.

12. This statement first appeared in Isaac Leeser's Jewish monthly *Occident* I, no. 10 (January 1844): 490. For textual background on this quotation, see Moshe Davis, "The South Florida History of the American Jewish History Center," *Proceedings of the Conference on the Writing of Regional History in the South* (New York: American Jewish History Center, Jewish Theological Seminary, 1956), 72–74.

13. Sarah Schmidt, "A Conversation with Horace M. Kallen: The Zionist Chapter of His Life," *Reconstructionist* (November 1975): 33.

14. Circular dated March–April 1898 (Nisan 5658).

15. *American Hebrew* 63 (10 June 1898): 173.

16. Solomon Schechter, *Seminary Addresses and Other Papers* (New York: Burning Bush Press, 1959), 91–92, 95.

17. See, for example, Abba Hillel Silver's ringing statement on "Mission" and "Restoration," *CCAR Yearbook*, 1935: 327. See Michael A. Meyer, "American Reform Judaism and Zionism: Early Efforts at Ideological Rapprochement," *Studies in Zionism* 7 (Spring 1983): 49–64. See also, Allon Gal, *The Changing Concept of 'Mission' in American Reform Judaism* (Cincinnati: American Jewish Archives, 1991), 10–21.

18. *CCAR Yearbook*, 1935: 103.

19. "Guiding Principles of Reform Judaism" (adopted by the Central Conference of American Rabbis, at Columbus, Ohio, May 27, 1937), *CCAR Yearbook*, 1937: 98–99.

20. *Reconstructionist* 9, no. 2 (March 3, 1944): 23.

21. For the sequence of the supportive evidence to this conclusion, see Appendix 2B. As further background, see Cyrus L. Sulzberger, "Patriotism and Zionism," *Maccabaean* (February 1904): 83–84; Julius Haber, "American Zionists Who Met Herzl," *American Zionist* (March–April 1960): 7; also his "When

Gottheil and Herzl Worked Together," *American Zionist* (January 1962): 8–9, especially the text of Gottheil's first letter to Herzl.

22. *Maccabaean* 9 (November 1905): 243.

23. Louis D. Brandeis, "The Jewish Problem—How to Solve It," *Maccabaean* (June 1915): 109; reprinted in *Brandeis on Zionism: A Collection of Addresses and Statements by Louis D. Brandeis* (Washington, D.C.: Zionist Organization of America, 1942), 28–29. See also "Address of Louis D. Brandeis," *Maccabaean* (June 1915): 31; Eisig Silberschlag, "Zionism and Hebraism in America (1897– 1921)," *Early History of Zionism in America*, ed. Isidore S. Meyer (New York: American Jewish Historical Society and Theodor Herzl Foundation, 1958), 326– 40, especially, 334–37; Bernard G. Richards, "The American Contribution to Zionism," *American Jewry: The Tercentenary and After*, ed. Eugene Kohn (New York: Reconstructionist Press, 1955), 84–93.

24. Dean Acheson, *Morning and Noon* (Boston: Houghton Mifflin, 1965), 47.

25. Compare Felix Frankfurter, "The Balfour Declaration and After: 1917– 31," *The Jewish National Home: The Second November 1917–1942*, ed. Paul Goodman (London: J. M. Dent, 1943), 47–81.

Chapter 3

American Christian Devotees in the Holy Land

Contemporary Christian Zionism has a long and honored tradition, with deep roots in biblical thought and millennialism.[1] In the United States, during the nineteenth century, there were varied manifestations of Restorationism. Among indigenous millenarian sects, some attempted to establish settlements in the Holy Land, thus declaring the imminent Advent of Christ. Individual proto-Zionist expression was manifest in theological schools, particularly among scholars of classical Hebrew and Scriptures.

Outstanding examples of such millenarian sects, though they failed, were the agricultural settlements near Jaffa of Clorinda S. Minor and Reverend G. J. Adams. A distinguished proto-Zionist scholar was Professor George Bush (1796–1859), author of *The Valley of Vision, or, The Dry Bones of Israel Revived: An Attempted Proof (From Ezekiel, Chap. xxxvii, 1–14), of the Restoration and Conversion of the Jews* (1844).[2]

Restoration also had its activist manifestation, as uniquely exemplified in the personality of Harriet Livermore (1788–1868), schoolteacher, itinerant preacher, and social belle. She moved among the Indians, whom she identified as descendants of the Ten Lost Tribes of Israel. Between 1836 and 1852, she visited Jerusalem in anticipation of the return of the Jews to the Holy Land.[3]

Toward the end of the nineteenth and into the early twentieth century, as political Zionism came to the fore, significant spokesmen in American Protestantism, as for example, the towering figure of Reinhold Niebuhr, identified with the Zionist aspiration and program.[4] They specifically urged American intercession for the return of the Jews to the Holy Land in order to alleviate their suffering in the lands of oppression. For individuals such as A. A. Berle, Jewish Restoration in the Holy Land was not a metaphor; it was the reality of a people's reformation on the soil of their history, leading to the "opportunity of world instruction in the religion of Israel, which has never been vouchsafed to any other cult in the history of mankind!"[5]

In the course of time there emerged perceptive figures of the diverse American Christian landscape whose vision was enlarged by direct physical touch with the Land of Israel. Several of these—William Eugene Blackstone, Edwin Sherman Wallace, William Foxwell Albright, John Haynes Holmes, and Walter Clay Lowdermilk—form the basis of this chapter.

WILLIAM EUGENE BLACKSTONE

"A Land Without a People, a People Without a Land"[6]

A century ago, William Blackstone (1841–1935) came as a pilgrim to the Holy Land. Accompanied by his only daughter, Flora, Blackstone left for a year-long tour of Europe and the Middle East in May 1888. Regrettably, as far as we know, he did not keep a journal. But the impress of the pilgrimage in the Holy Land can be felt throughout his subsequent writings, reflecting the immeasurable zeal it added to his humanitarian Christian Zionism. Then, as today, Zionists were concerned with the urgency of redeeming Russian Jewry. Appalled by the prospect that those expelled from Russia would be refused asylum, Blackstone asked, "What shall we see when the four millions are pushed out? . . . Will the Christian nations of this nineteenth century stand by this wreck and launch no life boat?"[7]

Blackstone's passionate dedication to a Jewish national home in the Holy Land was preceded by a rather diversified career. Beginning as a farm-insurance salesman and real-estate investor, he was eminently successful in business. However, it was his intensive study of the Bible that brought him at the age of thirty-seven to his life's consecration as "missionary evangelist." Blackstone rapidly became popular as a dispensationalist preacher and writer. His volume *Jesus Is Coming*, twice revised and expanded, was a "compact presentation of the pre-Millennialist view of the Second Coming in the context of the Jewish Dispensation, translated into some forty languages, including Yiddish, Hebrew, Chinese, Armenian, and Hindi."[8]

Only within this context of Blackstone's missionary belief can one comprehend his fervent advocacy of Zionism leading to the Memorial for America's intercession on behalf of the Jews, presented to President Benjamin Harrison and Secretary of State James G. Blaine on 5 March 1891.[9] Without entering into the details of the antagonism his teachings engendered within the Jewish community, suffice it to say that Blackstone's Zionist resolve was not shaken. He was determined to demonstrate to the Jewish world what enlightened Christian love could do for them.

Against this backdrop we can better understand Blackstone's motivation to go to the Land of Israel—to touch sacred soil and to be touched by it.[10]

Examination of one text illustrates how reality endowed sight with insight. That text is the singular article written shortly after Blackstone's return to Chicago and to rapid involvement in the Zionist cause: "May the United States Intercede for the Jews?" The following excerpts are taken from that text.

The argument of space (p.15): There is one spot toward which the eye of the Jew has turned. It has a territory of at least ten thousand square miles, with only six hundred thousand population. There is room there for two or three million more people. . . . The rains are returning, agriculture is improving, its location promises great commercial possibilities, and only an independent, enlightened, and progressive government is needed to afford a home for all Israel who wish to return. . . .

The argument of Jewry's incapability of self-government (p. 16): The names of Jewish statesmen are household words in every land. . . . Joseph, Daniel, Mordecai, Beaconsfield, Lasker, and Cremieux are only notable examples among a host of compeers. They have the brains and the wit to establish a state that shall be honorable and celebrated among the nations.

The argument that Jews do not wish to return (p. 21): *Chobebei Zion* (Lovers of Zion) Societies and *Shova Zion* (colonization) Societies have been formed by the Jews all through Russia and extended into Europe and the United States. . . . Twenty or more colonies are now established there, and they are giving the lie to the stigma, that they are not agriculturists, by actually cultivating the land as their ancestors did centuries ago.

The argument for American intercession (p. 23): A people that has freed millions of slaves, spent billions to suppress rebellion, revolutionized navies by its innovations . . . a nation that is sought by the overflow population of the world, will have no difficulty in securing respectful attention to its peaceable diplomatic efforts for oppressed Israel.

Recalling the pre-Herzlian decade in which Blackstone's Zionist espousal was published, and considering the condition of European Jewry at the time, may we not see him as opening a window to the future?[11]

By the turn of the century, the impact of Blackstone's Memorial and its argumentations was felt throughout the United States. The missionary aspects of his worldview dimmed, and the humanitarian, political implications increased. Remarkably, Blackstone's presentiments were incorporated in major statements and his visions were extolled. In 1891, President Harrison referred to Russia's cruel treatment of the Jews in his third annual message to the Congress in the spirit, if not in the actual words, of the Blackstone Memorial.[12] At the 1916 Convention of the Federation of American Zionists in Philadelphia, Blackstone was acclaimed "The Father of Zionism"—reflection of a popular view.[13] And, it is told, Justice Louis D. Brandeis himself called attention to similarities between some arguments advanced by Blackstone and Herzl's thoughts.[14] In one core argument, Blackstone preceded Herzl, as expressed in the document written after his return from the Holy Land: "And now, this very day, we stand face to face with the awful dilemma, that these millions cannot remain where they are, and yet have no other place to go. . . . This phase of the question presents an astonishing anomaly—a land without a people, and a people without a land."[15]

EDWIN SHERMAN WALLACE

"Heavenly Jerusalem . . . Jerusalem of Earth"[16]

Toward the end of the past century, Jerusalem was graced by the presence and devotion of U.S. Consul Edwin Wallace (1864–1960), "one of the most benign and well-meaning men who ever held the post in Palestine."[17] An ordained Presbyterian minister, Wallace came to Jerusalem in 1893. After five years of diligent service and study in the city, he departed, predicting that the Holy Land would inevitably be restored by the Jewish People to its ancient productivity.

In writing *Jerusalem the Holy*, Wallace had a double purpose: To awaken interest in the city's sacred memories and holy sites, and to describe Jerusalem's "present condition" as it existed in those years. Wallace's narrative is inspired by Christian commitment, but his text is factual, precisely as stated in the subtitle: "A Brief History of Ancient Jerusalem with an Account of the Modern City and Its Conditions Political, Religious, and Social."

The manner of Wallace's consular service, especially his humane intercession on behalf of those distressed people who were dispossessed under Turkish rule, may be described in the words of Rabbi Nahman of Bratslav: "Every shepherd has his own special melody according to the grass where he herds."

Wallace's "special melody" was his discernment, advocated in word and deed, that the "coming inhabitants of Palestine will be Jews."[18] This perception and his concrete acts for the well-being of the *Yishuv*, the Jewish community in the Holy Land, were promptly reported in the Hebrew press of the period with gratitude and admiration, made even more intense by the Turkish authorities' efforts to restrict Jewish immigration. Several illustrations reflect Wallace's sustained concern and ready support.

The *Havatzelet*, a newspaper appearing in Jerusalem, records an incident at the Western Wall on *Tisha B'Av*, the ninth day of the month of Av—the date of the annual commemoration of the destruction of the Temple in 70 C.E. A group of young hooligans and their parents broke in on the worshippers—among them an American rabbi from Boston—and put them to flight. Learning from the rabbi of the disturbance, and in characteristic fashion, Wallace protested to the Turkish authorities and received guarantees for future protection. Regrettably, constant vigilance could not be relaxed.[19]

Wallace's genial character also helped to placate tensions within the Jewish community, which was too often beset by inner, communal conflict. For example, he encouraged the founding of Kollel America. The agreement to elect Rabbi Moshe Yehoshua Lev Diskin, also known as the rabbi of the American Jewish community in Jerusalem, was signed in the presence of Consul Wallace: "Witness my hand and the consular seal this 26th day of January 1897."[20]

That Wallace's "special melody" had meaning for all who would listen was dramatically proclaimed by no less a figure than Eliezer Ben-Yehuda, champion of the Hebrew language reborn.[21] Wallace's distinctive statement had been made on a unique occasion in the city of Jerusalem on Sunday, 18 April 1897–a day on which Easter and Passover coincided. Gathered at the New Grand Hotel were the members of the Anglo-Jewish Maccabaean Pilgrimage led by Herbert Bentwich and a select general audience that included English Consul D. Bliss and American Consul Edwin Wallace. That evening, Israel Zangwill delivered a lecture on the subject "Life and Customs of the Ghetto." According to Ben-Yehuda, the hall was filled to overflowing, and Zangwill captivated the audience. Following Zangwill's presentation, Edwin Wallace summarized "how happy he was that he, a stranger, was privileged to hear in the mother-city of the Jews these words of one of the select of her sons." Then Wallace exclaimed, "O Christianity, how many monumental sins have my people, the Christians, sinned against this people, the Jews." And he continued, that in his country America, "there is no ghetto and never will there be a ghetto."[22]

On this triad—Christian belief, Jewish Holy Land experience, and American involvement—Edwin Wallace wrote his forceful volume, which stands to this day as a master work of research, acuity, and judgment. We select highlights of his course of reasoning.

The City as It Is Today (Chapter IV, pp. 86–87): The most careful estimate yet made was in 1892, by the missionary workers of the London Jews' Society. The result was as nearly exact as has yet been made and may safely be depended upon. According to this there are just about forty-two thousand Jews in the city and contiguous colonies, whose inhabitants are justly classed among Jerusalem residents. . . . Should the restrictions against the immigration of the Jews be removed they would come in ever increasing numbers, until the Christian and Moslem dwellers in the Holy City would be so few as to be conspicuous. As it is, nearly three-fourths of the entire population are descendants of Jacob.

Next in numerical strength are the Christians, including all sects who so call themselves. Of this part of the population nearly a half are adherents of the Greek Orthodox body. In wealth as well as in numbers this is the leading sect. The entire number of Christians is about 8,630. The Moslems number about 6,500 and though the smallest numerically, are the strongest officially.

Topography assists in the development of prophecy (Chapter V, pp. 98–99): Once the Turk gets over his animosity toward his elder brother, the Jew, there will be nothing in the way of the increase of the new city. The Jew wants to come. He is anxious to buy a plot of ground and build him a home in or near the city of his fathers. He simply asks to be let alone, freed from oppression and permitted to enjoy his religion. The land of the new city is ready for him. . . . Thus topography assists in the development of prophecy. . . .

Thus the new Jerusalem grows by accessions from every part of the globe. On its street 'all sorts and conditions' of Jews and Gentile meet and pass one another. They may be strangers to each other and ignorant of the part they are playing, but I cannot resist the belief that each is doing his part in God's plan for the rebuilding of the city and its enlargement far beyond the borders it has occupied in the past.

The Jewish national destiny (Chapter XVIII, p. 347): Jerusalem has now been practically in undisputed Moslem possession for six hundred years. How long it will continue to be is a question often asked. The weakness of the possessors is very evident. . . . Perhaps a compromise will be effected by the terms of which Palestine will be considered as neutral territory, where the Jew will be given an opportunity to work out his national destiny. The Jew has national aspirations and ideas, and a national future. Where, if not here, will his aspirations be realized and his ideas carried out?

Bringing his treatise to a climax in the final chapter "The Future of Jerusalem," Wallace triumphantly walked with the ancient prophets. He foresaw Jerusalem's centrality in a rising independent nation and proclaimed that the time had surely come "when Jew and Christian can live together without persecution on either side." For Wallace, past and present, prophecy and reality, were all parts of an organic whole: "The subject of Israel's restoration I freely admit is not a popular one now; but the unpopular of today is the universally accepted of tomorrow."[23]

WILLIAM FOXWELL ALBRIGHT

"The Near East Needs the Jews"[24]

Professor William Foxwell Albright (1891–1971), as a young scholar, labored in the Holy Land for thirteen years—1919–29, 1933–36—first as Thayer Fellow at the American School of Oriental Research in Jerusalem, then as acting director and, ultimately, as director and mentor of that institution.

In the decades that followed, even when serving at Johns Hopkins University, he never left the Land. As a mature scholar, Albright's studies led him to insist on the substantial historicity of the Mosaic tradition and the antiquity of Israelite monotheism—basic principles in his lifelong writing and teaching career.

Remarkably, however, his attachment to the Holy Land seems to have been ingrained from childhood. As Albright wrote in the third person, in his "spiritual autobiography" years afterward, he "was to live again in the Mediterranean climate of Palestine, which was in many ways so strangely reminiscent of his Chilean boyhood in La Serena and Antofagasta."[25]

Beyond the physical and climactic reminiscence, Albright's sentiments toward the Holy Land were rooted in the intensive religious experience and training he received at home. During those formative years, he was preparing in more than one sense for the distinguished scholarship that was to become the Albright hallmark. Raised in a Methodist missionary family, his religious environment was strictly evangelical Protestant. An omnivorous reader of church history and theology, he had a special interest in biblical archaeology and Oriental studies. Albright's mastery of the Hebrew language began at age sixteen, when he determined to study it on Sundays, using his father's library. Thus, by the time he came to Johns Hopkins at age twenty-two as a student and then as research fellow, the "bookworm turned archaeologist"—as Albright referred to himself—possessed "a fair elementary knowledge of Hebrew and Assyrian, together with a considerable reading knowledge of ancient history and related subjects."[26]

The rest of the scholarly odyssey over three continents is legend.[27] In his personal manner and conduct, Albright was, above all, the exemplar of scholarship. His phenomenal gifts continued to amaze his colleagues and disciples. Carl Hermann Voss wrote in a letter, dated 16 October 1987, about his " . . . unique knowledge and the light manner with which he carried the burden of being multi-lingual (26 languages, no less!) and untold centuries of history at his fingertips." Here we will deal with aspects of his spiritual biography that emphasize the Holy Land's impact on his views and intellectual approach. Albright proclaimed the solid basis of his views in primary tones: "The Ten Commandments cannot be violated with impunity by any people or any philosophical sect. The latest attempts of Nazis and Communists to set them aside and to replace the Commandments by their own party lines have resulted in orgies of slaughter almost unparalleled in history."[28]

More concretely, Albright's deep-rooted religious commitment as an active Methodist was fully supported by his wife, Ruth Norton Albright. She forged his sensitivities to problems of minorities everywhere.[29] These included his passionate interest in the fate of the pre–World War II Jewish communities in Europe and his intense interest in issues concerning the blacks in the United States. On all these matters, regardless of his position, Albright based his authoritative stance on historical analysis with special insight on contemporary affairs. While he initially maintained an intellectual neutrality to political Zionism, the cataclysmic events in Europe reshaped his views, which he expressed with great force. He evinced ardent respect for Zionist achievements, as indeed he was devoted to the State of Israel. Two texts testify: Albright's presentation to the National Conference for Palestine in Cleveland, Ohio, on 17–18 January 1947 and his essay "Israel—Prophetic Vision and Historical Fulfillment."[30]

From the Cleveland Address

Political Zionism as the only alternative to heartless cynicism (p. 12): I come before you as friend of the Arabs as well as the Jews. During my first months in the Near East, in 1919 and 1920, I oscillated rather violently between the causes of the two people, but after those first waverings I became an increasingly warm supporter of cultural Zionism, especially of the great institution on Mount Scopus. Until shortly after the outbreak of the Second World War, I remained strictly neutral on the subject of political Zionism. Recent events have made it impossible to continue this neutral attitude. The appalling situation of the Jewish people in Europe, and the steady widening of the zone in which they are declared to be an alien race with slave status, has changed my attitude. Like my friend Chancellor Magnes of the Hebrew University, who gave up lifelong pacifism when he was confronted with the monstrous reality of Hitlerism, I have been forced to adopt political Zionism as the only alternative to heartless cynicism.

The danger to the Christians from potential Moslem domination (p. 12): Palestine is, in fact, the only possibility, the only land where the Jewish people has a historical right to be, and where it has an internationally recognized legal right to dwell. . . .

The danger to the Christians from potential Moslem domination was brought home to me again and again during my fifteen years in the Near East. If Jewish Palestine must become a helpless pawn in the game of political diplomacy, so must also the Christian republic of Lebanon. What applies to the one applies remorselessly to the other.

The contributions of Jewish Palestine to civilization (p. 13): It is not easy to visualize Palestine as one of the greatest centers of medical research and practice in the world. Yet it is a fact—and a lambent fact situated in the heart of the Arab world. From Iran to Abyssinia and from Yemen to Turkey patients come to Palestine for treatment in Jewish hospitals and by Jewish physicians. Nor is it easy to imagine Jerusalem as one of the greatest centers of academic research in the world—yet it really is just that. Even in the early thirties it was possible to concentrate a greater number of investigators in almost any field of research in Jerusalem than it is, for example, in Cleveland or Baltimore, with five times the population. Now, thanks to the great influx of scholars from Europe, Jerusalem has become more of a research center in some respects than even Philadelphia.

From Albright's Essay on "Israel-Prophetic Vision and Historical Fulfillment"

What History Teaches (p. 31): No other phenomenon in history is quite so extraordinary as the unique event represented by the Restoration of Israel in the sixth and fifth centuries B.C.E. At no other time in world history, so far as is known, has a people been destroyed, and then come back after a lapse of time and re-established itself. It is utterly out of the question to seek a parallel for the recurrence of Israel's restoration after twenty-five hundred years of further history.

The vision fulfilled (p. 38): Both Jews and Christians have thus played a role in keeping alive the hope of Restoration. And so Restoration came. . . . I have never dreamed that there would be an actual Jewish State in Israel, and I must often have asserted its 'impossibility.' Yet Israel exists, and the vision has been fulfilled. . . . What is going to happen next? Are the words of the Prophets merely archaic survivals of a naive age? Not at all. God will keep His covenant with His people, if His people obey the Divine commands.

With all his appreciation for the People of Israel—ancient and contemporary—Albright's Christian belief was supreme. Yet that very deep-rooted Christian commitment, combined with his scientific approach to archaeology and the Bible, was marked by his need to seek new avenues of cooperation between the Muslims, Jews, and Christians.

> Surely it is not too much to hope for revival of Islam as a religion, in which *Ijtihad* will replace the traditional *jihad*, or holy war. The contributions which Moslems, Jews and Christians working together in peace, could make to the civilization of the west, which we jointly represent, are incalculable.[31]

JOHN HAYNES HOLMES

"This Zionist cause must succeed"[32]

For three weeks in February 1929, John Haynes Holmes (1879–1964) travelled the length and breadth of the Holy Land, together with his wife and son. The immediate purpose of the visit was to participate in the dedication of the Nathan and Lina Straus Health Center in Jerusalem, but the underlying motivation, as Holmes put it, was to inspect and inquire into the Zionist cause at its source. Together with his close friend Judah Magnes, Holmes travelled freely throughout the country by car and horseback and was received with open arms wherever he went. In settlements, towns, and cities, he conferred with spokesmen of the Arab, Jewish, and English communities. Zionist moderates with whom Holmes conferred, in addition to Magnes, were Hans Kohn and Henrietta Szold. The capstone of his experience was the publication of *Palestine Today and Tomorrow: A Gentile's Survey of Zionism*.[33] As the volume amply demonstrates, a lifetime of study and active concern had anticipated the mission.

For more than half a century, John Haynes Holmes was a distinctive, highly individualistic figure on the American religious scene.[34] Formally a Unitarian minister, Holmes was a pathfinder in the advancement of the Unitarian Universal fellowship. However, his intense involvement in varied and far-reaching social activities in the spirit of Christian socialism of the period led him toward the decision to become an "independent" as minister of the Community Church in New York City. From his free pulpit, he rose to the stature of foremost liberal minister in America, eloquent in speech and letters.

Of all the ideals Holmes espoused from the days of his youth to the very end of his years, his pacifism was unswerving. "From every point of view," he wrote during World War I, "from the standpoint of things spiritual as well as things material, from the standpoint of the future as well as the present— war is the antithesis of life . . . therefore, in the name of life and for the sake of life, do I declare to you that war must be condemned universally and unconditionally."[35]

Although deeply troubled by the turbulent events of the mid-twentieth century, Holmes remained steadfast in his pacifist conviction, parting in views from some of his noblest and devoted friends. It is remarkable to consider, for example, how he coped with such men as Mahatma Gandhi, Stephen Wise, and Judah Magnes, who were all equally tormented in those critical decades but who came to other conclusions, each in accordance with his own pacifist conscience.

Holmes's contact with Gandhi was not as frequent as with the others, but the shared commitment was intense and deep. In October 1947, when Holmes visited India, he met with Gandhi on the very day of his arrival. The overwhelming concern was the riots that had broken out following the establishment of the separate nations of India and Pakistan. Despite massacres, refugees, and human agony, Gandhi maintained his stance of nonviolence. For Holmes, this was the supreme virtue, making Gandhi, as he proclaimed, one of the half-dozen "spiritual saviours of the race."[36] Nevertheless, Holmes differed from Gandhi on the issue of Jewish self-determination in Palestine. Unlike his paragon of world pacifism, Holmes stood committed to Zionism and its implications for the Middle East. While he argued against a political state, he ardently supported a spiritual and cultural homeland in Zion.[37]

Holmes' affirmation of Zionism reached back to 1914 when he was influenced by Richard Gottheil, then president of the Federation of American Zionists. In Zionism, Holmes saw a "recovered, restored, regenerated Israel . . . for what the Jew is seeking in Zion is not only his country but his soul."[38] As a Unitarian Universalist, Holmes believed in trying to relate the Bible to the Holy Land.

These thoughts were further buttressed by Holmes's intimate association with Judah Magnes and Stephen S. Wise. In the case of Magnes, Holmes was inspired by his spiritual philosophy of Zionism and his concept of the need for a binational state. Although they were separated by vast distance, the men remained in active communication with each other. Holmes read and reacted to Magnes's addresses to the Hebrew University at the annual academic convocation. Again, in this special context, Magnes was a symbol of pacifism. Even when Magnes chose to adopt a prowar, nonpacifist stance, given the choice between battling the evils of Hitler and inviolate pacifism, Holmes's faith in Magnes's unique spiritual quality was not diminished.[39]

The relationship with Stephen Wise, although of a more intimate nature, was more complex. Even if Holmes could not agree with the seeming ambivalence of Wise's pacifist position, he did not hesitate to cooperate with many of his programs. Carl Hermann Voss recalls that when Wise announced a protest march of Jewish leaders and organizations against Hitlerism in the early spring of 1933, Holmes initiated a request to take part. Holmes—the only Christian participant—strode beside Wise on the march from Columbus Circle to Union Square. Silently they walked together, leading tens of thousands of Jews in this anti-Nazi manifestation.[40]

This was Holmes the pacifist and reformer Unitarian minister, and unmitigated Christian Zionist, who said on the eve of his departure for the Holy Land on 10 January 1929:

> I cannot say that I am going to Palestine with an open and unprejudiced mind. I am afraid I am a little prejudiced. Ever since the Zionist movement was started, the romance of the idea has appealed to me. Zionism thrills me and the romance of it all appeals to me most strongly. Therefore I say that I am not going out there unprejudiced. That is impossible for anyone who has any imagination and is the least bit farsighted. Yet Mrs. Holmes and I are going with open minds, and I think we will return as the messenger which Moses sent into the Holy Land. "Glad pilgrims with glad tidings."[41]

Holmes's perceptions are expressed at length in his volume *Palestine Today and Tomorrow: A Gentile's Survey of Zionism*. In essence, Holmes declared his position shortly before his departure from the Holy Land in a prescient interview given to the distinguished *New York Times* correspondent Joseph M. Levy: "Success of Zionism: a Matter of Time."[42] The following extracts are from that interview.

> *For the sake of humanity itself*: The Zionist cause must succeed for the sake of humanity itself. Here in Palestine I have discovered a laboratory in which are being worked out the problems of human kind. Here, in essence, is every problem and difficulty that is now baffling the world. Here, in its most intense form, is the problem of nationalism, here is the question of racial differences, prejudices and fears. Here there are religious divisions and hatreds in their most intense and bitter forms. Just because these problems in Palestine are of such enormous difficulty they present a perfect laboratory for solution, and the Jew has come like the scientist with a test tube, with his vision of justice, brotherhood and peace, to work it out.

> *Zionism's need of support from America*: The present situation is critical. Things done or not done now may determine all the future. I have come to feel intensely the pressing need of certain things, thus the support of Zionism in America and elsewhere must be greatly increased in everything that goes to making up a great constructive enterprise such as knowledge, skill, labor, devotion. When I get home, I shall plead with all men, Jews and Gentiles, to give to this cause as never before.

The destiny of the land is spiritual: Above all, what is needed in Palestine is patience, moderation and steadfast idealism of all good men. There must be no resort to violence, dictation, arbitrary rule. The law of justice and the spirit of love which I have found in the minds of many men and women must be made a force in the life of Palestine, and not merely a sentiment in the hearts of individuals. The destiny of this land is spiritual and not material. Here, as nowhere else, the Kingdom of God is possible, and the building of that Kingdom is the task of today and not of tomorrow.

With eyes open and heart attuned, John Haynes Holmes returned to America worried that his pacifist ideals would not be realized in Palestine, yet determined to help build its future: "I came away from Palestine knowing a darker side of Zionism than I had ever dreamed before, but with an assurance as to its future as firm-rooted as the everlasting hills. These great leaders of the cause . . . know what they are doing, and that it is not in vain."[43]

WALTER CLAY LOWDERMILK

"Thou shalt inherit the holy earth"[44]

Between the years 1939 and 1964, Walter (1888–1974) and Inez Lowdermilk came to the Holy Land seven times. That first work visit in 1939 was a dream come true for Walter Lowdermilk. His goal was to study the land record of Palestine, "because the Bible presents the most authentic and longest written record of any nation except China."[45] Early in the course of his inventive and prodigious labor, land conservationist Walter Lowdermilk laid to rest the myth about the limited absorptive capacity of Palestine, thus scientifically substantiating the Zionist argument. During those critical decades Lowdermilk was a clarion voice for reclaiming the "Bible lands," for Zion redeemed, for "recognition of great possibilities of development of the unique geographic feature of the Holy Land."[46]

Walter Lowdermilk was an inspiring scientist—a model of "intelligent service," to use Franklin Littell's description—and always remained to those who knew him the simple, unassuming, farmer-like person possessed of great strength, marked by fortitude "in both physique and in character."[47] In the span of fifty years, he travelled, worked, and studied in some thirty-four countries on four continents. Born in Liberty, North Carolina, the young Walter (of Methodist training and background) moved with his family to the West, where he was taught the art of combining lumbering, farming, and engineering. Later a Rhodes scholar at Oxford and a forestry student in Germany, Lowdermilk devoted his life to famine prevention. His steadfast dedication to this cause remained his guiding lodestar all the days of his life. "Civilization is running a race with famine, and the outcome is still in doubt"; he taught this to everyone he could reach. He sought to secure links between people, their land, and natural resources.

No wonder that in 1939 he became enamored at first sight with the Jewish colonists in the Holy Land who were reclaiming a man-made desert. Beyond the Jews who were the human instruments, mankind would be the beneficiary.

> In the midst of general decadence in the Near East, there is hope in Palestine: hope made real by the Jewish colonies which are showing the most remarkable devotion to reclamation of land that I have seen in any country of the New or Old World. The result of their efforts this far is an inspiration and splendid achievement. Unknown to themselves these colonies have laid the foundation for a Greater Palestine and have shown the way for the resurrection of the Near East as a whole.[48]

During that first contact with the Holy Land, Walter Lowdermilk learned another lesson. He witnessed the reality of persecution and homelessness, realizing that it could happen in our times. He saw the cargo boats, too often unseaworthy, floating on a steaming sea but unable to disembark their passengers who had fled the Nazi inferno. "The laws governing the transportation of animals for slaughter in the United States," he wrote, "do not permit conditions like those which some of the intelligentsia of Central Europe had to undergo in those old boats on the Mediterranean."[49] In Beirut, he interviewed refugees from Czechoslovakia at a quarantine station. He was astonished at their high level of European culture. While they had no passports, no country, no recourse to aid or advice, they had courage and fortitude.

With the dual perception of "Land and People," Lowdermilk introduced reclamation methods of farming, planting on the contour, rows of vineyards and orchards, with stone walls and broad bench terraces. Then came the vision of the "Jordan Valley Authority" inspired by the U.S. Tennessee Valley Authority.

Tangible and earnest application were the order of the day. Fortunately for scholarship, on several occasions Lowdermilk recorded in vivid language, yet with accent on detail, the remarkable scientific achievement begun in those years and carried forward over several decades.[50] By the time he had plotted out the inventory of land resources, trained his students and successors, and enjoyed the work of his hands, Lowdermilk could state with true satisfaction: "I had written my biography, not with words, but with land and water conservation on the slopes and fields of this sacred land."[51] As one of his listeners quipped at the 1946 sessions of the Anglo-American Committee of Inquiry on Palestine in Washington: "Now we know that Palestine is a land of 'Lowdermilk and honey.'"[52]

As the Lowdermilks themselves attested, the period they spent in Israel was the happiest time of their lives. Inez was the daughter of a Methodist minister and had served as a missionary in China in her early years. Fortifying her husband's spiritual insights as they worked together in the "Bible Lands," she was his "Comrade and Inspiration," to whom he dedicated his volume *Palestine Land of Promise*.[53] In a rare and as yet unpublished oral history document, Inez illuminates many of her husband's thoughts in the section entitled "Written Questions and Answers."[54] That magnificent, comprehensive text includes citations from Walter Lowdermilk's 7,000–page diary, also unpublished. Written on 17 May 1957, before their departure from Israel, this excerpt is a retrospective meditation characterizing the essential Lowdermilk as scientist, Christian Zionist, idealist:

Sabbath Meditations on our Balcony in our Haifa House: What a blessing Moses rendered humanity when he proclaimed this Seventh Day for complete rest. Israel keeps this commandment more strictly than any other nation I know. I thoroughly enjoy it.

Today is my last Sabbath in Israel before my retirement and emeritus status and my 70th birthday.

Again I visualize the terrible erosion of this Holy Land as I first [saw] it in 1939 and the human erosion of the people, who with their herds had brought to the Holy Earth such destruction and had created here a man-made desert.

Today as I think of my last trip around the country, I felt as if I had written my autobiography in the valleys and on the hills of Israel as I saw the many measures of conservation such as countless miles of contour terraces, grassed water ways, check dams to hold storm runoff, in great numbers large and small reservoirs and other water saving devices applied by my soil conservation 'boys' in drainage and irrigation. . . . Israel is already a Pilot Project for two thirds of mankind, who must change over from subsistence [agriculture] in economies to modern ways if they are to give their peoples a more abundant life.

Israelis realize that there is much to do to prepare the Good Earth to support present and future generations. In a larger sense everyone is a farmer for the stewardship of the Holy Earth is given to the Human Race.

When one gets out on the land as I do and work with farmers, there is some sort of a common denominator when one works with soils as they relate to welfare of humanity, one talks a common language.

Love of land and determination of these people to redeem the land has made Israel an example for emerging nations.[55]

To summarize, the essential quality of the select figures I discuss in this chapter is their Christian conviction, marked by inner awakening and heightened attachment to the Jewish Return, and stimulated by their service in the Land itself. Through their activities, they came to view the Holy Land not just as a place of refuge for the homeless, but as the physical center for the corporate spirit of the Jewish People. Following their experiences, each in his own way contributed of his specialized capacities and served as an exemplary figure on the wide American scene in the exposition of Jewish self-realization in the Holy Land. In the fullness of that dedication and achievement, these personalities passed into history, but history has not passed them by.

NOTES

1. For an insightful interpretation of the term "Christian Zionism," see Carl Frederick Ehle, Jr., "Prolegomena to Christian Zionism in America: The Views of Increase Mather and William E. Blackstone Concerning the Doctrine of the Restoration of Israel" (Ph.D. diss., New York University, 1977), 339–45. See also, his wide-ranging bibliography, which includes important primary sources on Christian Zionism and Jewish Restoration, pp. 358–75. In this chapter, I distinguish between those American Protestant spokesmen who served as standard-bearers of Jewish Restoration and the proportionally smaller numbers of Protestant biblical scholars and theologians who had their "Christocentric piety renewed" by personal contact with the Holy Land. See Robert T. Handy, "Holy Land Experiences of Two Pioneers of Christian Ecumenism: Schaff and Mott," *Contemporary Jewry: Studies in Honor of Moshe Davis*, ed. Geoffrey Wigoder (Jerusalem: Institute of Contemporary Jewry, 1984), 65–78.

2. See Shalom Goldman, "Professor George Bush: American Hebraist and Proto-Zionist," *American Jewish Archives (AJA)* 43, no. 1 (Spring/Summer 1991): 58–69.

3. For a more detailed characterization of Harriet Livermore, see Ehle, Jr. (see note 1 above), pp. 213–15.

4. David A. Rausch and Carl Hermann Voss, "A Heritage of Prophetic Ministry: A Seventieth Birthday Tribute to Franklin Hamlin Littell," *Christian Jewish Relations* 20, no. 2 (1987): 5–17. Other contemporary scholars, such as Ronald R. Stockton, posited the view that "Christian Zionism is more a mainstream cultural theme linked to American self-identity and to perception of America as a moral community." See Ronald R. Stockton, "Christian Zionism: Prophecy and Public Opinion," *Middle East Journal* 41, no. 2 (Spring 1987): 251.

5. A. A. Berle, *The World Significance of a Jewish State* (New York: Mitchell Kennerly, 1918), 16.

6. "May the United States Intercede for the Jews?" *Our Day* 8, no. 46 (October 1891). Appended to *Palestine for the Jews: A Copy of the Memorial*

Presented to President Harrison, March 5, 1891 (Illinois, 1891), 17; reprinted in the Arno Press anthology *Christian Protagonists for Jewish Restoration* (New York: Arno Press, 1977).

7. Ibid., p. 15.

8. William E. Blackstone, *Jesus Is Coming* (Chicago: Fleming H. Revell; Los Angeles: Bible House, 1908): "Preface to the Third Revision," p. 5. It is interesting to note, as Yaakov Ariel points out in his volume, *On Behalf of Israel: American Fundamentalist Attitudes Toward Jews, Judaism and Zionism, 1865–1945* (Brooklyn, N.Y.: Carlson Publishing, 1991), 59: "The Hebrew version of *Jesus Is Coming*, published in 1925, carries a different title from the original one. In Hebrew it is called *Hofaat Ha-Mashiach Ha-Shnia (The Second Appearance of the Messiah). . . .* The Hebrew title stresses the fact that the Messiah had already come once before, while in the original title this point is taken for granted."

9. The Memorial is reprinted in *Christian Protagonists for Jewish Restoration* (see note 6 above), pp. 1–14. For a perceptive analysis of Blackstone's evangelical Christian commitment to Zionism, see David D. Brodeur, "Christians in the Zionist Camp: Blackstone and Hechler," *Faith and Thought* 100, no. 3 (London 1972–73): 284–98. See Yaakov Ariel's comprehensive discussion of Blackstone's Zionist and missionary activity in his volume (see note 8 above). See also, Gershon Greenberg, "Fundamentalists, Israel and Theological Openness," *Christian Jewish Relations* 19, no. 5 (September 1986): 29–31. It is of interest to note that in a series published in Eretz Israel for young readers, Dr. N. M. Gelber wrote a volume entitled *The Righteous of the Peoples of the World as Heralds of the Jewish Renascence* (Tel Aviv: Omanut, 1931, Hebrew). For the section on Blackstone, see pp. 151–59.

10. The literature on Blackstone is not sparse, and the primary sources are available. See Anita Libman Lebeson, "Zionism Comes to Chicago" (note 3), *Early History of Zionism in America*, ed. Isidore S. Meyer (New York: American Jewish Historical Society and Theodor Herzl Foundation, 1958), 155–90. For editorial sources relating to the controversy around Blackstone, including citations from the Hebrew press, see Marnin Feinstein, "The Blackstone Memorial," *Midstream* 10, no. 2 (June 1964): 89. Examples of how opposition mounted and fluctuated are the leaders in *Hapisgoh* 3, nos. 1 and 4 (Maryland, 8 and 29 May 1891). See also Abraham G. Duker, "Reverend William Blackstone—Zionist," *New Palestine* 31, no. 21 (7 March 1941): 9–11.

11. See "The Jews returning," in W. E. Blackstone (see note 8 above), pp. 210–11.

12. M. Feinstein (see note 10 above), p. 89.

13. A. L. Lebeson (see note 10 above), pp. 169–70.

14. I. L. Kenen, "Blackstone: Forgotten American-Zionist Tradition," *Jerusalem Post*, 4 March 1966. See Brandeis's letter to Blackstone, 22 May 1916, *Brandeis Papers*, University Archives and Records Center of the University of Louisville. We thank Janet B. Hodgson for the courtesy of sending to Jerusalem that letter and other Blackstone correspondence.

15. Perhaps it is this allusion by Brandeis that led to widespread belief that the oft-quoted formulation—"a land without a people and a people without a land"—originated with Herzl. My own examination of the sources led me to the conclusion that the statement is genuinely Blackstone's. I consulted Alex Bein, the authoritative Herzl scholar, who informed me that he had pursued this question at Ben-Gurion's request. It was Bein's conclusion that the reference could be found in Israel Zangwill's writings. The closest source suggested by Bar Ilan University scholar Stuart A. Cohen is to be found in Zangwill's "Zion, Whence Cometh My Help": "Palestine needs a people; Israel needs a country," *Speeches, Articles and Letters of Israel Zangwill*, ed. Maurice Simon (London: Soncino Press, 1937). However, Zangwill's address was delivered in 1903, while Blackstone published his statement in 1891. In concluding that this formulation originated with Blackstone, I am not unmindful of Adam W. Garfinkle's study "On the Origin, Meaning, Use and Abuse of a Phrase," *Middle Eastern Studies* 27, no. 4 (October 1991): 539–50. Garfinkle maintains that the earliest known reference of this concept is found in Lord Shaftesbury, in a letter written in 1853. See Garfinkle, p. 543 and note 38. He further suggests the possibility that there was a second inventor of the phrase in the United States, namely John Lawson Stoddard of Brookline, Massachusetts. According to Garfinkle, Stoddard first used the thought in a public lecture in 1891, the very year Blackstone published his statement. Whether Stoddard garnered his statement from Blackstone, or vice versa, it is intriguing to ponder that indeed Blackstone's contact with the Holy Land brought forth his unique formulation.

16. From Edwin Sherman Wallace's dedication page of *Jerusalem the Holy* (Edinburgh: Oliphant, Anderson & Ferrier, 1898).

17. Frank E. Manuel, *The Realities of American-Palestine Relations* (Washington, D.C.: Public Affairs Press, 1949), 88.

18. E. S. Wallace (see note 16 above), p. 358. See the unpublished dissertation of Ron Bartur, "American Consular Aid to Jews in Eretz Israel in the Twilight of the Ottoman Rule, Until the Outbreak of the First World War, 1856–1914," pp. 145–51.

19. David Menahem Deinard, "Expressing Thanks," *Havatzelet* (17 Elul 1895, Hebrew): 405.

20. See Simcha Fishbane, "The Founding of Kollel America Tifereth Yerushalayim," *American Jewish Historical Quarterly* 44, no. 2 (December 1974): 120–36.

21. See *Hazvi*, 26 Shevat 1897 (Hebrew).

22. I am indebted to David Geffen who brought this source to my attention in his article "A 'new literature' of Jewish pilgrimage," including excerpts of Wallace's remarks. See *Jerusalem Post Supplement*, 13 April 1987: 18–19. For a study of the Maccabaean pilgrimage, see Stuart A. Cohen, "The First Anglo-Jewish Pilgrimage to Palestine: 1897," *Zionism* 3 (April 1981): 71–85.

23. E. S. Wallace (see note 16 above), p. 355.

24. *New Palestine* 32, no. 9 (23 January 1947): 12–13.

25. Louis Finkelstein, ed., *American Spiritual Autobiographies: Fifteen Self Portraits* (New York: Harper & Bros., 1948), 158.

26. Ibid., 163–66.

27. See *Eretz Israel* 9, "W. F. Albright Volume" (Jerusalem, 1969), particularly the editor's note and the tribute by Y. Yadin. See also, an earlier appraisal, Samuel I. Feigen, "Professor William Foxwell Albright," *Bitzaron* (February 1947, Hebrew): 303–13.

28. L. Finkelstein (see note 25 above), p. 177.

29. Ruth Albright was not averse to criticize certain activities of the Church. See, for example, David Klatzker, "American Catholic Travelers to the Holy Land, 1861–1929," *Catholic Historical Review* 74, no. 1 (January 1988): 61–62.

30. Moshe Davis, ed., *Israel: Its Role in Civilization* (New York: Harper & Bros., 1956), 31–38.

31. "Palestine in a Brave New World," *New Palestine* 32, no. 17 (11 September 1942): 12.

32. *New York Times*, 17 March 1929: 8.

33. John Haynes Holmes, *Palestine Today and Tomorrow: A Gentile's Survey of Zionism* (1929; reprint, New York: Arno Press, 1977). See David Klatzker, "American Christian Travelers to the Holy Land 1821–1939" (Ph.D. diss., Temple University, 1987).

34. See the definitive works of Carl Hermann Voss, ed., *A Summons Unto Men: An Anthology of the Writings of John Haynes Holmes* (New York: Simon & Schuster, 1971); his *Rabbi and Minister: The Friendship of Stephen S. Wise and John Haynes Holmes* (Cleveland: World Publishing, 1964). Beyond the primary and interpretive sources in those major works, I am indebted to Carl Voss for his friendship in sharing with me the wealth of his knowledge.

35. "Is War Ever Justifiable?" Sermon, *The Messiah Pulpit*, cited in C. H. Voss, ed., *A Summons Unto Men* (see note 34 above), p. 116.

36. Ibid., p. 71.

37. See C. H. Voss, "John Haynes Holmes: Through Gentile Eyes" (ms., pp. 5–6); *They Were Not Silent: American Christians For and Against Israel, From the Wilson Era To The Present* (Valley Forge, Pa.: Trinity Press International, in press).

38. J. H. Holmes (see note 33 above), p. 81.

39. In 1940, in his address "Hard Thinking—A University Task," Magnes stated: "The military victory over the German Satan must be overwhelming, and we must all of us, young and old, do what we can to bring this about. There must be no equivocation about this. No sacrifice can be too great for this." Quoted in C. H. Voss, "John Haynes Holmes: Through Gentile Eyes" (see note 37 above), p. 24. See Arthur A. Goren, ed., *Dissenter in Zion* (Cambridge: Harvard University Press, 1982), 205. I am grateful to Professor Goren for showing me his file of the Holmes–Magnes correspondence, particularly the "Dear Magnes" letter of 29 May 1939.

40. C. H. Voss, *Rabbi and Minister* (see note 34 above), pp. 285–86.

41. "Nathan Straus," *Hadassah Newsletter* 9, no. 4 (January 1929).

42. "Success of Zionism: A Matter of Time," *New York Times*, 17 March 1929: 8.

43. J. H. Holmes (see note 33 above), pp. 88–89. For Holmes' analysis of the Arab-Jewish conflict of interests and his suggestions for conceivable solutions to the problem, see pp. 249–54. See also the passage on the "Gifts of Zionism to American Jewry," cited in *A Summons Unto Men* (see note 34 above), pp. 198–99.

44. From "The Eleventh Commandment," written in biblical cadence and broadcast over the radio by Dr. Lowdermilk in Jerusalem, June 1939, and dedicated to the Palestinian Jewish villages whose good stewardship of the earth inspired this idea: "Thou shalt inherit the holy earth as a faithful steward, conserving its resources and productivity from generation to generation. Thou shalt safeguard thy fields from soil erosion, thy living waters from drying up, thy forests from desolation, and protect thy hills from overgrazing by the herds, that thy descendants may have abundance forever. If any shall fall in this stewardship of the land, thy fruitful fields shall become sterile stony ground or wasting gullies, and thy descendants shall decrease and live in poverty or perish from off the face of the earth." *Palestine Land of Promise* (New York: Harper; London: V. Gollancz, 1944), frontispiece.

45. Ibid., p. 2.

46. Speech at ground-breaking ceremony of Samuel Brody building in the "Lowdermilk School of Agricultural Engineering," Haifa, 15 June 1964.

47. In letters from Franklin Littell, January 1987, and Carl Hermann Voss, October 1987.

48. *Hadassah Magazine* 24, no. 3 (May 1944): 13.

49. W. C. Lowdermilk (see note 44 above), pp. 8–9.

50. See especially his "Jewish Colonization in Palestine," *Menorah Journal* 28, no. 3 (October–December 1940): 311–25; "The Right to Land Use with Particular Reference to Palestine," ibid. 29, no. 2 (April–June 1941): 104–10. His "The Land," *Assignment in Israel*, ed. Bernard Mandelbaum (New York: Harper & Bros., 1960), 168–83; also his "Israel, A Pilot Project for Total Development of Water Resources," *The Time of Harvest: Essays in Honor of Abba Hillel Silver*, ed. Daniel Jeremy Silver (New York: Macmillan; London: Collier-Macmillan, 1963), 215–26. See also, Emanuel Neumann, *In the Arena* (New York: Herzl Press, 1976), 175–82; Inez Marks Lowdermilk, *All in a Lifetime: An Autobiography* (California: n.p., 1985), chapters 13, 19, 20.

51. W. C. Lowdermilk, "The Land" (see note 50 above), pp. 182–83.

52. E. Neumann (see note 50 above), p. 182. See also, on same page, Neumann's story of President Roosevelt and the Lowdermilk volume.

53. See her pamphlet, *Modern Israel: Fulfillment of Prophecy, A Christian Speaks Out* (Berkeley, Calif.: Christian Committee for Israel, 197?).

54. Interview conducted by Malca Chall, *Walter Clay Lowdermilk: Soil, Forest, and Water Conservation and Reclamation in China, Israel, Africa and the United States* (in two volumes), at University of California Bancroft Library, Berkeley Regional Oral History Office. I am grateful to Carl Alpert for his advice

and help in attaining this text and other primary sources pertaining to this book. Copies of the text are available at the Technion Library in Haifa; also at the Jewish National and University Library in Jerusalem.

    55. Ibid., p. 623a.

PART II

REPRESENTATIVE
JEWISH PERSONALITIES

Chapter 4

Isaac Leeser of the Historical School

During the nineteenth century, the American Jewish community was more beneficiary than benefactor of world Jewry. The rapidly developing Jewish community in America was preoccupied with problems of its own growth, and urgent local needs were given prior consideration. Overseas aid was, therefore, limited. To the extent that the Jews of America felt an obligation to their brethren, this sense of responsibility embraced primarily those who had emigrated to the United States.

Appeals from Eretz Israel fell into another category entirely. The love and dedication of generations had its impact even upon people who were culturally and geographically far removed from Palestine. Printed circulars in Hebrew had found their way to responsive Jews in Colonial times, and direct contact with the Holy Land increased as the Jews in America grew in numbers and in strength.[1] Already in the formative years of the American Jewish community, activities for the benefit of Eretz Israel stemmed from a variety of spiritual and practical reasons.[2] Some were motivated by the traditional belief in the coming of the Messiah, while others were moved by the desire to provide a place of refuge for those leaving Europe. Some thought in international political terms, beginning to hope for the resettlement of Jews in Eretz Israel as a result of the changing political events in Europe; still others began to dream of the realization of the Return as a fulfillment of Jewish aspirations for the redemption of the Jews and mankind. These views, which found appeal across the Jewish community as a whole in the United States in the nineteenth century, came to the fore in the views of the Historical School of Judaism, especially through the personality, thought, and action of Isaac Leeser.

There are abundant studies of Isaac Leeser's pioneer leadership on the American Jewish scene in mid-nineteenth century.[3] However, the fullness of his vision with respect to Eretz Israel has not been sufficiently accentuated.[4] In those decades, questions connected with the transmission and distribution of money to Eretz Israel—rather than those questions with social and political connotations for the restoration of the Jews in the Holy Land—aroused the greatest interest. Mordecai Noah's political formulation of America's role in the possible Restoration was still in the nature of a "discourse." The problem at hand was practical aid to the residents in Zion. The Jews of the *galut*, whether religious or not, felt it incumbent to give financial support to the communities in Jerusalem. Whoever appealed on their behalf was not turned away indiscriminately. And such appeals were not lacking.

The settlements in Jerusalem had sent representatives to the United States as far back as the eighteenth century. Among the first of these were Moses Malki (1758) and Haim Isaac Carigal (1771). Their success stimulated others, including frauds and swindlers who appropriated for themselves the money they had collected. Furthermore, echoes of the disputes about the division of the sums reached America. Eretz Israel Sephardim quarreled with Ashkenazim, and Ashkenazim argued among themselves. In addition, Jews in America began to realize that the salaries and expenses of the solicitors were deducted from the collections, resulting in smaller proceeds to the inhabitants of Jerusalem. American Jews, not wishing to see their contributions squandered, and attempting to secure transfer of the sums *in toto*, organized the *Hebrat Terumat haKodesh* (Society for Offerings to the Sanctuary) in 1833 under the presidency of Israel B. Kursheedt, an outstanding figure from Congregation B'nai Jeshurun in New York City. The purpose of this society was to raise annual gifts from its members and to transfer the money directly to the inhabitants of the "four holy cities"—Jerusalem, Hebron, Safed, and Tiberias. In this way they hoped to put an end to unnecessary expenditures. When they collected a sizable sum, they transmitted it directly to Rabbi Hirsch Lehren—the original founder of *Hebrat Terumat haKodesh* in Amsterdam who was to transfer and allocate the monies at his discretion.

In time of peace it might have been possible to supply the needs of Eretz Israel from European sources, without resorting to aid from the United States. But, when revolutionary disturbances engulfed European Jewry, collections failed. The wars of 1848–1849 in Europe substantially reduced the contributions by European Jews for Eretz Israel. Thus, the Jews in Eretz Israel turned to their coreligionists in free and peaceful America.

Two messengers, Joseph Schwarz and Zadok Levy, were dispatched in 1849. Joseph Schwarz, whose works are still studied, was the first modern scholar of Palestinography. Isaac Leeser translated Schwarz's first volume into English in 1850 and published it under the title *A Descriptive Geography and Brief Historical Sketch of Palestine.*

For Leeser this task was in every way a labor of love and dedication. In his conclusion to the "Translator's Preface," he wrote:

> It is hoped that this book will contribute to extend the knowledge of Palestine, and rouse many to study the rich treasures which our ancient literature affords, and also to enkindle sympathy and kind acts for those of our brothers, who still cling to the soil of our ancestors, and love the dust in which the many saints of our race sleep in death awaiting a glorious resurrection and an immortal life.[5]

The two distinguished emissaries were eagerly welcomed by the American leaders. Their mission, according to Isaac Leeser's testimony, was to help set up a society that would collect annual contributions. Leeser explained that, unlike the situation in 1833 when the *Hebrat Terumat ha-Kodesh* had been organized, "communication by steam-packets has made every country easily accessible, and commercial connexions have now been formed all over the world, so that remittance can be made promptly from here to Palestine, in a manner formerly impossible."[6] The messengers issued proclamations in the name of the inhabitants of Jerusalem. Leeser calculated that, if each of the forty organized congregations in the country were to contribute from ten to twenty-five dollars annually, it might be possible "to protect the poor of Palestine, and to snatch them from the necessity of receiving aid from the missionaries, those inveterate foes of our religion."[7] Lesser announced the formation of a committee of eight whose members would receive donations.[8] But the proposal by Leeser and his friends was not realized for two reasons. First, the Jews of America were not yet experienced in collecting funds. They intuitively responded to immediate needs rather than to future plans. Second, each faction in Eretz Israel felt it necessary to protect its own interests by sending its own messengers.

In 1849, Rabbi Aaron Selig Ashkenazi, a representative of the chief Ashkenazi group that called itselves the *Perushim* of Jerusalem, arrived in America. Rabbi Ashkenazi, systematic and enterprising, succeeded in rallying wide support, even though many forces on the American Jewish scene were opposed to his methods. One of his main achievements was to attract Samuel Myer Isaacs to his project. Isaacs was the prominent Rabbi of

Shaarey Tefila Congregation in New York City; among his manifold activities on behalf of the American Jewish Community, he founded in 1857, together with his sons, *The Jewish Messenger*, and supported all Leeser's endeavors. Leeser, who was generally opposed to the system of messengers, agreed to aid Ashkenazi's mission on the condition that all the money collected would be transferred to Sir Moses Montefiore in London, while Ashkenazi himself would receive specific sums for his expenses.

In time, Isaacs became the mainstay of efforts on behalf of Eretz Israel, responsible to the congregations. He was in constant correspondence with Moses Montefiore, with whom Isaacs, an English Jew, felt a special sense of kinship. Isaacs transferred the funds to Montefiore for distribution. Before long, Isaacs began to investigate carefully the private affairs of the messengers, a step that Ashkenazi did not like at all. Isaacs complained about the disproportionate expenses of the messengers. In the *Asmonean* of 26 April 1850, he announced:

Notice is hereby given. To the Presidents and Members of the various Societies organized throughout the United States, in support of the mission of Rabbi Aaron Selig for the Poor of the Holy Land, *not* to pay any *monies* whatever either to Messengers or through any channel except through the only accredited agents. . . .[9]

Isaacs' firm stand brought about an improvement in the situation. A majority of the Historical School congregations in New York and in Philadelphia participated in a meeting in New York, whose purpose was to determine division of future contributions.[10] The main spokesmen were Isaacs and Leeser. In charitable matters for Eretz Israel, they argued, direct contact is preferable to transfer of funds through intermediaries. It was clear from the outset that the recipients in Eretz Israel would gain if the expenses of the messengers were eliminated.

Plans for systematization had little effect. Somehow the Jewish public could not be persuaded of its obligations for the indigent of Eretz Israel without hearing pathetic and heartrending accounts by the messengers as they described existing poverty and suffering. Nevertheless, in 1854, Isaacs succeeded in collecting a fund of $5,000 for the relief of famine-stricken areas in Eretz Israel. One year earlier he had organized the North American Relief Society for Indigent Jews in Jerusalem and Palestine, of which he became treasurer. The Society benefited from bequests by Judah Touro in the amount of $10,000, which when invested, yielded an annual income of $700. This sum was sent directly to Jerusalem. A contribution by Moses Montefiore was added to the income from Touro's legacy. With this money a row of houses for the poor was built in 1860 outside the Old City's walls. Thus was created the first residential quarter of the new Jerusalem, *Mishkenot Sha'ananim*.

It is, therefore, no surprise that the various communities in Eretz Israel continued to send messengers in the attempt to stimulate the generosity of American Jews. In 1861, Abraham Nissan Ashkenazi was dispatched. Isaacs and Raphall, old and loyal friends of the cause of Eretz Israel, though pained by the failure of their goals for better organization, could not, as faithful supporters of Jewish settlement, withhold their help. Despite the economic depression in America on the eve of the Civil War, many who were solicited rallied to the cause. Isaacs' weekly publication, *The Jewish Messenger*, was an important vehicle for bringing Ashkenazi's mission to public attention. When Isaacs saw that Ashkenazi conducted himself as others had previously, he pleaded with him to leave America. Isaacs tried once more to establish a central organization, but this effort, too, was unsuccessful.

In 1867, the Jews of America witnessed a significant development in Palestine requests. A group of twelve persons, former American Jews who had settled in Eretz Israel, complained that neither the German nor the Russian Jews wanted to appropriate to them a single cent of the money that had been received from America. They further complained that the Jews of the United States had no knowledge of the existence of American Jewish settlement in Jerusalem. The American consul in Jerusalem, Victor Beauboucher, sent separate letters to Rabbi Max Lilienthal in Cincinnati and to Samuel Isaacs in New York:

> The number of American Jews residing in Jerusalem is very limited, a dozen altogether; but these unfortunates are the most miserable of all and do not receive pecuniary succor from any one, the German committees never having given a cent, and those of America perhaps do not know them at all.
>
> I have done all I could to relieve these poor people ever since two years that I am in Palestine: and seeing their increasing misery, I this day address myself to you, in order that something may be done in their favor by the Committee of which you are a member.
>
> One of them, Benjamin Lilienthal, whom I know as an honest man, left yesterday for the States, and will be able orally to make to you the lamentable narration of the position of his coreligionists and fellow-citizens in Palestine. I have remitted to him the necessary recommendations for the success of his travel, and beg you to receive him with the attention due to a good and honest father of a family. . . .[11]

Every new source of America–Eretz Israel relations reveals how deeply involved the Historical School was in Jerusalem's destiny. Not only the rabbis, but also the members of their congregations aided each new enterprise and were among its organizers. In addition to their endeavors to supply the continuing needs of the inhabitants of Jerusalem, they were concerned with the long-range development of Jewish settlement in Eretz Israel. In many of their appeals, Leeser and Isaacs expressed the hope that the day would come when Jerusalem would be so firmly established as to be able to care for its own needs and redeem itself by its own efforts. Writing in the *Occident* as early as 1853, Leeser argued: "Among the means for promoting the independence of the Jewish people, and thereby advancing the best interests of Jerusalem, one of the most likely to be efficient appears to be the establishment of industrial institutions."[12]

The members of the Historical School did not believe that Eretz Israel could be rebuilt without hard and exhausting labor. In the eleventh volume of the *Occident* (1853–1854), Leeser wrote three basic articles about Eretz Israel in which he discussed the possibility of agricultural development of the land. He wished to see the inhabitants of Jerusalem as farmers, vinegrowers, and tillers of the soil. He was, therefore, pleased when Gershom Kursheedt, president of the Society for Offerings of the Sanctuary and the executor of Touro's will in matters connected with Eretz Israel, returned from the Holy Land and gave an account of the state of manual labor there. He said the widespread opinion that manual labor was not acceptable to the *Yishuv* was essentially erroneous. On the basis of this information, Leeser proposed that the workers build their own institutions: libraries, hospitals, and the like. From the profit thus made, they could conceivably expand their building activities. He wrote:

> Let it not be imagined that Palestine even now is what it was twenty years ago; on the contrary, many changes for the better have taken place already, and the arts of European civilization, and the requirements, luxuries and comforts attending them, are gradually making their way, at least in Jerusalem.[13]

Leeser wanted to see the rapid establishment of agricultural settlements in Eretz Israel. The Jews of the Diaspora should not go to die in the Holy Land or live there on charity. The aged and the sick should not be sent, but rather those who are able to work. At the time Isaacs and Raphall were attempting, in the face of apathy, to collect money to help the needy in the Holy Land, Leeser began to work in other directions. In 1853 he supported the effort of Moses Sachs to organize an agricultural settlement in Jaffa. He served as president of the central committee in America, whose aim was to collect a fund for the support of this undertaking.[14] Isaacs, too, in various articles, urged that those who were active in support of Eretz Israel should give priority to agricultural funding rather than charitable aid. He appeared before the Board of Delegates with such a proposal, and he was also largely responsible for convincing the board to apportion funds for an agricultural school in Jaffa.[15]

What has not sufficiently come forth from the various studies on Leeser were his bold views regarding Jewish self-defense. In many instances, he stressed Jewish self-protection as a requisite for his agricultural program. Yet careful examination of the sources reveals the force of Leeser's argument so many years before it became a basis for Zionist colonization in Eretz Israel. His views went beyond economics and stressed the very heart of permanent settlement. He wrote:

> Peace is the greatest blessing which God has ever bestowed on the world: but it is no peace where the proud oppress the humble without redress; where the weak have to submit to exaction without any one to do them justice. Hence, we say, that could the Jews in Palestine organize themselves for mutual protection; could they but obtain the privilege from the Sultan to form themselves into regular companies of national guards, for the defence of their own firesides and homesteads, should they be able to acquire them, they would do much to procure themselves a respite from the constant annoyance to which they have been so often subjected by the Arab chieftains, such as Abdarachman, the Sheikh of Hebron.[16]

What moved the builders of the Historical School in the United States, with Leeser in the forefront, to such continuing efforts on behalf of the *Yishuv* in Eretz Israel? The foundation of their belief in the Restoration is, of course, expressed in the tradition which they taught to their generation.

But Leeser posed the question unequivocally. Referring to the mourning laws of Tisha B'Av, he said:

> Again it is asked: "Why should we mourn at this distance of time?" But let me ask in return: Does distance of time lessen the evil? Are we less exiles, because we have been exiles for near eighteen hundred years? or, do you wish it said, that Jews have lost their national feelings because they no longer live in Palestine, and because the punishment inflicted has been so long continued on account of their obduracy in not repenting?[17]

Leeser slowly embraced the conviction that the dream of the Return might be a practical reality. Beginning as a practitioner of charity for the needy in the Holy Land, he moved on to constructive programs. He began to consider the twofold goal that was much later to be defined as Zionism: The practical building of Eretz Israel as the home of the Jews, and the dedication of the Land to the spiritual and cultural regeneration of the entire

Jewish people, in the Diaspora as well as in Eretz Israel.[18] His words, haltingly but surely, point the direction which the Historical School took in later decades:

> Will this dream be speedily realized? We cannot tell indeed; events occasionally creep slowly over the face of the world; but at other times they rush rapidly forward, and one great development follows closely on the heels of the other. The same may be the case with the now apparently distant restoration of Israelites to Palestine. . . . Is it then so unlikely that an effort will be made to place in Palestine and the countries immediately north, south, and east of it an enterprising race, which shall keep it as a highway of all nations, and thus prevent the occupation of it by any great power, to become a clog to the commerce of the world? . . . whereas, possessed by Israelites, feeble as they would be politically, disinclined to control others if they even could, it would be a highway of nations, and men could meet there to exchange the products of all climates in perfect security, and without injury to any other land or government. . . . One thing is certain, whether our views be realized or not, whether speedily or tardily, that it is no silly wish for us to pray for a national restoration, if we have any love for the triumphant though peaceful rule of our religion over our people, and to free them from the moral and physical yoke which will necessarily rest upon us, while we have a permanent home nowhere.[19]

As we review the thoughts and actions of the members of the Historical School regarding Eretz Israel, especially the forthright expression of Isaac Leeser, we learn much about their understanding of Judaism and Zionism, for the Return to Zion was integral to Historical Judaism. Moreover, they had unusual insight into the American spiritual tradition with respect to Zion. They knew that every American regarded himself as possessing a portion in Zion, and that the dream of the Restoration was part of the thought pattern of America. As America was a highway of peoples, so the Holy Land, in the age of a third Jewish Commonwealth, could become, to use Leeser's phrase, a "highway of nations."

NOTES

1. Maxwell Whiteman records that a number of items relating to Palestine are found in the papers of the Philadelphia Land Grants, 1684–1772, Penna. Mss., VII, 39. The oldest reference, dating back to 1763, is a response to an appeal by the Jews of Hebron. "Zionism Comes to Philadelphia," *Early History of Zionism in America*, ed. Isidore S. Meyer (New York: American Jewish Historical Society and Theodor Herzl Foundation, 1958), 191, 207.

2. From the study by Salo and Jeannette Baron on messengers sent from Eretz Israel to the United States, we gather a clear picture, based on records and periodicals, of the developing relationship between the leaders of the communities in Palestine and America in that period. See "Palestinian Messengers in America, 1849–79," *Jewish Social Studies* 5 (April 1943): 115–62; (July 1943): 225–92; republished as a monograph in the *America and the Holy Land* reprint series (New York: Arno Press, 1977).

3. For a listing of some of these studies, see Jeffrey Gurock, *American Jewish History: A Bibliographical Guide* (New York: Anti-Defamation League of B'nai B'rith, 1983), 37.

4. The essay by Maxine S. Seller, "Isaac Leeser's Views on the Restoration of a Jewish Palestine," *AJHQ* 58 (1968–1969): 118–35, is an outstanding exception. To see how little the Eretz Israel dimension of Leeser's thought is represented, one need but review the eulogy of Leeser by Mayer Sulzberger, "No Better Jew, No Purer Man," reprinted in *American Jewish Archives (AJA)* 21 (1969–1970): 140–48.

5. Joseph Schwarz, *A Descriptive Geography and Brief Historical Sketch of Palestine*, tr. Isaac Leeser (Philadelphia: A. Hart, 1850), viii-ix.

6. *Occident* 7 (October 1849): 344.

7. Ibid., p. 345.

8. Members of the committee were Dr. Max Lilienthal, Samuel Isaacs, Mordecai M. Noah, Jacob J. M. Falkenau, Simeon Abrahams (who had just returned from Palestine), Henry Moses (president of Anshe Chesed congregation of New York), L. Bomeisler, and Isaac Leeser.

9. Salo and Jeannette Baron (see note 2 above), pp. 136–37.

10. Among the participants were Isaacs of Shaarey Tefila; Noah and Abrahams of Shearith Israel; Jacob M. Falkenau and Amsel Leo of B'nai Jeshurun; Henry Moses of Anshe Chesed; Jacob Weinschenck of Rodeph Shalom; Isidore Raphael of Shaarey Zedek; Abraham Schwartz of Shaarey Hashamaim; Max Lilienthal, Isaac Leeser, and Abraham Hart of Philadelphia.

11. Salo and Jeannette Baron (see note 2 above), p. 241. For a brief description of the first American Jewish society in Eretz Israel, see Frank E. Manuel, *The Realities of American-Palestine Relations* (Washington, D.C.: Public Affairs Press, 1949), 34–35. For additional material on Benjamin Lilienthal, see Judah Aaron Segal Weiss, *Bi-Shearaikh, Yerushalayim* [In Thy Gates, O Jerusalem] (Jerusalem: Halevi, 1949, Hebrew), 60–61, 71, 265–75.

12. *Occident* 10 (February 1853): 604.

13. "Palestine and Its Prospects," *Occident* 13 (February 1856): 523. See also, G. Kressel's article on Leeser's interest in agricultural settlements in Eretz Israel, *Davar*, 8 January 1954 (Hebrew).

14. See Joseph L. Blau's description in his essay, "The Spiritual Life of American Jewry 1654–1954," *AJYB* 56 (1955): 157–59.

15. *Jewish Messenger* 23 (22 May 1868): 4–5. See also, Max J. Kohler, "The Board of Delegates of American Israelites, 1859–1878," *PAJHS* 29 (1925): 99.

16. *Occident* 11 (December 1853): 433.

17. Isaac Leeser, "The Restoration of Israel," *Discourses, Argumentative and Devotional, on the Subject of the Jewish Religion* I (Philadelphia: Haskell & Fleu, 1837), 189.

18. Compare Maxwell Whiteman, "The Legacy of Isaac Leeser," *Jewish Life in Philadelphia 1830–1940*, ed. Murray Friedman (Philadelphia: ISHI Publications, 1983), 40: "Although no formal plan was ever expressed by Leeser that was comparable to latter-day Zionism, his emphasis on agriculture, commerce, and small industries to turn Jews into mechanics and farmers paralleled his immutable, traditional beliefs in the restoration of the Holy Land and in the concept of a modern Jewish commonwealth."

19. *Occident* 22 (April 1864): 13.

Chapter 5

Abraham I. Rice: Pioneer of Orthodoxy in America

In their illuminating study of Eretz Israel emissaries, cited in the previous chapter, Salo and Jeannette Baron referred to an unpublished manuscript in the Jewish National and University Library in Jerusalem from which we can glean important data both on the sparse *Yishuv* (Jewish community) in Eretz Israel and on the evolving Jewish community in the United States.[1] This manuscript, listed in Issachar Joel's catalogue, contains records of three emissaries to America—Aaron Selig Ashkenazi, Abraham Nissan, and Nathan Neta Notkin—in 1848, 1860, 1866, and 1870.[2] The authors aptly stressed that such record books not only constitute primary sources for the history of the organizations they describe in the United States, but they also bring to the fore those individuals whose chief desire was to strengthen the *Yishuv* in Eretz Israel.

Another mostly unpublished source for America–Holy Land Studies is to be found in the letters of the *Pekidim* and *Amarcalim* of Amsterdam (*PAA*).[3] In this chapter I focus on one aspect, namely, the devotion to Eretz Israel of Rabbi Abraham Rice, the first ordained orthodox rabbi who served in the United States.[4] To better comprehend the historical setting in which Rabbi Rice sought to function, it is necessary to introduce the institution through which he was able to serve the needs of the *Yishuv*.

The *PAA* was founded in Amsterdam in 1809, and its officers were given the honorary title of *Pekidim ve-Amarcalim* (officials and managers) by the rabbis of the Sephardi and Ashkenazi communities in Jerusalem. Among the important officers of this organizaton was Isaac Guteinde, who was succeeded after his death in 1817 by Solomon Baruch Rubens, Abraham Prinz, and Zvi Hirsch Lehren, who became the dominant figure. Zvi Hirsch and his brothers, Meir and Akiva, were prominent businessmen and communal leaders who were particularly concerned with the needs of the *Yishuv* in Eretz Israel.[5]

Initially, the *PAA* aided the emissaries from Eretz Israel and fully cooperated with them. The lay leaders would note the sums raised in the emissaries' ledger books, the money would be transferred to the *PAA*, and the *PAA* in turn would forward the money to Eretz Israel. Its position later changed; the *PAA* began to oppose strongly the entire system of appointed emissaries from Jerusalem. This policy was not uniformly honored by the appointed heads of the organized communities [the *kollels*] in Eretz Israel. Emissaries continued to arrive from time to time, despite the opposition of the *PAA*.

In 1824, the head of the London rabbinical court, Rabbi Solomon Hirschell, established standing societies and appointed special officials to collect donations, hoping in this fashion to abrogate the need for emissaries.[6] He called the voluntary society *Hebrat Terumat haKodesh*.[7] The *PAA* viewed this favorably, and also began to establish branches of volunteers committed to annual donations. In 1832, under Rabbi Hirschell's influence, a branch of the *Hebrat Terumat haKodesh*, named the "Society for Offerings to the Sanctuary," was founded in New York. The new group undertook to collect the donations, transmit them directly to London and Amsterdam, and refrain from aiding the emissaries who would come or be sent to America.[8] One of the founders of the New York society was Israel Baer Kursheedt, who was lavishly praised in the contemporary Jewish press for his spiritual leadership and public initiatives.[9] In 1847, the New York branch of *Hebrat Terumat haKodesh* undertook a special effort, publishing the following circular, a copy of which is in the archives of the American Jewish Historical Society:

EXTRACT FROM THE CONSTITUTION
Section 5

The money raised by this Society shall be remitted, at stated times, to some responsible Agent in Europe or Asia, to be distributed by him, fairly and equitably, amongst the different Congregations in the Holy Land; but in no instance whatever to be paid to any Messenger or Agent of any of the Congregations there who may be sent here to collect the same.

*   *   *

The *Hebrat Terumot ha-Kodesh* [sic] has received recent intelligence that our Brethren in the Holy Land are suffering from the horrors of Famine, the consequence of the continued drought for near two years. They appeal to the sympathies of their more prosperous Co-religionists.

This Society has just received the acknowledgement of their last remittance made to Mr. Hersch Lehrens, and other gentlemen in Amsterdam, composing the Distribution Committee, and calling on us for all the additional aid in our power. With this view, the Hebra has appointed Messrs. Solomon I. Isaacs, I. B. Kursheedt, and Simeon Abrahams, to solicit aid from all well-disposed Yehudim, in this city and elsewhere; the amount collected to be sent in accordance with the above Extract from the Constitution, with the names of the donors, and the amount subscribed by each individual.

I. B. KURSHEEDT, President.
N. PHILLIPS, Clerk.

New-York, 18 Kislef, 5607.

With this background, we may appreciate the importance of the correspondence in the copybooks of the *PAA*. It also enables us to clarify certain events in American Jewish history. The letters relating to the United States, extending over more than three decades, from 1835 through 1870, are interlaced in ten of the fifteen volumes, offering evidence of the activity of the *PAA*. Most were written in English, and others were in Hebrew, German, or Yiddish. The *PAA* repeatedly emphasized the necessity to aid the poor in Eretz Israel. Generally it depicted the sorry state of affairs there, complaining of emissaries who visited America despite the *PAA*'s opposition or that the money sent to London did not arrive in Amsterdam, etc. A picture both compelling and instructive of America and its Jewish community emerges between the lines of these letters.[10]

In the source material on American Jewry in this correspondence, we find information on Rabbi Rice's activities and his various contacts with Eretz Israel before the advent of the Hibbat Zion movement. Selections from these letters supplement the archival material on Rice found in the collection of the American Jewish Historical Society and in the library of the Jewish Theological Seminary of America.

The letter dated 11 Tammuz 5602 (18 June 1842) sent by Hirsch Lehren to the president of Rabbi Rice's congregation in Baltimore demonstrates the spiritual condition of the community at the time. This Orthodox congregation even lacked copies of the Pentateuch, which the *PAA* undertook to supply.[11]

Biographical details about Rabbi Abraham Rice are scattered throughout the contemporary Jewish press. He is regarded as the first ordained rabbi to arrive in the United States.[12] Born in 1800 in Gagesheim, near Würzburg, Germany, he studied in his youth under Rabbi Abraham Bing. Later he drew close to Rabbi Wolf Hamburger, the head of the Furth *yeshivah*, and remained his disciple. Rabbi Rice arrived in America in 1840. A brief description in a manuscript (which has fortunately survived) by William S. Rayner, the president of the Reform Har Sinai congregation in Baltimore, provides information about Rice's early days in America.[13] Rayner and Rice had sailed together from Hamburg in the spring of 1840, arriving in New York on July 20. Rayner relates that in his inaugural sermon in the synagogue on Henry Street in New York, Rabbi Rice proclaimed to his audience, his first in the New World, that his goal in the United States was "to establish pure Orthodox belief in this land."[14]

A short time later, it was suggested to Rice that he explore the possibility of being appointed to serve a congregation in Newport, Rhode Island. The hope was that he would succeed in reestablishing the original congregation in that city, which had been abandoned at the end of the eighteenth century. Rice found that the small number of Jews in Newport could not maintain a congregation, and he returned to New York. Shortly thereafter, he accepted the invitation of Aaron Waglein, a compatriot, then chairman of the Nidchei Israel congregation in Baltimore (also known as the *Stadt Schul*), to serve as its rabbi. In 1849, Rice left that post to establish a small but poor congregation that was incapable of supporting a rabbi. He opened a fabric store, which appealed to him, because he had never wanted to earn his living as a rabbi. Rather, as he wrote in 1862, "Regarding my work as a rabbi, you already know that I never wanted to be a rabbi and leader in such backwater cities, but necessity is a cruel master. . . ."[15]

Rice's widespread reputation is attested by an extremely favorable letter of recommendation sent by Lehren to Kursheedt in New York. The bond between Rice and Kursheedt was strengthened by their joint role on behalf of the *Yishuv* and the *Hebrat Terumat haKodesh*. In his letter, Lehren asked Kursheedt to welcome the new immigrant "because he has no friend or acquaintance there. A man must not be judged by his appearance, and therefore a person cannot favorably judge the nature of a visitor who has come from a foreign land. And, so that it would not be necessary to exceed the bounds [of propriety], the wise king [Solomon], may he rest in peace, directed us by saying, 'Let the mouth of another praise you, not yours' [Proverbs 27:2]. . . ."[16]

Rice's strictures about the state of American Jewish life did not diminish even as time went on. He was bitterly disappointed by the Jews in the United States. Not only was he unsuccessful in fulfilling his purpose to establish Orthodox belief in the United States; the very opposite took place.[17] The desire to escape this condition disturbed him endlessly. His complaints, both in private and in letters to his friends in Europe, the moralizing tone of his sermons, and his incessant labors on behalf of the Jewish community in

Eretz Israel helped him somewhat to lessen his anguish. Rabbi Rice came to appreciate the meaning of freedom in America. However, like many others after him, he foretold the "kiss of death" awaiting the Jews in the United States. In one of his sermons, he warned that Jews were incapable of properly appreciating freedom in America. To paraphrase his language, they regarded liberty as something that would free them from the yoke of the Torah and commandments while they danced around the Golden Calf. In each city where he preached, a new Moses arose, who sculpted tablets, in accordance with the spirit of the times. "But these tablets are the work of man, who comes from dust and to dust will return."[18]

Reflecting his candor and apprehension, Rice asked whether "it is permissible for a Jew to live in such a country" in which "the majority eat forbidden foods, and publicly desecrate the Sabbath . . . they have intermingled with the [non-Jewish] nations and have taken foreign wives. . . ."[19] In a letter to Kursheedt, he warned of the "baseness of the generation" and its leaders:

> Another plague shall soon come upon this land, that is, people are coming who know not their right from their left, who mutter and chirp in insolent voice. They will arise at the head of the mass and people will stream after them. In this manner, what little knowledge remains will be consumed by these people in their heresy. The scholar, the man of faith, will be forced to sit in darkness, without bread to eat, and the wisdom of the learned shall vanish. Those who fear sin will be despised. Truth is absent, and all that is left for us is to rely upon our Father in Heaven. . . .[20]

However, above and beyond his gloomy perception of Jewish reality in America, Rabbi Rice's career was marked by a unique turn in his personal plans. From the letter sent to him by Lehren regarding the possibility of Rice's *aliyah* to the Holy Land, it is possible to draw a picture of the path he set for himself: to personally fulfill the heavenly commandment to settle in Eretz Israel. What emerges from this correspondence is Rice's deep involvement with Eretz Israel, hopefully through personal fulfillment.

Rice's outlook on Eretz Israel was expressed in one of his sermons about the coming of the Messiah, a topic to which he frequently returned. In discussing the topic "What Is a Jew?" he pointed to three foundations on which the Jewish religion is based: belief in the Unity of God and in Divine Providence; belief in the Torah of Moses; and belief in the Messiah, who shall lead us to rebuild the Temple in the Promised Land.[21] Rice expanded on this basic principle at every opportunity. In speaking to his American audience, Rice alluded to the "breaking of the tablets" by Reform Judaism in the extreme form it took at the time. However, his basic intention was to provide a rationale for the centrality of Eretz Israel in Jewish tradition. Rice stressed that the very essence of Judaism is the fulfillment of all the commandments. This could only be accomplished in Eretz Israel, for, according to Jewish law, a considerable portion of the *mitzvot* could only be observed in the Holy Land.[22]

Unlike many other observant Jews, who also obviously awaited the final Redemption, Rice did not regard his activity on behalf of the Return to Zion as connected to a future Messianic age. The Jewish press of those years lavishly praised his success in raising contributions for the rescue of the *Yishuv* in Eretz Israel. Rice, who sought donations among Jews and non-Jews alike, was always in the forefront of fund-raising activities. During the difficult years of the Crimean War, in which contributions from Russian Jews to Eretz Israel ceased, in the course of only a few months (between June and October 1854), Rice forwarded $1213. He based this on the principle that the poor of the land of Israel should receive precedence in charitable aid, as opposed to the normative rule that the poor of one's own city have priority.[23] The letters of the *PAA* reflect its trust in Rice. Already in 1837, when "a great calamity befell the holy cities of Safed and Tiberias, may they speedily be rebuilt, in the earthquake that struck them on 24 Tevet past," the *PAA* urgently requested aid, "and after we saw that our call went unanswered in New York," they decided to rely upon the committee in Baltimore, which sent "a new contribution for help in the calamity of this earthquake. . . ."[24] After Rice came to serve the Baltimore congregation, the *PAA* turned to him in these urgencies.

Rice's commitment toward personal fulfillment in Eretz Israel can be discerned in his aid in the *aliyah* of Benjamin Lilienthal. We learn about Lilienthal from a detailed letter he sent to his brother in Germany and from contemporary newspaper acccounts.[25] Lilienthal was of German extraction, having lived for several years in Bavaria. Once in America, he moved from Cincinnati to Baltimore in 1846. There he met Rice, who provided him with recommendations to Rabbi Isaac Dov (Seligmann Baer) Bamburger in Bavaria and to Rabbi Eliezer Bergmann of Heidenheim (a fellow student of Rice's in the *yeshivah* of Rabbi Wolf Hamburger in Furth), resident in Jerusalem. Bergmann was one of the first German Jews to emigrate to Eretz Israel. The following sentence in Rice's letter to Rabbi Bamberger alludes to the writer's own aspirations: "I have greatly longed many days to reply to my master . . . and now I have encountered someone who is surely pure, for Rabbi Benjamin Lilienthal has offered to leave the foreign land and go to the Holy land, may it be rebuilt. . . ."[26]

Lilienthal's personal example undoubtedly influenced Rice. It was during this period that Rice apparently wrote to Lehren, asking his advice about his own immigration. I could not find the original letter, but we learn of Rice's query from Lehren's reply in the copybooks of the *PAA*, wherein he distinguishes between the commandment to support the *Yishuv* and the obligation to further the Ingathering of the Exiles.

The following passage from Lehren's letter in Hebrew reveals not only Rice's wish to immigrate, but also Lehren's wide knowledge and contacts with the American Jewish community of the day.

To Baltimore

With the help of God,
Monday, 18 Kislev 5607
[30 November 1846]

May Heaven add to you length of days and years of life, and blessings without end; and may we see the consolation of Zion and Jerusalem. The great sage, his excellency, my distinguished and beloved friend, the rabbi great in Torah whose fear of the Lord is his treasure, the perfect scholar, the source of knowledge, the crown of Torah, our master and teacher, Rabbi Abraham Rice, may God preserve and protect him, may his light endure. . . .

Now, regarding your second question, I cannot clearly express my view, for several years I have refrained from telling anyone to go up to the Land, for I was aware of the poverty and hardship there, and afterwards the immigrant would complain, and the fear of his excellent majesty, may his light endure, also is related to my reluctance to counsel him to immigrate.

Lehren continues his rather forceful argument with the thought that if, indeed, Rabbi Rice is convinced that his efforts among the American Jews are fruitless, why should he persist in work in the *golah*? In that case, Lehren proposes that Rice move decisively to the Holy Land, fully determined in advance not to enter into disputes, because peace is the greatest of blessings. He goes into great detail, advising him to be circumspect with regard to travel arrangements, and urges Rice to keep him informed of his progress. It would be excellent, Lehren writes, if Rice would succeed to bring with him a large purse . . . it would do him well.

Once in the Holy Land, Lehren reminds Rice in his practical vein, he should devote himself exclusively to aid the needy. Lehren does not hesitate to detail his difficulties with I. B. Kursheedt, for the New York community has hardly contributed to Eretz Israel through the *PAA*, nor have other communities such as Charleston.[27]

Rabbi Rice was destined to remain in America. His talents, moral stature, and learning did not spare him trials and tribulations. Writing to his pupil in the spring of 1862, he revealed the truth of his condition, namely, that it was pointless to move from city to city without certain guarantee of income. Citing Ecclesiastes [10:4], "Don't give up your post," he writes: "I have heeded the cry of the Jews around me, and I decided to dwell here for the present, and I will see the pattern of their behavior towards me."[28]

That spring, Rice returned to his first congregation, Nidchei Israel, serving as its rabbi for only a few months before his death. In the fall of that year, on 23 Heshvan 5623 [5 November 1862], he passed on to his eternal rest. Religiously scrupulous to the end, Rice directed that he be interred without a coffin, so that his body be returned to the earth as was the *minhag*, the burial custom in the Holy Land.

APPENDIX 5: RABBI SOLOMON HIRSCHELL'S MANIFESTO

With the Help of the Lord! Amen.

To the worthy members of the several holy Congregations of Israel in England, may the beauties of the Lord shine upon them and establish the works of their hands. AMEN

ATTEND DEAR BRETHREN,

I have heretofore often had occasion to rouse your hearts and excite your attention to the miserable state of our fellow brethren, who are wandering about the precincts of the Holy Land, and particularly towards those of the German Congregation who have attached themselves to the soil of our fore-fathers, and are praying for your happiness and success. Be it known unto you my brethren that their cries have again reached me, cries excited by distress, by hunger, by wretchedness unassisted and unrelieved, by miseries bringing tears from every commisserating [!] eye, and sorrow to every feeling heart.

It is true that messengers arrive from time to time commissioned to collect relief for these unfortunates, and thanks be to Heaven that they do not return empty handed, yet all their exertions fall very short of effecting any efficient good, notwithstanding the benevolence of all classes of our Brethren whose sympathy is ever alive to this holy Charity; for the expence [!] unavoidably attached to travelling absorbs too great a proportion of the little stock they may have collected, more especially if their stay be by any accident unusually prolonged: these circumstances have induced me to point out the expediency, nay even the necessity of establishing a Society under the management of religious and respectable persons who shall occupy themselves in this holy measure and become the depositaries of an annual Subscription for the relief of these our distressed Brethren, and thus save expence and trouble to messengers and ourselves from their importunities; surely there are persons whose pious hearts will prompt them to collect benevolences for the purpose, surely there are many, who for the honor of God and his Law will transmit their annual Subscription, and all my exertion shall be employed to secure their correct application.

The following is the plan on what the Society is supposed to be Founded.

1. The Society ahall [!] be called, [HEBREW - *hevrat terumat hakodesh*].
2. Subscriptions to consist of any sum the liberality of the Subscribers may be pleased to give annually.
3. The affairs of the Society to be managed by a Committee of gentlemen appointed from the several Congregations.
4. Should the amount of the Subscriptions allow the same, it is promised to institute an accumulating fund for permanent support.

Such are the principles on which I propose to establish a Society for so sacred and so charitable a purpose, in the mean time shall be happy to receive any subscription whatever in aid thereof, well do I know my Brethren, the liberal spirit that prevails in this country and that charity lies treasured in your hearts, let me conjure you to seek the peace of the holy city of Jerusalem and other towns in the land our former glory, to use your exertions for the establishment of a permanent Society for their aid. The Almighty will surely bless your endeavours, and the merits of our pious fore-fathers, who lic interred in that holy land will prove a support for you and your posterity for ever, AMEN. Such are the prayers and desires of your sincere well wisher,

SOLOMON HIRSCHELL

London, Thursday, the 17th of Sivan, A.M. 5584.

NOTES

1. Salo W. and Jeannette M. Baron, "Palestinian Messengers in America, 1849–79; A Record of Four Journeys," *Jewish Social Studies* 5 (April 1943): 115–62; (July 1943): 225–92; (reprint: New York: Arno Press, 1977).

2. Issachar Joel, *List of the Hebrew Manuscripts in the Jewish National and University Library in Jerusalem* (Jerusalem: Jewish National and University Library, 1934, Hebrew), 52, no. 517.

3. Fifteen manuscript volumes of these letters were originally obtained in Jerusalem by Joseph Joel Rivlin. With the assistance of the Society for the History of the Old Yishuv in Eretz Israel, which he headed, Professor Rivlin, together with Benjamin Rivlin, edited two volumes encompassing the years 5586–5588 (1825/26–1827/28). A third volume, covering the year 5589 (1828/29), was edited by Benjamin Rivlin and published by Yad Izhak Ben-Zvi. The other volumes remain unpublished and are deposited in Yad Izhak Ben-Zvi. The significance of this correspondence as a historical source is discussed by Arieh Morgenstern, "The Correspondence of the *Pekidim* and *Amarcalim* as a Source for the History of Eretz Israel," *Cathedra* 27 (March 1983, Hebrew): 85–108.

4. For a recent study of Rice, see I. Harold Sharfman, *The First Rabbi: Origins of Conflict between Orthodoxy & Reform-Jewish Polemic Warfare in pre-Civil War America, a Biographical History* (Malibu, Calif.: Joseph Simon, Pangloss Press, 1988).

5. See Jozeph Michman, "The Beginnings of the *Pekidim* and *Amarcalim* of Amsterdam," *Cathedra 27 (March 1983, Hebrew): 69–84. See also, Rivlin (see note 3 above), 11–23; Avraham Yaari, Messengers of Eretz Israel* (Jerusalem: Mossad Ha-Rav Kook, 1951, Hebrew), 183–84, 783–85; Mordehai Eliav, *The Love of Zion and the People of HOD [Holland and Germany]: German Jewry and the Settlement of Eretz Israel in the Nineteenth Century* (Tel Aviv: Hakibbutz Hameuchad, 1971, Hebrew), esp. 14–16.

6. For biographical material about Hirschell, see Cecil Roth, "The Chief Rabbinate of England," *Essays in Honour of the Very Rev. Dr. J. H. Hertz* (London: E. Goldston, 1943), 377–81; idem, *History of the Great Synagogue* (London, 1950), 181ff. For examples of Rabbi Hirschell's ties with the Jewish Community in America in that period, see Moshe Davis, "The First Ashkenazi Synagogue in New York: B'nai Jeshurun," *Beit Yisrael Be-Amerikah: Studies and Sources* (Jerusalem: Magnes Press, 1970, Hebrew), 6–9; Israel Goldstein, *A Century of Judaism in New York* (New York: Congregation B'nai Jeshurun, 1930), Appendix 323–30; *The Jews of the United States 1790–1840: A Documentary History* 2, ed. Joseph L. Blau and Salo W. Baron (New York: Columbia University Press, 1963), 588–90.

7. A manifesto in Hebrew and in English distributed by Rabbi Hirschell is extant in a file of eighteen unpublished documents relating to the *Hebrat Terumat haKodesh* in the American Jewish Historical Society. These documents, including certificates from rabbis in Eretz Israel, presumably linked the centers in Amsterdam, London, the United States, and the Holy Land. The text of Rabbi Hirschell's manifesto is published as an Appendix.

8. In his journal, *The Occident*, Isaac Leeser diligently chronicled the *Hebrah*'s activity, thus obtaining for it a great deal of publicity. See, for example, *Occident* 4 (March 1847): 601–603; 5 (April 1847): 50–52; (August 1847): 276; 6 (June 1848): 155; (August 1848): 263–64; 7 (October 1849): 340, 347; 8 (December 1849): 475; 9 (July 1851) 226; 10 (June 1852): 170. For a detailed description of the *Hebrat Terumat haKodesh* and its activity during its approximately twenty years of existence, see Hyman B. Grinstein, *The Rise of the Jewish Community of New York 1654–1860* (Philadelphia: Jewish Publication Society of America, 1945), 441–47. See also Yitzhak Rivkind, "A 'Zionist Campaign' in America a Hundred Years Ago (On the One Hundredth Anniversary of *Hebrat Terumat haKodesh*)," *Der Tog* (12 April 1933): 4; (15 April 1933): 4 (Yiddish). Rivkind appended to his article the first report of the *Hebrah* in New York, dated 20 November 1832.

9. Israel Baer Kursheedt (1766–1852) was born in Germany and studied in the *yeshivah* of Rabbi Nathan Adler in Frankfurt am Main. He came to America in 1796, married the daughter of Gershom Mendes Seixas, the *hazan* (cantor) of the

Shearith Israel Congregation in New York, and was one of the founders of the B'nai Jeshurun congregation, the first Ashkenazi synagogue in New York. In addition to his business career, he devoted himself to the synagogue and public affairs, helping to establish educational and welfare institutions. For lack of rabbinical leadership in the United States, people turned to Kursheedt with questions pertaining to religious life and accepted his decisions. He referred complex queries to Rabbi Hirschell in London. In 1840, he headed an assembly organized by New York Jews to protest against the Damascus Blood Libel. For biographical details, see *Occident* 10 (June 1852): 162–67; Grinstein (see note 8 above), 48–49, 220–91, 317ff., 420–21.

10. A manuscript annotated list of congregations to whose "Parnassim and Elders" the *PAA* sent letters was prepared by Francine Schnitzer and deposited in the library of Yad Izhak Ben-Zvi, Jerusalem.

The following letter, sent on 24 Nisan 5598 [29 March 1838] to the Parnassim and Elders of the congregation in Charleston, South Carolina, is representative both of the style of the period and the manner of approach to the hearts of the recipients:

> You, protected by the liberal constitution of Amerika, living in freedom, opulence and prosperity: turn your eyes to the horrible state of slavery and misery, under which our brethren are weeping in the holy land! and your compassionate hearts will be deeply affected. Oh, certainly you will not refuse to grant a support to them, and by this religious work turn thanks to Heaven, who, in his incomprehensible wisdom has lead you to a happier situation. (Correspondence of the *PAA*, vol. 7, 283)

A letter in Hebrew sent to Kursheedt on 19 Heshvan 5598 [17 November 1838] claims that the poor of Eretz Israel should take precedence even over the impoverished immigrants newly arrived in America. The translation of one section follows:

> Let him lift his eyes to what he himself wrote to me, that a few months ago about two hundred poor came there from Bavaria, and our co-religionists there, may our Rock and Redeemer preserve them, expended more than four hundred dollars on them, and they do not know the nature or the deeds of those guests who came to them; in contrast, the holy congregations in Eretz Israel, may it speedily be rebuilt, are renowned in name, in praise, and in glory, among them are famous men, great in Torah and in holiness, pillars and defenders of the generation. . . . (Ibid., vol. 8, 72)

11. Ibid., vol. 9, 264.

12. Details about Rice are found in the contemporary press, primarily in the *Occident* (see, especially, Leeser's eulogy, vol. 20 [December 1862], pp. 424–25) and in his unpublished sermons, which are in the library of the Jewish Theological Seminary of America, together with several manuscript letters. See also A. Guttmacher, *A History of the Baltimore Hebrew Congregation Nidchei Israel* (Baltimore: The Lord Baltimore Press, 1905), 65–67; Sharfman (see note 4 above), esp. 479–535. For additional primary sources on Rabbi Rice and his times, see Isaac M. Fein, *The Making of an American Jewish Community: The History of Baltimore Jewry from 1773 to 1920* (Philadelphia: Jewish Publication Society of

America, 1971). See also, Israel Tabak, "Rabbi Abraham Rice of Baltimore: Pioneer of Orthodox Judaism in America," *Tradition* 7 (Summer 1965): 100–20; idem, "The First Ordained Rabbi in America, and a Fighter for the Integrity of Judaism, against Reform: Rabbi Abraham Rice, of Blessed Memory," *Or ha-Mizrah* 11 (Nisan 1963, Hebrew): 34–36; Isidor Blum, *The Jews of Baltimore* (Baltimore and Washington, D. C.: Historical Review Publishing, 1910), 11–13. The stalwart orthodoxy of Rice in various situations is described by Jacob R. Marcus in his monumental *United States Jewry 1776–1985*, 4 vols. (Detroit: Wayne State University Press, 1991–93), I, 228, 275; II, 225 and esp. 231–32; III, 66, 70, 400.

13. William S. Rayner was a successful merchant and philanthropist. Born in Bavaria in 1822, he immigrated to the United States in 1840. He settled in Baltimore, where he played a role in the development of the city and its Jewish institutions. He assisted David Einhorn in the publication of the first Reform prayerbook.

14. "The History of the Har Sinai Congregation," English ms. by Rayner, in the Rice papers at the Jewish Theological Seminary library.

15. A letter dated 1862 to Meir Dov, in the Jewish Theological Seminary collection, reflects Rice's own modest evaluation of his influence on Baltimore Jewry, especially with the leading figures of the community. Thus does Dr. Harry Friedenwald describe his father's attitude toward Rabbi Rice:

> An important influence upon the formation of his character was that exerted by the late Rev. A. Rice, the first rabbi of the Baltimore Hebrew Congregation and an intimate friend of the family. Rice was a very pious man, whose congenial nature and religious fervor attracted the thoughtful boy, and it is to his influence rather than to any other that I should ascribe the consistent religious views which marked the whole course of my father's life. His loving veneration for Rice appeared in his frequent references to him and in his unvarying custom of having the prayer for the dead recited in his memory on the Day of Atonement. He mentioned on several occasions his intention of publishing a biography of the rabbi, together with a selection from his sermons, some of which my father transcribed; this intention, however, was never carried out. . . . (Harry Friedenwald, *Life, Letters and Addresses of Aaron Friedenwald, M.D.* [Baltimore: The Lord Baltimore Press, 1906], 23)

16. Correspondence of the *PAA*, vol. 8, 197. After a lengthy introduction, extolling both Kursheedt and Rice, Lehren concludes:

> As regards the exalted rabbi . . . [he] asked me to provide him with some lines to his exalted highness, may our Rock and Redeemer protect him, so that he may become acquainted with him and learn of his nature. Accordingly, I find myself duty bound to put my signs in his hand and to tell men of his integrity and righteousness, and the attribute of the wisdom of his Torah [scholarship]; I shall add also his perfection and innocence. He is fit for any religious post, and if it is possible to place him in one of the positions, how good and pleasant this will be. Happy will be the man who supports him with his righteous right hand. He will be blessed by Heaven and his future will be most splendid. Peace and blessing be with you, etc.

In another letter to Kursheedt, from 21 Sivan 5600 [****1840], Lehren adds the following (ibid., vol. 9, 177):

I am aware of the emigration of many of our Brethren from Germany and hope in time North America will have a *Kehillah Kedoshah* especially when such man as the Rev. Abm. Reiss [sic] comes among you, who is fit as by his diploma to be a *rav* among you, indeed the present time requires all of us *Yehudim* to be upon our guard respecting our holy Religion. . . .

17. In his volume *Response to Modernity: A History of the Reform Movement in Judaism* (New York: Oxford University Press, 1988), 236, Michael Meyer correctly imputes the dissatisfaction of many of Rice's congregants with what seemed to them to be an extreme Orthodox stance. See also, C. A. Rubinstein, *History of Har Sinai Congregation of the City of Baltimore* (Baltimore: Kohn and Pollock, 1918), the section: "The Founding of Har Sinai: Its First Development." See also, Hasia R. Diner, *A Time for Gathering: The Second Migration, 1820–1880, The Jewish People in America*, 2 (Baltimore and London: Johns Hopkins University Press, 1992), esp. 161 and also 122, 229. Not quite in character, on some issues Rabbi Rice took a liberal position, such as urging Jewish schools to emphasize the teaching of English and the production of reading material for the children so that the service would be understood by those who knew only English. Ibid., 220. Arthur Hertzberg, *The Jews in America: Four Centuries of an Uneasy Encounter—A History* (New York: Simon & Schuster, 1989), 126–27, etches Rabbi Rice's travail:

Rice's face, in the only portrait of him that remains, is wan and sad. His eyes seem to be looking across the Atlantic to the vibrant academy of Talmudic learning in Pressburg (Bratislava), in Slovakia, where he had studied under Moses Schreiber, one of the great rabbinic authorities of that generation. Rice resigned his position as rabbi [in Baltimore] in 1849. He wrote in utter despair to a friend in Germany: "I dwell in darkness without a teacher or companion. . . . The religious life in this land is on the lowest level; most people eat forbidden food and desecrate the Sabbath in public. . . . Under these circumstances my mind is perplexed and I wonder whether it is even permissible for a Jew to live in this land."

18. From the collection of Rice's sermons, 227–28. The sermons are written in German, in Hebrew letters.

19. Letter to Rabbi Isaac Dov Bamberger, Landrabbiner (district rabbi) of Wurzburg, appended to the book of sermons, 236.

20. From a letter to Kursheedt, ibid., 235.

21. Ibid., 116–17.

22. Ibid., 42–43. See also, the sermon on the Messiah delivered by Rice on the Sabbath preceding Passover 5602 (1842), published in the *Occident* 1 (September 1843): 271–80.

23. *Occident* 12 (June 1854): 168; (August): 264; (October): 374.

24. Correspondence of the *PAA*, vol. 8, 48; also see vol. 12, 69.

25. See A. M. Habermann, "The Journey of R. Benjamin Lilienthal to Eretz Israel a Hundred Years Ago," *Sinai* 25 (1948, Hebrew): 235–47. There was a tradition in the Lilienthal family "that R. Benjamin warned his sons that none should agree to leave the land, and whoever would violate his command would not be forgiven." See also, Yuda Aaron Weiss, *Within Your Gates, O Jerusalem* (Jerusalem: Halevi, 1949, Hebrew), 72. In 1867, Lilienthal was sent to the United States as an emissary on behalf of the small community of American Jewish immigrants in Jerusalem. Compare S. W. Baron (see note 1 above), 240–42.

26. Letter to Rabbi Isaac Dov Bamberger, appended to the book of sermons, 236.

27. Letters of the *PAA*, vol. 11, 188.

28. Letter dated Friday, the eve of the Sabbath of Vayikra 5622 (1862).

Chapter 6

Sir Moses Montefiore: American Jewry's Ideal

Moses Montefiore never set foot on America's shores. Yet, Sir Moses, already in his lifetime, was perceived both as symbol and reality within American Jewish life; indeed as a hero-type of American Jewry. Why did he succeed so much more than others in entering the group consciousness of American Jewry? How did he, quite literally, become an image for American Jewry, his portrait displayed in communal institutions and synagogues throughout the land? How were the achievements of Sir Moses compounded into a rationale whereby he came to be the quintessential role model of a modern, emancipated, yet totally committed traditional Jew? The answer, I suggest, can be found in the all-embracing involvement of Sir Moses in the Holy Land. As the Jews and the world sensed, his *neshama*—the breath of his being—was Zion Restored. The peace of Jerusalem was his vision; its good fortune his chief joy.

The symbols are too well known to enter into detail: The Coat of Arms "inscribed Jerusalem in Hebrew characters gold"; the lion and the hart, as in "Teachings of the Fathers" (5:20); the letterhead stamped Holy Land, the biblical verse over his bed: "If I forget Thee, O Jerusalem, Let my right hand forget its cunning." It is symbolism that reflects the driving force in his conception of world Jewry's responsibilities for the Holy Land. If there is more than a touch of contemporary allusion to the points I raise, it only reflects on the continuities in history, as well as on some of the problems of post-Emancipation Jewish life that have remained unresolved.

This proposition can best be examined in the fullness of Sir Moses' personality and life work in three lodes of source materials: institutions bearing Montefiore's name; primary historical—not hagiographical—sources; Montefiore's correspondence and a vast testimonial literature. In addition, of course, relevant material can be found in the periodical press and miscellaneous books and articles.[1]

Those strands, when combined, clarify how Moshe Haim ben ha-gvir Yosef Eliahu Montefiore was declared, not by vote, but by a people's instinct, as the ideal to which American Jews aspired. In a word, it was Sir Moses' performance on the world scene, and especially his ultimate dedication to the Holy Land.

INSTITUTIONS BEARING SIR MOSES' NAME

An excellent introduction to the special relationship between American Jewry and Moses Montefiore is Bertram W. Korn's keystone article entitled "A Preliminary Checklist of American Jewish Institutions and Organizations Named in Honor of Sir Moses Montefiore."[2] Regarding Sir Moses as "the most revered leader of the American Jewish community," Korn chose to document through his compilation "the power of the name and reputation of one man" on the nineteenth-century American scene as "a symbol of aristocracy, capitalistic wealth, public recognition and dignity, philanthropic benevolence, religious observance, championship of equal rights for Jews and support for modern Jewish development in Israel." Dr. Korn summarizes: "Unless we count each individual Hillel Foundation as a separate entity, the institutions and organizations which were named for Montefiore probably equal all of those named for other Jews of historic importance added together."

In his listing, Korn specified seventy-seven Montefiore-named institutions, some fifty of which were proclaimed in Montefiore's lifetime. Malcolm Stern and I add twenty-one places in our supplementary findings, thus indicating that the combined inventory is still incomplete (see Appendix 6A). Still, Bertram Korn's master list is a fascinating Jewish institutional map of the mid- and late-nineteenth century, spanning the continent. It is built around the inspiring Montefiore name, covering fifty-one cities in twenty-seven states, and reflects the mobility, communal growth, and social development of American Jewry. The check list includes synagogues (17); cultural and literary associations (11); Hebrew free schools (5); benevolent societies and lodges (12); social clubs (9); aid organizations (12); old-age homes (3); hospitals (2); burial associations and cemeteries (4); and for the benefit of the new Eastern European immigrants, two agricultural-aid institutions.

A more searching look into the manifold services to which these institutions were dedicated, and into the way each institution approached Sir Moses in letter, testimony, and appreciation, reveals the multifaceted qualities that the American Jewish community saw in him. For American Jewry, then, Moses Montefiore was the *summum bonum* of religio-cultural, communal, and social Jewish interest—above all, World Jewry and the Holy Land. What aspects of that totality were expressed in the records of the period?

HISTORICAL RECORD

Turning to the literature on Moses Montefiore, one is mindful that scholars of nineteenth-century Jewish history, primarily in Great Britain and Israel, have brought forth a more balanced evaluation of Sir Moses' life and person.[3] Separating wheat from chaff, carefully measuring successes and critically analyzing failures, they depict a less idealized and far less glorified personality. Myth has to be corrected so that it does not become historical reality. While I certainly respect every concern for historical revision, I delve here into Montefiore the living legend as projected on the American Jewish scene—a projection that, in essence, assumed its own reality.

Accordingly, most of my documentation is from American sources. At the same time, one must take into full account pertinent European materials, particularly British, that permeated the Jewish community in the United States, even in a century that did not know instant transcontinental communication. The Jews in America were the beholders. What were the distinctive elements that constituted the composite portrait of Sir Moses as he captivated the American Jew?

Clearly, the most prominent feature was the conflation of British-Jewishness. The hyphen both separates and unites. It is important to recall the historical setting: The Victorian age in the century when Jews were granted civil rights, public office, and position in the countries of Emancipation and Enlightenment. In this ambience, Montefiore appeared in court with equanimity in the scarlet gown appropriate to the High Sheriff of London and Middlesex, and at prayers in Ramsgate and Jerusalem in a fringed *Tallit*.[4] The impressive pictures portraying the bearded Montefiore crowned with a large *yarmulke* were proudly placed in Jewish households in many countries. They bespoke the grandeur of an English gentleman who would not shed any of the rituals of British Orthodoxy. Yet a mere glance at the painting in the Ramsgate Museum reveals that, indeed, Reb Moses' head was covered, but with a British smoking cap, even to the tassel! Neither contradiction nor meshing marked the separate yet seemingly compatible relationship of the Order of the British Empire with the *Shulhan Arukh* of a Sephardi Jew. It was the (seventh) Earl of Shaftesbury, one of the great philanthropists of Christian England and a believer in Jewish restoration to the Holy Land, who wished to see Montefiore elevated to the peerage. Writing in 1868 to Prime Minister Gladstone, he concluded: "It would be a glorious day for the House of Lords when that grand old Hebrew were enrolled on the lists of the hereditary legislators of England."[5] To all, then, Montefiore was exemplar of this harmonization.

The argument in Shaftesbury's letter was that "the Jewish question has now been settled. The Jews can sit in both houses of Parliament." But this reason was not accepted, and the vote failed. Actually, Shaftesbury had made the suggestion to the previous prime minister, namely the Jewish-born Benjamin Disraeli. Although Disraeli approved in principle, he stated that for obvious reasons, he would not be the first to raise a Jew to the peerage.

More than a century later, the *Times* of London celebrated Montefiore's 200th birthday in a feature article wherein the thesis of harmonization is repeated; "Montefiore demonstrated by his life that it was possible to be both a passionate Jew and a passionate Englishman." The writer, Philip Howard, captioned the piece, "Thanks Moses, you were a real Brit."[6]

No less characteristic of the style of Sir Moses and his Lady Judith—Yetta bat Joshua Levi HaCohen—was their public display of scrupulous Jewish observance in court, in travel, and in their relations with the Christian world.[7] Two citations from American testimony demonstrate Montefiore's authoritative Jewish stance in his contact with Christians.

A rare book, printed in Philadelphia by the Presbyterian Board of Publication, *Narrative of a Mission of Inquiry to the Jews from the Church of Scotland in 1839*, contains an "interview with Sir Moses Montefiore." These Scottish missionaries came, as they put it, to see the true condition and character of God's ancient people; and they chose to call upon Sir Moses "who had come on a visit of love to his brethren in the Holy Land . . . and his tent was now pitched on one of the eminences of the hill," the Mount of Olives.

Their description of the meeting in this imposing setting and the ensuing conversation speaks vividly:

> Sir Moses and his lady received us with great kindness, and we were served with cake and wine. He conversed freely on the state of the land, the miseries of the Jews, and the fulfilment of prophecy. He said that the Bible was the best guidebook in the Holy Land; and with much feeling remarked, that, sitting on this very place, within sight of Mount Moriah, he had read Solomon's prayer (I Kings viii) over and over again. He told us that he had

been at Saphet and Tiberias, and that there were 1500 Jews in the latter town, and more in the former; but they were in a very wretched condition, for first they had been robbed by the Arabs, then they suffered from the earthquake, and now they were plundered by the Druses. When Dr. Keith suggested that they might be employed in making roads through the land, as materials were abundant and that it might be the beginning of the fulfilment of the prophecy, 'Prepare ye the way of the people; cast up the highway, gather out the stones;' (Isa. lxii 10), Sir Moses' acknowledged the benefit that would attend the making of roads, but feared that they would not be permitted. He seemed truly interested in the temporal good of his brethren, and intent upon employing their young people in the cultivation of the vine, the olive, and the mulberry.[8]

Sir Moses was approached not only by missionaries in Zion, but by Christians of all denominations who sought his beneficence for their churches and institutions. Archival lists show requests from all corners of the United States. Montefiore's deeds were noted in the local American press, for example, in the item that appeared in the Delaware Gazette on 10 September 1850, under the heading "Jewish Liberality":

A foreign paper states that lately a deputation waited on Sir Moses Montefiore, to ask his assistance in the efforts to build a church. 'You know my religious opinion,' replied the excellent Jew, 'I cannot give you money to build a church—there are five hundred guineas for you to do what you like with.'[9]

Without underestimating the power of Montefiore's British-Jewishness and forthright Jewish religious position vis-à-vis the Christian denominations, a third factor that elicited the adulation of the Jewish masses was undoubtedly his intercession on their behalf in lands where they suffered indignities and suppression. In recognition of these endeavors and of the respect Montefiore earned among his coreligionists, Queen Victoria bestowed her "especial mark of our Royal favor" on Sir Moses in 1841, granting him the privilege to inscribe "Yerushalem" in Hebrew characters on his Arms. The citation therein reads: "In commemoration of these his unceasing exertions on behalf of his injured and persecuted brethren in the East, and the Jewish nation at large. . . ."[10] The paramount feature of Sir Moses' profile was "*mitzvah be-gufo,*" giving of one's self to help, in the words of the prayer, toward the deliverance of "the household of Israel . . . from darkness to light, from oppression to freedom."

A headline description suffices: Extensive travels to Russia, Morocco, and Rumania as Jewish entreator; seven journeys to the Holy Land as beneficent *parnass*; champion of Jewish rights as long-term president of the

London Board of Deputies of British Jews; prominent international Jewish figure in the trials of the Damascus Affair (1840) and Mortara case (1858); philanthropic dispenser of alms, aid, and relief literally to thousands; patron of scholars, learning, and institutions; and on, and on!

In this context, the lesser-known American record also offers interesting supportive evidence. An entry in the *Diaries* (September 1881) reveals the concrete Jewish reason for Sir Moses' high regard for Americans and their "noble institutions." "How many millions of our fellow beings . . . found a happy home there when all hope for an honourable maintenance in their own country had to be given up, because the land which gave them birth ceased to give them shelter and protection?" In the very same vein, Sir Moses had given vent to his deeper feelings about America as he spoke with pain about the assassination of Abraham Lincoln:

> Abraham Lincoln has broken the chains of the slaves and succumbed. I wish that God would grant me the strength and energy of this man to break the chains of my people, and I should have willingly endured death like this Abraham—this righteous man. Henceforth the Negroes are free, and will remain so, God willing. O, that I could say the same of Israel! In the territories of the Czar, in Morocco, and in a thousand other countries, my brethren are still waiting for their Abraham Lincoln![11]

Pogroms spread in the towns and villages of Russia. Moses Montefiore was in his ninety-seventh year, but the need for Jewish emigration and salvation occupied him, fortifying him in his determination. Hence, his sincere appreciation for each letter from America informing him of the absorption of the Russian emigrants. The 30 December 1881 notation in the *Diaries* states that: "At New Orleans every assistance was given to the emigrants numbering about a hundred, and the president of the West End Railway placed a special train at their disposal. The local Committee leased the Continental Hotel, capable of lodging over five hundred persons, and placed it under the Ladies' Hebrew Sewing Society. . . . I wish facilities like those offered by the committee at New Orleans could be secured for the emigrants who select the Holy Land for colonization."[12]

Clearly, then, Sir Moses' actions show that of his manifold goals, commitment to his people's amelioration received highest priority. Still, he was no less concerned with the Jewish quality of their life. For him, Jews and Judaism were indivisible. Thus, while he was never certain of the developing character of American Judaism, he responded to many calls for cultural and educational support. In 1851, he sent a *Sefer Torah* to the newly established synagogue Emanuel in San Francisco; to the congregations

Shearith Israel and Chizuk Amuno in Baltimore he also sent a Torah, on the condition that they share with one another, in recognition of their aid to the indigent in the Holy Land.[13]

Interestingly enough, as the evidence shows, while Sir Moses was unwavering in his adherence to traditional Judaism, he always found a quiet way to assist even those who did not share his views. A singular example is his gift to the library of the Hebrew Union College and the accompanying letter explaining his views. On December 30, 5635 (corresponding to 1874), Montefiore wrote, probably to M. Loth, Esq., president of the Union of American Hebrew Congregations, Cincinnati:

Dear Sir—Allow me the pleasure of depositing in the library of the College to be established by the Union of the American Hebrew Congregations, a copy of a bible in five folio volumes, containing thirty-two commentaries of our most ancient and most celebrated authors, accompanied by a copy of the statutes for the regulation of the college, 'Ohel Moshe ve Yehoodit,' in Hebrew and English, which I beg the Council of the Union will be pleased to accept and regard as a manifestation of the high esteem in which I hold the zealous exertions of our brethren in America for upholding and vindicating our holy law, as revealed on Sinai, and expounded by the revered sages of the Mishna and the Talmud.

It will always be a source of high gratification to me to learn the satisfactory progress the students in your college are making in their noble pursuits of our sacred writings, so as to enable them, when necessary, boldly to rise and defend the cause of our holy religion. 'Speak of God's testimonials in the presence of kings and be not ashamed.'

I have no doubt, in the course of time, your noble example will be followed by many of our brethren, who, under the pressure of circumstances and the influence of unwise teachers, allowed themselves hitherto to deviate from the path of truth, which alone leads man to lasting felicity, and you will, with God's blessing, be permitted to enjoy the pleasing consciousness of having been the originator of so holy a cause.

With sincere wishes for the welfare of every member of the Council, including yourself and your family, and with fervent prayers for the prosperity of all the Hebrew Congregations in America, and the restoration of glory to Zion.

I remain, dear sir, yours very truly,
Moses Montefiore
M. Loth Esq., member of the Council of the Union
of American Hebrew Congregations, Cincinnati.

On motion the Secretary was instructed to tender the thanks of the Executive Board to Sir Moses Montefiore for his generous donation.[14] (See Appendix 6B)

Our portrait cannot be complete without reference to a profound and continuing issue which pervaded people's thought and action, namely the issue of "dual loyalty." A fascinating example appeared in *The American Israelite* of 4 December 1885. The subject of the article (reprinted from the *Jewish Chronicle*) was antisemitism. Its substance was an interview with the then Prince of Wales, later Edward VII; and the canard discussed was the standard view that "the Jews cannot be patriots, because their eyes are always lovingly turned toward the Holy Land—the country regarded by them as their only fatherland." In his response, the Prince unequivocally extolled Sir Moses:

> It is universally acknowledged that there never was a greater lover of Zion than Sir Moses Montefiore, who, when he was Sheriff, had his coat of arms, with the word 'Jerusalem,' placed on the raiment of all his servants.[15] Yet England has no truer patriot than he; not a man throughout the kingdom exceeded him in the love he bore for his adopted country. It was in recognition of his universal acts of philanthropy that my august mother, the Queen, raised him to the dignity of a Baronet, and Sir Moses Montefiore may best serve as a proof to anti-Semites in Hungary and elsewhere that a Jew can at one and the same time be attached to the land of his ancestors, and loyal to the ruler of the country of his adoption.[16]

Reports such as these regularly found their way into the general and Jewish periodical press in the United States, and appeared especially in such publications as *The Occident* and *The Jewish Messenger* as well as *The American Israelite*. Sir Moses' passion for Zion exhilarated the entire Jewish community. Every statement and action in this regard enhanced his authority as a guiding figure and leader. His relations with the Board of Delegates of American Israelites, which have been traced by Yaakov Kellner,[17] are an example of his unique influence with that body (see Appendix 6C). Other areas of Sir Moses' involvement were the *Hebrat Terumat haKodesh* and the North American Relief Society for the Indigent Jews in Jerusalem, and especially the Judah Touro legacy.[18]

Recent archival research on these aspects, as on others, warrants sober reevaluation of Montefiore's institutional activities in and for the Holy Land: Sources that call for authoritative reexamination are the Moses Montefiore Testimonial Fund (for which Ismar Elbogen's study can serve as a model)[19] and Montefiore's relations with Gershom Kursheedt, who was one of the executors of the Judah Touro Trust. (See Appendices 6D and 6E.) In any definitive history of Mishkenot Sha'ananim, the first Jewish quarter outside the walls of old Jerusalem founded by Sir Moses in 1860, the events of its founding will have to be reconsidered.

Notwithstanding indispensable corrections of fact and interpretation with respect to concrete historical situations in which Sir Moses was engaged, his intuition of the place of Eretz Israel in the Jewish future was unequivocal. And this is the second issue with contemporary overtones: the impact of Sir Moses' abiding belief in the eternal mission of Zion, that *Shivat Zion* (Return to Zion) is the fundament of Jewish continuity.

Sir Moses knew full well the realities of the Jewish diasporas and the negative, or at best neutral, reaction to personal settlement in Eretz Israel. But his vision was not diminished. In his eightieth year, he wrote: "I am quite certain of it; it has been my constant dream and I hope will be realized some day when I shall be no more. . . . I do not expect all Israelites will quit their abodes in those territories in which they feel happy, even as there are Englishmen in Hungary, Germany, America, and Japan; but Palestine must belong to the Jews. . . ."[20]

Moses Montefiore was of another century and another stamp. But his views anticipated the pragmatism of American Jewry's involvement in Eretz Israel and World Jewry. (See Appendix 6F.) "Begin in the first instance," he said, "with the building of houses in Jerusalem; begin at once."[21]

TESTIMONIAL LITERATURE AND CORRESPONDENCE

By what standard can we measure an individual's influence on his contemporaries and his times? One measuring rod is, of course, authenticated source materials. In the case of Sir Moses, testimonials to him on various anniversaries are a storehouse of illuminating information, as are minute books from congregations and Jewish organizations throughout America.

One of the archival resources is American testimonials to Sir Moses Montefiore, catalogued by the Montefiore Endowment Committee.[22] Beyond the value of such documents for any Montefiore study, important leads for American Jewish historiographers can be gleaned from the letters sent to London from all sections of the United States: The West Coast—Los Angeles, San Francisco, Portland (Oregon); the Midwest—Detroit, Milwaukee; the South—Paducah (Kentucky), New Orleans; and in the East—Buffalo, Brooklyn.

Another quite remarkable source is the publications of the many centennial anniversary services in major American cities, as, for example, the addresses delivered at the Thanksgiving Service of Temple Emanu-El in New York (22 October 1884). Special services were prepared, music was composed, and poems were written in English and Hebrew for the extraordinary occasion.[23]

A unique illustration is the acrostic poem in Hebrew of one hundred words (a word for each year), by Reverend Dr. M(oses) Mielziner of the Hebrew Union College. Dr. Mielziner served as Professor of Talmud and

Rabbinical Literature at the College from 1879—and upon the death of Isaac M. Wise (26 March 1900), he became president of the College until his passing in 1903.[24]

> In Honor* Sir Moses Montefiore, may his light shine,
>   Prince, Epitome of this generation, and
>   Elder of the House of Israel!
>   On the Anniversary of his One Hundredth Birthday
>   Sunday, 7 Heshvan, 5645 (1885)
>
>   From the ends of the earth let this day's song resound—
>   Paean and Psalm of Thanksgiving in God's holy places.
>   All lips shall declare your glory and majesty
>   All Israel shall pray on your behalf.
>
>   Today you have reached a hundred years.
>   May you flourish mightily as in days of youth,
>   Chief and Prince; with fealty and generosity
>   You have faithfully sought the welfare of Israel
>
>   In times of trouble, you went forth to rescue your brethren
>   You've redeemed them in Damascus and saved them from
>   blood libel.**
>   You came before Kings and Princes of the earth
>   As a guardian angel for the silent and oppressed.
>
>   You have favored the Holy Land, our father's land.
>   Travelling to and fro accompanied by Judith—
>   To see Zion and Examine the state of our brethren:
>   You have been a blessing and Salvation to the remnant of Judah
>
>   May God reward your many faithful deeds
>   And in return for your mercy and loyalty to your people
>   May he extend his mercy towards the centarian
>   And may your days be as numerous as Amram's son.***
>
>   Words of your servant who from the distance bows before your honor
>   Moshe son of our teacher and Rabbi Benjamin, may the
>   memory of righteous be blessed, [Signed] Mielziner

---

*   The poem contains the Acrostic: Long Live Moshe (Moses) Montefiore.
**   Reference to the Damascus blood libel.
***   That is, Moses (120 years).

APPENDIX 6A: INVENTORY OF INSTITUTIONS IN THE UNITED STATES BEARING THE NAME OF MOSES MONTEFIORE

1. Bertram Wallace Korn's Checklist

Altoona, Pennsylvania, Moses Montefiore Lodge of B'nai Brith, 1878.

Appleton, Wisconsin, Moses Montefiore Social Club, 1903.

Atlantic City, N. J., Montefiore Social Club, 1894.

Baltimore, Maryland, Montefiore Literary and Pleasure Assn., 1897.

Baltimore, Maryland, Ohel Moshe School, 1884.

Bloomington, Illinois, Moses Montefiore Congregation, 188?

Boise, Idaho, Ladies Judith Montefiore Society, 1896.

Boston, Massachusetts, Montefiore Home and Aid Society, 1887.

Braddock, Pennsylvania, Montefiore Society, 1888.

Buffalo, New York, Montefiore Lodge of B'nai B'rith, 1866.

Buffalo, New York, Montefiore Club, 1920.

Cairo, Illinois, Congregation Montefiore, 1894.

Chicago, Illinois, Congregation Moses Montefiore, 1875.

Chicago, Illinois, Moses Montefiore Hebrew Free School, 1883.

Chicago, Illinois, Moses Montefiore Night School for Hebrew and German, 1884?

Chicago, Illinois, Montefiore Literary Assn., 1892.

Cincinnati, Ohio, Montefiore Mutual Benefit Soc., 1883?

Cleveland, Ohio, Montefiore Lodge of B'nai B'rith, 1864.

Cleveland, Ohio, Montefiore Home, ?

Detroit, Michigan, Montefiore Lodge of Free Sons of Israel, 1864.

Duluth, Minnesota, Moses Montefiore Congregation, 189?

Duluth, Minnesota, Moses Montefiore Hebrew Institute, 1905.

Hoboken, New Jersey, Congregation Moses Montefiore, ?

Houston, Texas, Montefiore Hall in Beth Israel Synagogue, 1885.

Indianapolis, Indiana, *Montefiore Magazine*,?

Kansas, Montefiore Agricultural Colony, 1884.

Lafayette, Indiana, Montefiore Street, ?

Las Vegas, New Mexico, Congregation Montefiore, 1884.

Leavenworth, Kansas, Montefiore Literary Society, 1883.

Los Angeles, California, Moses Montefiore Congregation, 1886.

Lowell, Massachusetts, Congregation Montefiore, ?

Marinette, Wisconsin, Moses Montefiore Congregation, ?

Milwaukee, Wisconsin, Moses Montefiore Congregation, 1886.

Marshall, Texas, Temple Moses Montefiore, ?

Minneapolis, Minnesota, Montefiore Burial Assn., 1876.

Montreal, Canada, Montefiore Social and Dramatic Club, 1880.

Newark, New Jersey, Montefiore Mutual Aid Assn., 1885.

New York, New York, Montefiore Society for the Relief of Widows and Orphans, 1841.

New York, New York, Montefiore Literary Assn., 185?

New York, New York, Montefiore Benevolent Union, 1869?

New York, New York, Montefiore Agricultural Aid Society, 1882.

New York, New York, Lady Montefiore Relief Assn., 1883?

New York, New York, Montefiore Hospital, 1884.

New York, New York, Montefiore Square, ?

New York, New York, Moses Montefiore Benevolent Society, 1884?

New York, New York, Moses Montefiore Lodge, Kesher Shel Barzel, 1884?

New York, New York, Montefiore Sewing Circle, 1884?

New York, New York, Moses Montefiore Lodge, B'rith Abraham, 1887.

New York, New York, Montefiore Hebrew School, 1889.

New York, New York, Montefiore Brotherly Beneficial Assn., 1897.

New York, New York, Montefiore Hebrew Congregation, 1884?

New York, New York, Montefiore-Dreyfus Lodge, Order of United Hebrew Brothers, 1915?

New York, New York, Montefiore Social and Literary Union,?

Norfolk, Virginia, Montefiore Literary and Social Assn., 1887?

Orange, New Jersey, Ladies Montefiore Aid Society, 1884?

Pensacola, Florida, Montefiore Auxiliary Lodge, 1897?

Peoria, Illinois, Moses Montefiore Lodge, Kesher Shel Barzel, 1876.

Philadelphia, Pennsylvania, Montefiore Cemetery, 1911.

Philadelphia, Pennsylvania, Montefiore Congregation, 1915.

Pittsburgh, Pennsylvania, Montefiore Hospital, 1888.

Providence, Rhode Island, Montefiore Lodge Ladies Hebrew Beneficial Assn., 1885.

Providence, Rhode Island, Moses Montefiore Association, 1889.

Providence, Rhode Island, Young Mens Moses Montefiore Society, 1891.

Richmond, Virginia, Montefiore Literary Assn., 187?

Richmond, Virginia, Sir Moses Montefiore Congregation, 1887.

Salt Lake City, Utah, Montefiore Congregation, 1899.

San Francisco, California, Montefiore Lodge of B'nai B'rith, 1864.

San Francisco, California, Montefiore Lodge, Kesher Shel Barzel, 1884?

St. Paul, Minnesota, Montefiore Burial Assn., 1876.

Seattle, Washington, Ladies' Montefiore Aid, 1901.

Springfield, Illinois, Montefiore Cemetery, ?

Syracuse, New York, Moses Montefiore Lodge, Kesher Shel Barzel, 187?

Toronto, Canada, Ladies Montefiore Benevolent Society, 1878.

Trinidad, Colorado, Montefiore Literary Society, 1894.

Wheeling, West Virginia, Montefiore Literary Society, 1875.

Wilmington, Delaware, Montefiore Beneficial Society, 188?

Woodville, Mississippi, Montefiore Literary Assn., 1884?

Note: In his paper, Dr. Korn stated that his "preliminary checklist is published now in the hope that students of local American Jewish history will assist the compiler in correcting inadequate or erroneous data and in adding new names to the list." See also his "Request for Information," *AJHQ* 64, no. 3 (March 1975): 267. In keeping with this testament, both Dr. Malcolm Stern and I have tried to continue this work. Further corrections, revisions, and additions should be sent to the American Jewish Archives in Cincinnati, marked for the Bertram W. Korn literary estate.

2. Supplementary List—Malcolm Stern

Corrections

Cincinnati, Ohio, (1871).

Cleveland, Ohio, Sir Moses Montefiore (*Kesher* Home for Aged and Infirm Israelites), (1889).

Hoboken, New Jersey, (1892).

Marinette, Wisconsin, (1888).

Providence, Rhode Island, Montefiore Lodge Ladies Hebrew *(Benevolent)* Association, (1878).

Wilmington, Delaware, Montefiore *(Benefit)* Society, (1884).

Additions

Baltimore, Maryland, Montefiore Club, 1892.

Baltimore, Maryland, Congregation Moses Montefiore Amenus Israel, 1889.

Chicago, Illinois, Lady Montefiore Lodge, Sons of Benjamin.

Chicago, Illinois, Montefiore Charity Society No. 1.

Detroit, Michigan, Montefiore Pleasure Club, 1897.

Indianapolis, Indiana, Montefiore Society.

New York, New York, Lady Montefiore Auxiliary of B'rith Abraham.

New York, New York, Moses Montefiore Lodge of Sons of Benjamin.

Oakland, California, Montefiore Youth Auxiliary of B'nai B'rith.

San Antonio, Texas, Montefiore Benevolent Society, 1856.

Seattle, Washington, Judith Montefiore Society.

Tacoma, Washington, Judith Montefiore Society, 1890.

3. Supplementary List—Moshe Davis

Corrections

Bloomington, Illinois, (1889).

Cleveland, Ohio, Montefiore Home *(for the Aged),* (1884).

Wilmington, Delaware, (1879).

Additions

Atlanta, Georgia, Montefiore Relief Association, 1896.

Boston, Massachusetts, Moses Montefiore Asociation, 1890(?).

Cleveland, Ohio, Montefiore Lodge No. 13 of B'rith Abraham.

Des Moines, Iowa, Montefiore Old Folks Home.

Hartford, Connecticut, Moses Montefiore Lodge No. 365 of Brith Abraham.

Meriden, Connecticut, Montefiore Circle, Order B'nai Zion.

New York, New York, Montefiore Society for Tenement House Reform, 1884.

New York, New York, Montefiore Home for Chronic Invalids, 1884.

Philadelphia, Pennsylvania, Montefiore Agricultural Aid Society, 1882.

An example of a synagogue that originally planned to name itself after Montefiore and then reversed its decision is Congregation B'nai Amoona of St. Louis, Missouri. See Rosalind Mael Bronson, *B'nai Amoona for All Generations*, St. Louis, 1982, p. 5. I thank Rabbi Baruch Lipnick who brought the source to my attention.

APPENDIX 6B*

East Cliff Lodge
Ramsgate 22 September 5638

Dear Sir,

It is a source of much gratification to me to have again the opportunity of handing you enclosed £3: the amount of my subscription to your excellent Journal "The Jewish Record": for the year 5639, the receipt of which I beg you will kindly acknowledge. I fervently hope you will continue disseminating the principles of our holy Religion and promote, as much as may be in your power, the Study of the Hebrew language and its sublime literature.

We must now more than ever make every effort to support our Schools and Colleges where the word of God is taught in its purity, so that the rising generation may learn to understand the prophecies conveyed unto Israel by the mouth of the Seers of Old.

With sincere wishes that the approaching New Year may bring unto yourself and family, as well as unto every member of your esteemed congregation perfect health and lasting prosperity.

I remain, Dear Sir
Yours very truly
Moses Montefiore

Alfred T. Jones Esq.
Editor of "The Jewish Record"
Philadelphia

APPENDIX 6C**

East Cliff Lodge
Ramsgate November 3rd, 5636–1875

To: P. J. Joachimson Esq. & Myer S. Isaacs Esq.

Dear Sirs,

I have much pleasure in acknowledging the receipt of an Address through you, from the Board of Delegates of American Israelites, of which you are the esteemed Representatives, in which they most kindly offer their Congratulations on my obtaining by the mercy of God, the advanced age of Ninety-one years.

*   From: American Jewish Archives, Cincinnati, Ohio.
**   From: American Jewish Historical Society Archives, Waltham, Mass.

I beg you will offer to the Board the assurance of my grateful sense of the Kindness with which they have testified to their approbation of my conduct, and have recognized my humble efforts for the interest and welfare of our Coreligionists in all parts of the World, and I am thankful to say that the few petitions I have been permitted to present to some of the Great Rulers of the Nations have been invariably received with the kindest consideration, and perhaps I may express a hope that some of the obnoxious laws to which you refer have been removed or somewhat ameliorated.

I am very sensible of the kind manner in which the Board alludes to my recent visit to the Holy Land, and most thankful to Almighty God for causing me to surmount the great difficulties attending so long and fatiguing a journey and for the success with which he has so mercifully crowned it.

May I request you to do me the favour to tender to the Board my heartfelt wishes for their prosperity and for the happiness of its individual members and the various Congregations which they so ably represent

I remain
Dear Sirs
Yours very faithfully
Moses Montefiore

APPENDIX 6D*

East Cliff Lodge, Ramsgate
6th February 5615
1855

Duplicate (To Gershon Kursheedt Esq.)

My dear Sir

I have been most anxiously expecting to hear the good news of your having reached home in safety and in good health, I trust that such is the case and that I shall soon have the pleasure of learning of your welfare.

It is my intention (P.G.) to proceed to the holy [sic] Land, accompanied by Dr. Loewe, the week after the ensuing Passover Holidays when I hope it may be my happy privilege greatly to contribute by personal exertions towards the amelioration of the condition of our brethren through the means so liberally entrusted to me for that purpose.

I hope with the blessing of God to establish such institutions as shall elevate generally their position; and to secure to them the blessings of labour, the cultivation of the soil, so that they may truly realize the blessings of God in the labour of their hands. How greatly should I rejoice to be able to embrace

*   From: American Jewish Archives, Cincinnati, Ohio

so favorable an opportunity, an opportunity not likely ever again to occur to lay the foundation stone of the intended Hospital, and see the good work in progress intended by the munificent bequest of your late lamented friend Mr. Judah Touro, may his soul rest in peace.

To see in a state of progress the Testators benevolent intentions, and the realization of some of my fondest hopes, for the benefit of our good brethren of the Holy Land, will indeed make my visit a blessing to the peoples, (happiness) to myself and I hope will prove a glory to God.

Hoping yourself and circle are in the enjoyment of health and that I shall soon have satisfactory accounts from you,

I am with every good wish
Your faithful & obt. servant
Moses Montefiore

Lady Montefiore begs to add her kind wishes.

APPENDIX 6E*

Ship Hotel
Thursday Night
8th July 5618
1858

To: Gershon Kurscheedt, Esq. (excerpt)

. . . I have not had the pleasure of receiving a line from you during the whole time of our absence. I hope you and your family have been quite well. I wish I could prevail on you to come and pass a couple of months with us in East Cliff we could then conclude on the best plan for carrying our Mr. Touro's benevolent intentions without that delay which a correspondence across the Atlantic would occassion [sic]. I cannot defer any longer the erection of the Building but it would be of the greatest possible satisfaction to me to have the advantage of your advice on every point concerning the matter, pray let me know can you without great inconvenience come (and come as soon as possible). We shall indeed be happy to have you.

Lady Montefiore writes with me in kindest regards to you and beg you to make our good wishes acceptable to your esteemed family.

Mr. and Mrs. Cohen also desire me to add their best compliments.

I have the pleasure

from M. Montefiore

---

*   From: American Jewish Archives, Cincinnati, Ohio

APPENDIX 6F: HOLY LAND*

Sir Moses Montefiore, Bart.
East Cliff Lodge
Ramsgate, Rosh Chodesh
Kislev 5640

Dear Sir,

My attention has recently been drawn to a notice you have given in the *Jewish Record* of the 95th Anniversary of my Birthday, accompanied by a prayer referring to some important event in the History of Israel which occurred in our time.

It is not with the purpose of conveying my special thanks to you for the flattering expressions you thought proper of introducing on that occasion, that I trouble you with these lines; knowing such to have been dictated to you by the good opinion you entertain of my humble efforts to serve in a good cause: overrating the little merit, I may, to a certain degree, have thereby earned: but I am promoted to address you, by a desire of manifesting to you my appreciation of the important service you render to all Hebrew Communities, when recalling to their memory, from time to time, the comforting assurance that "the Guardian of Israel neither slumbereth nor sleepeth," that He shows mercy to the innocent sufferer at times when all hope had been abandoned by him, and the Omnipotent will never withdraw his protecting grace from all who strictly abide by the law He revealed on Sinai.

Our Brethren, I am happy to say, still evidence that ardent love towards one another, as in times of old,—they constitute, as it were, all over the world, one body; and the sufferings of those who live in the remotest part of the globe, as soon as they become known to them, touch their heart, and find sympathy in every Jewish family. The Hebrew communities in America are preeminently distinguished by that characteristic trait of Israel. On all occasions, when the cry of anguish reaches their ear, promptly and most generously, they offer their noble contributions to assuage the sufferings of the Brother. And I ascribe the cause of it to their innate feeling of benevolence, intensely roused by the eloquent addresses they hear from men of great learning and piety, re-echoed from house to house by the powerful appeals from learned and conscientious Editors of Journals, raising high the banner of Israel for the vindication of our holy Religion.

You, my dear Sir, are one of those zealous brothers who stand in the breach to defend the sacred cause; great is your merit, and greater still the reward you earn by the consciousness of cordially associating yourself with all the earnest laborers in the vineyard of God. Your heart surely must be full with joy.

---

*   American Jewish Archives, Cincinnati, Ohio

Permit me, Dear Sir, to entertain the hope that you will continue to avail yourself of every opportunity to present, and where necessary to rekindle that spirit of devotion, that holy zeal which constitutes the life of Israel. Continue to retain in the heart of our Brethren that indomitable courage which made our forefathers plead the cause of our religion in the presence of Kings, and never felt ashamed of performing those Heavenly commandments which were binding upon them as Israelites.

You will have no difficulty among our American Brethren to execute so pleasing a task. I know many instances of their devotion to all that is good and holy, and have every reason to believe that they will gladly avail themselves of the opportunity to follow any of your suggestions, by which the children may be enabled to follow the footsteps of their fathers and forefathers in the fear of God.

As for myself, as long as God will bless me with health and strength, as long as my hand is able to move, my feet to walk and my eyes to see, I will not cease to remember all the mercies God has shown to Israel, and the promises he vouchsafed unto us.

Zealously and cheerfully, I will, conjointly with your faithful Brethren, hold high the Banner of Jerusalem, always praying that we may live to see the great day when the name of God as One God will be adored among all the nations of the earth.

> with best regards,
> I am, Dear Sir,
> Yours very truly,
> /s/ Moses Montefiore

Alfred T. Jones, Esq.
Editor of the Jewish Record
Philadelphia

NOTES

1. For a bibliography of Montefiore testimonial literature, see Pinhas Ya'akov Cohen, "A List of Books and Articles Published in Honor of Moses Montefiore," *Sinai* 32–33 (1953, Hebrew): 97–102, 254–55. A comprehensive bibliography is Ruth P. Goldschmidt-Lehmann, *Sir Moses Montefiore 1784–1885: a Bibliography* (Jerusalem: Misgav Yerushalayim, 1984). Some of this material was graciously shown to me in the private library of Mr. A. Schischa in London. Periodical cuttings were reviewed through the courtesy of the Kressel Collection at the Oxford Centre for Postgraduate Hebrew Studies.

For American references, see, especially, Salo W. and Jeanette M. Baron, "Palestinian Messengers in America, 1849–79: A Record of Four Journeys," S. W. Baron, *Steeled by Adversity* (Philadelphia: Jewish Publication Society of America, 1971), 158–266; Joseph L. Blau and Salo W. Baron, eds., *The Jews of the United*

States, 1790–1840 (New York: Columbia University Press, 1963); Arnold Blumberg, *A View from Jerusalem, 1849–1859: The Consular Diary of James and Elizabeth Ann Finn* (London: Farleigh Dickinson University Press, 1980); Moshe Davis, *The Emergence of Conservative Judaism* (New York: Burning Bush Press, 1963); Hyman B. Grinstein, *The Rise of the Jewish Community of New York, 1654–1860* (Philadelphia: Jewish Publication Society of America, 1945); Leon Huhner, *The Life of Judah Touro* (Philadelphia: Jewish Publication Society of America, 1946); Bertram Korn, *Eventful Years and Experience; Studies in Nineteenth Century American Jewish History* (Cincinnati: American Jewish Archives, 1954); idem, *The American Reaction to the Mortara Case* (Cincinnati: American Jewish Archives, 1957); Morris U. Schappes, *A Documentary History of the Jews of the United States, 1654–1875*, 3d. ed. (New York: Schocken, 1971).

2. Bertram Wallace Korn, "A Preliminary Check List of American Jewish Institutions and Organizations Named in Honor of Sir Moses Montefiore," *Gratz College Annual of Jewish Studies* 2 (1973): 60–64. A piquant reference to Montefiore's impact on American Jewry was the occasional practice of naming children after him, similar to a custom prevalent among North African Jews. See Gershon Greenberg, "A German-Jewish Immigrant's Perception of America, 1853–54," *AJHQ* 67 (1978): 319, where he quotes from an anonymous report: "Incidentally, children receive names of living fathers or which are neither biblical nor traditional. As the Jews of the Talmud named their children after Alexander [the Great], Sephardi children have names like Washington and Montefiore."

3. The important studies of Judge Israel Finestein are excellent examples of such analysis. See "The Uneasy Victorian: Montefiore as Communal Leader," in his *Jewish Society in Victorian England: Collected Essays* (London: Valentine Mitchell, 1993), 227–56; "Anglo-Jewish Opinion during the Struggle for Emancipation," ibid., 1–53; "The Jews and English Marriage Law during the Emancipation," ibid., 54–77; "The Anglo-Jewish Revolt of 1853," ibid., 104–29. In truth, critical evaluations of Montefiore's activities by American Jews appeared in the course of his lifetime. See, for example, the summary of Leeser's views in Jacob Kellner, *For Zion's Sake: World Jewry's Efforts to Relieve Distress in the Yishuv 1869–1882* (Jerusalem: Yad Izhak Ben-Zvi, 1976, Hebrew), 57–63; a highly subjective negative appraisal is Ephraim Deinard, *Megillat Setarim* (New York: [Author], 1928). See also, *The Century of Moses Montefiore*, ed. Sonia and V. D. Lipman (London: Oxford University Press, 1985); *The Age of Moses Montefiore: Collection of Essays*, ed. I. Bartal (Jerusalem: Misgav Yerushalayim, 1987).

4. Compare the description of a specific day in the life of Montefiore, as cited in V. D. Lipman, "The Age of Emancipation 1815–1880," in *Three Centuries of Anglo-Jewish History*, ed. V. D. Lipman (London: Jewish Historical Society of England, 1961), 69, 95.

At noon on the last day of July 1838, a tall man left a house in Prescott Street, on the south-eastern fringe of the City of London. The house he was leaving was doubly in mourning since he had been attending service on the Fast of Ab and it was the house of mourning of his wife's half-brother. The tall man of 53, who had 'a commanding figure, deportment dignified but not arrogant, a voice manly but gentle,'* walked briskly into the City to Guildhall. There he was transformed from the worshipper and mourner into one of the two Sheriffs of London and Middlesex; after donning the scarlet gown appropriate for the occasion, he attended sessions of the Court of Hustings and of the Court of Aldermen. He then called at the City offices of the Provincial Bank of Ireland and the Alliance Insurance Company, both of which he was a director. Finally he returned to Prescott Street at seven for evening prayers—after which he broke his fast.**

See also, Cecil Roth, "Sir Moses Montefiore," *Great Jewish Personalities in Modern Times*, ed. Simon Noveek (Clinton, Mass.: B'nai B'rith, 1960), 43–58.

5. The full text of the letter appears in Paul Goodman, *Moses Montefiore* (Philadelphia: Jewish Publication Society of America, 1925), 223–24.

6. *Times*, 19 October 1984.

7. For an insightful biographical appraisal of Judith Montefiore, see Sonia L. Lipman, "Judith Montefiore First Lady of Anglo-Jewry," *Transactions of the Jewish Historical Society of England* 21 (1968): 287–303.

A charming comment on Sir Moses' "gallantry," relating to taking Judith for his wife "from among the females of a congregation whose genealogical tree did not show the *Dons* and the *Hidalgos*," is found in Henry Samuel Morias, *Eminent Israelites of the Nineteenth Century* (Philadelphia: Stern, 1880), 241. Morias concludes: "On the 10th of June, 1812, he wedded a Jewess who had not read her prayers in the Bevis Marks Synagogue."

8. *Narrative of a Mission of Inquiry to the Jews from the Church of Scotland in 1839* (Philadelphia: Presbyterian Board of Publication, 1845), 43.

9. Quoted by David Geffen, "Delaware Jewry: the Formative Years, 1872–1889," *Delaware History* 16 (1975): 271.

10. S. U. Nahon, *Sir Moses Montefiore* (Jerusalem: Bureau for Jewish Communities and Organizations of the Jewish Agency, 1965), 95–96.

11. For the two citations, see (a) *Diaries of Sir Moses and Lady Montefiore*, ed. Louis Loewe, facsimile of the 1890 edition (London: Jewish Historical Society of England, 1983), vol. 2, 301. All further citations are from this edition, impressively introduced by Raphael Loewe. (b) *American Jewish Archives* 13, no. 2 (November 1961): 230, which reprinted the report published in *The Jewish Chronicle*, 30 June 1865, itself based upon the *Archives Israélites*.

12. *Diaries* . . . , v. 2, 302.

13. Fred Rosenbaum, *Architects of Reform* (Berkeley: Western Jewish History Center, 1980), 5; Isaac M. Fein, *The Making of an American Jewish Community* (Philadelphia: Jewish Publication Society of America, 5371 [1971]), 174. See also, Wolfgang Gunther Plaut, *The Jews in Minnesota* (New York: American Jewish Historical Society, 1959), 103. A further insight into Sir Moses' abiding

---

*   William Thornborrow, *Advocacy of Jewish Freedom* (2nd edition, 1848), 30, so describes Montefiore at this date.

**   *Diaries of Sir Moses and Lady Montefiore*, edited by L. Loewe, 1, 143.

interest in American Jewry is the reference in the report of the Western Jewish History Center to the effect that "It had the good fortune to obtain the bound volumes of *The Hebrew*, a San Francisco weekly newspaper, that Sir Moses Montefiore collected in London during the nineteenth century. The run is from January 1864 to June 1876. . . ." *AJHQ* 58 (1968–1969): 273.

14. *Proceedings of the Union of American Hebrew Congregations 1 (1873–1879) (Cincinnati, n.d.), 130. For background to this exchange see ibid., 74.*

15. For example, see Alfred Rubens, "Anglo-Jewish Coats of Arms," *Anglo-Jewish Notabilities* (London: Jewish Historical Society of England, 1949), 88, 109–10; Franz Hubmann, *Le grand album de la famille juive* ([Paris]: Hachette, 1974), 181.

16. *American Israelite* 32, no. 23, p. 6.

17. Jacob Kellner, "The Formative Years of American Support for the Jewish Community in Palestine, 1833–1881," *Shalem* 1 (1974, Hebrew): 377–426; idem, *For Zion's Sake* (see note 3 above).

18. On Touro, see L. Huhner (see note 1 above); Max J. Kohler, "Judah Touro: Merchant and Philanthropist," *PAJHS* 13 (1905): 93–111; Ruth Kark, "Notes on 'Batei-Tura'," *Cathedra*, no. 18 (January 1981, Hebrew): 158–67. Both Huhner and Kohler cite the full text of Touro's will.

19. Ismar Elbogen, "The Montefiore Testimonial Fund and American Israel," *PAJHS* 37 (1947): 95–101.

20. Cited in Lucien Wolf, *Sir Moses Montefiore: A Centennial Biography* (London: John Murray, 1884), 276.

21. Quoted by Barbara Tuchman, *Bible and Sword: England and Palestine from the Bronze Age to Balfour* (New York: New York University Press, 1956), 193–94.

22. I recall with gratitude my debt to the lamented Vivian Lipman who advised me in many phases of this study. He brought materials to my attention unknown to me, and in this particular instance, he served as gracious intermediary with the Endowment Committee, securing permission to review the American names from the catalogue prepared by Ms. M. Lehrer. Special thanks are due to Professor Raphael Loewe. Among those letters are two testimonials from Oliver Wendell Holmes and John Greenleaf Whittier, published in *AJA* 6, no. 2 (June 1954): 166.

23. As examples, see: "Centennial Anniversary," *Sir Moses Montefiore*, United Hebrew Services, Rodeph Shalom Synagoguge, Philadelphia, 26 October 1884; Addresses delivered at the Thanksgiving Service, Temple Emanu-El, New York, 22 October 1884. I am grateful to Professor Abraham Karp for copies of these rare pamphlets. An imposing American portrait of Sir Moses in his later years was painted by George da Maduro Peixotto (1859–1937), son of Benjamin Franklin Peixotto. It was reproduced by courtesy of the Jewish Museum of New York in *AJA* 13, no. 2 (November 1961): 198.

24. Copy of the original poem is also among the papers of the Montefiore Endowment Foundation and was printed in *American Israelite* 31, no. 17 (24 October 1884). The present translation of the original Hebrew is by Professor Ezra Spicehandler.

PART III
"NAMES ON THE LAND"

Chapter 7

Biblical Place-Names in America

My eyes were first opened to place-names as a guide to historical insight by George R. Stewart's masterwork *Names on the Land*.[1] He demonstrated that "the thing and the name were almost one" and that the heritage of names often outlives men and nations, and even languages.

There are literally millions of names on the multicolor American landscape of mountains, valleys, and rivers, people and events of Indian, Dutch, British, Spanish, French, and German flavor. My natural bent was to search out biblical place-names as manifestations of America's spirit. From the very beginning of European settlement, place-names of biblical context appeared on the face of America's map along her expanding frontiers.[2] In the American tradition, it was indeed the origin of the common faith.

Regrettably, much of this story is still unwritten. There is so much to be gleaned from the biblical source that the time is ripe for more comprehensive information and interpretation. Our research on biblical or, as generally referred to, Old Testament place-names has brought together an abundance of material on the inception of many cities, towns, and hamlets. These are of particular interest to those concerned with the history of American thought and character as well as the topography of the United States. Several examples, high on the current geopolitical agenda—Jerusalem/Salem, River Jordan, and Zion—suffice to illuminate the name-placing process.[3]

Jerusalem in Stevens County, Washington, evidently arose from the respect for biblical parity at home base. According to Edmond S. Meany, "Some said there was an Egypt on one side of Spokane River, and there ought to be a Jerusalem on the other side. In that way the name came into use."[4]

Salem, the short form of Jerusalem, is the anglicized version of the Hebrew *Shalom*. The name stretches across the American continent in some twenty-seven localities from Massachusetts to Oregon. As early as 1629, the Indian name "Naumkeag" near Plymouth in Massachusetts (some heard it as Nahum Keick: corrupted Hebrew meaning of comfort-haven) was changed to Salem when a new church was founded. Did it not say in Scriptures in the opening verses of Psalm 76?

> God has made himself known in Judah,
> > His name is great in Israel,
> > Salem became His abode;
> > Zion his den.[5]

Later, the capital of Oregon state, the present Salem, was also transposed from an Indian name "Chemeketa," meaning resting or meeting place, by David Leslie in 1844. Leslie came to Oregon from Salem, Massachusetts, thus entrenching the name of Salem from sea to sea.[6]

Jordan (Jordan River) is also woven into the language and culture of America. In Alabama it is a lake and a dam; in California's Sequoia National Park, it is a mount; in Minnesota, it is a city in Seth County. In black-slave litany, "Roll, Jordan, Roll" was a prayer of destiny, wherein the name was endowed with contemporary meaning.[7] The Mormons, to judge from the biblical names they left in their wake on their pilgrimage westward, seemed to have a penchant for the name. In August 1847, a month after the pioneers arrived in Great Salt Lake Valley, according to a communication from Earl E. Olsen, librarian of the Church of Jesus Christ Latter-Day Saints, it was moved "that we call the river running from the place, The Western Jordan." The motion was carried, and the river was so designated, later to become known as the Jordan River.[8]

Zion as simile for the Holy Land and Jerusalem continued to pervade the mind-soul of various ethnic subcultures in America, as for example, evangelical Protestants, black believers, and Jews. In the earliest days of American settlement, the Puritans determined the tone. To the Puritans, Lester Vogel succinctly states: "The consummate polity was theocratic in form and symbolically associated with Zion." For them, America was the New Zion.[9] John Alexander Dowie, founder of the Christian Catholic Church in 1896, built Zion City, Illinois, in 1901, with all its streets given biblical names. Dowie identified Zion with the Kingdom of God.[10] Blacks conceived the Holy Land as a Zion-centered scriptural drama that helped them transcend their existential plight.[11] The Jews rose to chant Naftali Herz Imber's *Ha'Tikva* (Hope) with the concluding refrain "Land of Zion and Jerusalem."

About one thousand names of biblical derivation appear on the map of the United States. Not all of them, however, stem from biblical sources. In order to ascertain the origins of these place-names, Lottie K. Davis collated a master list from official gazetteers, postal guides, state reference maps, W.P.A. (Work Projects Administration) sources, local histories, and place-name studies. A questionnaire was addressed to every village, town, or city on the master text. The following, authenticated list of 384 biblical names and their county locations is a result of this research. Every name listed is based upon a standard source. Many names have been omitted because of our reluctance to include places named for individuals or where we lacked definite verification.

Alabama

Boaz, Marshall
Goshen, Pike
Jericho, Perry
Joppa, Cullman
Mt. Carmel, Jackson
Mt. Carmel, Montgomery
Mt. Hebron, Greene
Mt. Olive, Jefferson
Pisgah, Jackson
Ruhama, Birmingham

Arizona

Eden, Graham

Arkansas

Bethel, Greene
Damascus, Faulkner
Hebron, Clark
Jericho, Grittenden
Jerusalem, Conway
Mt. Olive, Izard
Shiloh, Clebourne
Zion, Izard

California

Edenvale, Santa Clara

Goshen, Tulare
Havilah, Kern
Jerusalem (Lake)
Joshua, San Bernardino
Mt. Ararat, El Dorado
Mt. Hebron (Peak), Siskiyou
Mt. Hebron (Town), Siskiyou
Mt. Hermon, Santa Cruz
Ophir, Placer
Pisgah, San Bernardino
Pisgah Crater, San Bernardino

Colorado

Ephraim, Conejos
Hebron, Jackson
Lebanon, Montezuma
Manassa, Conejos

Connecticut

Bethel, Fairfield
Bethlehem, Litchfield
Bozrah, New London
Canaan, Litchfield
Goshen, Litchfield
Hebron, Tolland
Lebanon, New London
Mt. Carmel, New Haven

New Canaan, Fairfield
New Salem, New London
North Canaan, Litchfield
Salem, New London
Sharon, Litchfield

Delaware

Bethel, Sussex
Lebanon, Kent
Mt. Moriah, Kent
Rehoboth, Sussex
Rehoboth Bay, Sussex

Florida

Canaan, Seminole
Lebanon, Levy
Shiloh, Brevard

Georgia

Bethel, Rabun
Bethlehem, Barrow
Hebron, Sanderville
Hephzibah, Richmond
Naomi, Walker

Idaho

Eden, Jerome
Goshen, Bingham
Salem, Madison
Samaria, Oneida

Illinois

Bethel, Clay
Carmi, White
Goshen, Stark
Hebron, McHenry
Joppa, Massac
Jordan, Whiteside
Lebanon, St. Clair
Moriah, Clark
Mt. Carmel, Wabash
Nebo, Pike
New Salem, Menard
Pisgah, Jacksonville
Salem, Marion

Zion, Carroll
Zion City, Lake

Indiana

Bethel, Wayne
Bethlehem, Clark
Canaan, Jefferson
Carmel, Hamilton
Eden, Hancock
Gilead, Miami
Goshen, Elkhart
Hebron, Porter
Lebanon, Boone
Merom, Sullivan
Mt. Carmel, Franklin
Mt. Carmel, Gibson
Nineveh, Johnson
Zoar, Pike

Iowa

Bethel, Van Buren
Bethlehem, Wayne
Egypt, Van Buren
Goshen, Ringgold
Hebron, Adair
Jordan, Harrison
Kedron, Harrison
Lebanon, Van Buren
Mt. Moriah, Van Buren
Mt. Zion, Van Buren
Pisgah, Harrison
Salem, Henry
Sharon, Appanoose
Shiloh, Des Moines
Solomon, Mills
Tabor, Fremont
Zion, Adair
Zion, Van Buren

Kansas

Lebanon, Smith
Sharon, Barber
Sharon Springs, Wallace

Kentucky

Bethel, Bath
Goshen, Oldham
Jericho, Henry
Lebanon, Marion
Mt. Carmel, Fleming
Nebo, Hopkins
Zion, Grant

Louisiana

Ararat, Calcasieu
Ebenezer, Acadia
Eden, La Salle
Nebo, La Salle

Maine

Bethel, Oxford
Carmel, Penobscot
Gilead, Oxford
Hebron, Oxford
Hiram, Oxford
Jerusalem, Franklin
Lebanon, York

Maryland

Bethlehem, Caroline
Damascus, Montgomery
Ebenezer, Cecil
Joppa, Harford
Zion, Cecil

Massachusetts

Goshen, Hampshire
Mt. Horeb, Berkshire
New Salem, Franklin
Rehoboth, Bristol
Salem, Essex
Sharon, Norfolk
Zoar, Franklin

Michigan

Benzonia, Benzie
Bethel, Branch
Eden, Ingham

Gilead, Branch
Sharon, Kalkosha

Minnesota

Aaron (Lake), Douglas
Bethel, Anoka
Eden, Dodge
(and seven additional names in the state)
Hebron, Aitkin
Jordan, Fillmore
Jordan, Scott
Kedron Brook, Fillmore
Mamre, Kandiyohi
Mizpah, Koochinching
Moses (Lake), Douglas
Mt. Nebo, Todd
Nimrod, Wadena
Sharon, Le Sueur
Zion, Stearns

Mississippi

Bethel, Newton
Damascus, Scott
Ebenezer, Holmes
Mt. Zion, Simpson
Pisgah, Charles
Sharon, Madison

Missouri

Bethel, Shelby
Canaan, Gasconade
Jericho Springs, Cedar
New Salem, Newton
Nineveh, Adair
Pisgah, Cooper
Salem, Dent
Zion, Madison

Nebraska

Bethel, Kimball
Elim, Nemaha
Gilead, Thayer
Hebron, Thayer
Lebanon, Red Willow

Salem, Richardson
Zion, Burt

Nevada

Mizpah, Elko

New Hampshire

Bethlehem, Grafton
Canaan, Grafton
Gaza, Belknap
Goshen, Sullivan
Hebron, Grafton
Lebanon, Grafton
Salem, Rockingham

New Jersey

Carmel, Cumberland
Genesis Bay, Cape May
Goshen, Cape May
Jericho, Cumberland
Jericho, Gloucester
Jericho, Salem
Lebanon, Hunterdon
Mizpah, Atlantic
Mt. Bethel, Warren
Mt. Gilboa, Hunterdon
Mt. Hermon, Warren
Mt. Horeb, Somerset
Mt. Nebo, Sussex
Mt. Pisgah, Sussex
Mt. Tabor, Morris
New Egypt, Ocean
New Sharon, Gloucester
New Sharon, Monmouth
Salem, Salem
Siloam, Monmouth
Zarephath, Somerset
Zion, Somerset

New Mexico

Bethel, Roosevelt
Rehoboth, McKinley

New York

Bethel, Dutchess

Bethel, Sullivan
Bethlehem, Albany
Canaan, Columbia
Carmel, Putnam
Eden, Erie
Ephrata, Fulton
Gilboa, Schoharie
Goshen, Orange
Hebron, Washington
Hermon, St. Lawrence
Jericho, Nassau
Lebanon, Onondaga
Moriah, Essex
Nineveh, Broome
Sharon, Schoharie
Shushan, Washington

North Carolina

Ararat, Surry
Bethel, Pitt
Eleazer, Randolph
Mt. Gilead, Montgomery
Mt. Olive, Wayne
Ophir, Montgomery
Pisgah, Randolph
Pisgah Forest, Transylvania
Salem, Forsyth
Salemburg, Sampson
Tabor City, Columbus

North Dakota

Hebron, Morton
Mt. Carmel, Cavalier
New Salem, Morton
Sharon, Steele
Zion, Towner

Ohio

Ai, Fulton
Bethel, Clermont
Canaan, Wayne
Carmel, Highland
Gath, Highland
Gilboa, Putnam

Goshen, Clermont
Hebron, Licking
Lebanon, Warren
Mt. Carmel, Clermont
Mt. Carmel, Sandusky
Rehoboth, Perry
Salem, Columbiana
Sharon, Trumbull
Shiloh, Montgomery
Shiloh, Richland
Sodom, Trumbull
Zoar, Tuscarawas

Oklahoma

Gideon, Cherokee
Jonah, Garfield
Kedron, Cherokee
Lebanon, Marshall
Nebo, Murray
Sharon, Woodward

Oregon

Bethel, Polk
Damascus, Clarkamas
Goshen, Lane
Lebanon, Linn
Mt. Horeb, Marion
Mt. Moriah, Union
Mt. Pisgah, Polk
Mt. Tabor, Multnomah
Ophir, Curry
Salem, Marion
Selah, Marion

Pennsylvania

Ararat, Susquehanna
Bethel, Allegheny
Bethlehem, Northampton
Canaan, Wayne
Damascus, Wayne
Ephrata, Lancaster
Goshen Heights, Chester
Hebron, Potter
Jericho Mt. and Creek, Bucks

Lebanon, Lebanon
Mt. Carmel, Northumberland
Mt. Nebo, Lancaster
New Salem, Fayette
Nineveh, Greene
Sharon, Mercer
Zion, Lucerne

Rhode Island

Eden Park, Providence
Elisha, Little Compton, Newport

South Carolina

Ebenezer, Florence
Mt. Carmel, McCormick
Sharon, York
Shiloh, Sumter
Zion, Marion

South Dakota

Lake Sinai, Brookings
Lebanon, Potter
Salem, McCook
Sinai, Brookings

Tennessee

Joppa, Grainger
Lebanon, Wilson
Mt. Horeb, Jefferson
Sharon, Weakley

Texas

Bethlehem, Hill
Egypt, Wharton
Goshen, Parker
Hebron, Denton
Jonah, Williamson
Joshua, Victoria
Nineveh, Leon
Salem, Johnson

Utah

Eden, Weber
Ephraim, Sanpete
Goshen, Utah

Jordan, Salt Lake
Mt. Carmel, Kane
North Eden Canyon, Rich
Salem, Utah
South Eden Canyon, Rich
Zion Canyon, Washington
Zion National Park, Washington

Vermont

Bethel, Windsor
Canaan, Essex
Goshen, Addison
Goshen Corners, Addison
Jericho, Chittenden
Jericho Center, Chittenden

Virginia

Damascus, Washington
Lebanon, Russell
Mt. Carmel, Smyth
Zion, Louisa

Washington

Eden, Wahkiakum
Jericho, Grant
Jerusalem, Stevens
Sharon, Spokane
Tekoa, Whitman

West Virginia

Bethlehem, Ohio

Boaz, Wood
Canaan, Upshur
Damascus, Marshall
Ebenezer, Fayette
Edray, Pocahontas
Gilboa, Nicholas
Hebron, Pleasant
Joppa, Braxton
Kedron, Upshur
Mt. Carmel, Preston
Mt. Nebo, Nicholas
Mt. Pisgah, Clay
Mt. Zion, Calhoun
Nebo, Clay
Pisgah, Preston
Salem, Harrison

Wisconsin

Bethel, Wood
Eden, Fond du Lac
Hebron, Jefferson
Lebanon, Dodge
Mt. Horeb, Dane
Salem, Kenosha
Siloam, Milwaukee
Sharon, Walworth

Wyoming

Eden, Sweetwater
Goshen County

Thus did America express itself. In this expression we find another manifestation of the biblical impress that stamped America's spirit.

Figure 1
Western United States

Figure 2
Eastern United States

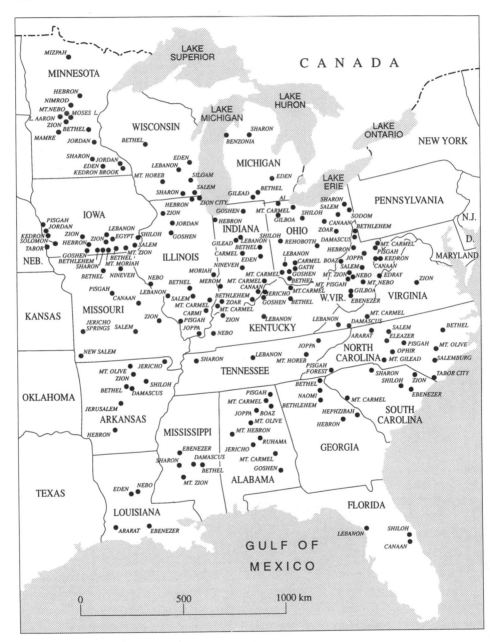

Figure 3
Northeastern United States

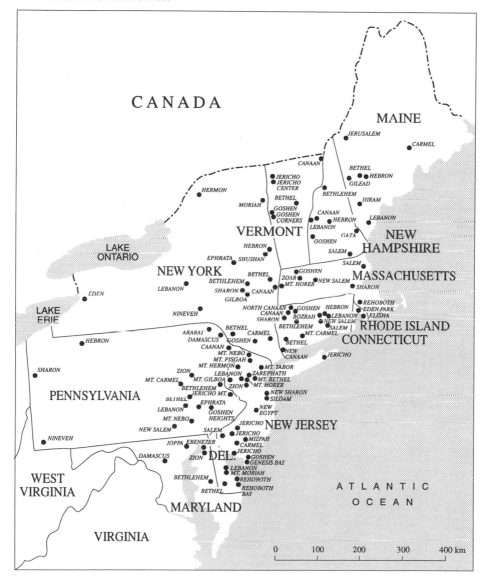

NOTES

1. George R. Stewart, *Names on the Land*. A historical account of place-naming in the United States (New York: Random House, 1945).

2. Lottie and Moshe Davis, *Land of Our Fathers: Guide to Map of Biblical Names in America*, illustrated by Charles Harper (New York: Associated American Artists, 1954). See also "Land of our Fathers" in *TV Version* by Morton Wishengrad, *Frontiers of Faith*, 28 November 1954.

3. See "Biblical Heritage" section in chapter 1, especially notes 5 and 6.

4. *Origin of Washington Geographic Names* (Seattle, 1923), 123.

5. G. R. Stewart (see note 1 above), pp. 39–41.

6. Lewis A. McArthur, *Oregon Place Names* (Portland, 1944), 37–38.

7. On religious symbolism derived from the Holy Land via the Bible, see Lawrence N. Jones, "Afro-Americans and the Holy Land," *With Eyes Toward Zion* I, ed. Moshe Davis (New York: Arno Press, 1977), 58–60.

8. Lottie K. Davis, "Jordan–Bible Names in the U.S.A.," in *Land of the Bible Newsletter* 1, no. 7 (August–September 1959): 1–3.

9. L. Vogel, *To See a Promised Land: Americans and the Holy Land in the Nineteenth Century* (University Park, Pa.: Pennsylvania State University Press, 1993), 32–33, 221.

10. Robert T. Handy, "Zion in American Christian Movements," *Israel: Its Role in Civilization*, ed. Moshe Davis (New York: Harper & Bros., 1956), 296–97.

11. See Gershon Greenberg, "Christianity and Blacks," *The Holy Land in American Religious Thought 1620–1948* (Lanham, Md.: University Press of America, 1994), 169–73.

Chapter 8

America in Zion:
Settlements and Institutions

The dynamics of history propelled American interaction with Zion Restored through diverse stages. In the beginning of New World–European settlement in the seventeenth century, the Puritan metaphor of America as Zion prevailed. The nineteenth century brought Christian messianism to the shores of the Holy Land; in later years, as the Jewish national renaissance evolved, colonization, primarily agricultural, emerged. After the Balfour Declaration in 1917, the American penchant for health and welfare found expression in Eretz Israel. With the establishment of the State of Israel, socioeconomic, cultural, and educational bridges were strengthened. Currently, all strands interweave, attesting to the enduring involvement of America and Americans in Zion.

Distinctive facets of the American role in Zion rebuilt are settlements and institutions founded and named by Americans; places established in honor of Americans; and others sustained by Americans, although they do not bear their names. The following succinct examples illustrate the rubrics of metaphor, messianism, colonization, health and welfare, culture, *halutziut*/pioneering, ecumenism, and "sub-urban" settlement in which Americans were involved. They also cast light on the periodization of America's developing interest in the Holy Land societal framework.[1]

METAPHOR: MOUNT HOPE (1855)

Clorinda Minor, native of Philadelphia and a Sabbath-observing Christian belonging to a Congregational church of Puritan ancestry, came on pilgrimage to the Holy Land in 1849 with other members of the Adventist sect, followers of William Miller. Their mission was to establish the "Manual Labor School of Agriculture for Jews in the Holy Land," which would assist Jewish settlers in productively working the land. Remarkably, the pioneers of modern agricultural settlement in the Holy Land were Christians. For the realization of her project, Minor and her son collaborated with a British convert from Judaism, John Meshullam, in the village Artas near Bethlehem. After she returned from a visit to the United States where she sought support for her project, in 1851, Minor settled again in Artas with other followers. When an internal dispute broke out two years later, the Americans separated from the British group and moved to a leased tract of land in the environs of Jaffa. In 1855, Minor bought the site, calling it Mount Hope. She was later buried there.

Despite its failure, the Artas experience had considerable importance in the history of agricultural settlement in mid-nineteenth century Eretz Israel. During her stay in the Holy Land, Minor's activity was profusely described in *The Occident* of Isaac Leeser in Philadelphia, the first major Jewish publication in the United States.[2]

MESSIANISM: ADAMS COLONY (1866)

George Washington Joshua Adams, a descendant of the renowned Adams family, was founder of the Church of the Messiah sect in New England. He preached that the End of Days was near and that the Jews would return from the four corners of the earth to the Holy Land. A group of his followers, pilgrims from Maine, landed on the shores of Jaffa to establish an agricultural settlement on a site about one kilometer northeast of the Old City of Jaffa. The settlement bore the name of Adams, but it is sometimes referred to as the "American colony." Prefabricated wooden houses were shipped from Maine, and some of these structures have been preserved and restored.

During their first year, the settlers were confronted with many hardships, essentially administrative and legal. Unable to maintain the community through their farming, they travelled to America and Europe to solicit funds, but with little success. The Adams colony was the subject of much intercession by American diplomatic agents in Palestine, Turkey, and Egypt during 1867–1868, and its survivors troubled the consuls in later years.[3] By 1868, most of the settlers, including Adams and his family, had left the Holy Land. The colony was sold to German Templars in 1869.[4]

COLONIZATION: PORIYYAH (1910)

The first years of the twentieth century, until the outbreak of World War I, marked a new thrust of American Jewish settlement in Eretz Israel. Those years, defined by Alexander Bein as "the most decisive period of colonization" in the Holy Land, correspond to the immigration wave, mostly from Russia and Poland called the *Second Aliyah*. American Jews attempted several settlement projects. The first was prompted by students of the Jewish agricultural college at Woodbine, New Jersey. Calling themselves *HaIkkar HaTzair*, "The Young Farmer," they planned to build a working collective farm on land leased to them near Lake Kinneret by the Jewish National Fund. While this American Jewish enterprise foundered, a *moshav ovdim*, the first cooperative, small-holders' settlement at Nahalal in the Jezreel Valley, was later founded in 1921.

Another, somewhat more effective colonization experiment was part of the Achooza (estate) movement designed to bring middle-class American Jews to settle in Eretz Israel. Individuals formed associations and made payments on an installment plan in the hope that they would later come to settle.[5] The first group, organized in 1908 by Simon Goldman in St. Louis, Missouri, purchased land that they called *Poriyyah* (fertile) as a symbol of their desire to make the abandoned, desolate land fruitful. The nearby settlements were very pleased with the new venture in their midst. They built houses for workers who began to plant almond trees, which, they expected, would bear fruit in the seventh year; it was the prime planting. The war, however, put an end to the venture; the orchards were destroyed, but title to the land was retained. Today, the name Poriyyah is borne by a village, hospital, and hostel in the Upper Galilee region.[6]

HEALTH AND WELFARE: HADASSAH (1912)

With the motto "The Healing of the Daughter of My People" (based on Jeremiah 8:22), suggested by Professor Israel Friedlaender of the Jewish Theological Seminary of America, Hadassah grew from a small Zionist group called "The Daughters of Zion" to become the largest Zionist organization in the world. In common Israeli parlance, the name Hadassah became a synonym for "hospital." The source of the eponym, Hadassah, is the book of Esther 2:7. Judah Magnes conferred the name; he was then rabbi of Temple Emanu-El in New York City where the founding meeting took place on 24 February 1912, which corresponded that year to the Feast of Purim (Hadassah was the name of the biblical Queen Esther). Its leading spirit, Henrietta Szold, had a rich fund of experience upon which she could draw. In her youth, Henrietta had learned in her father's house that Hebrew was the authentic voice of Judaism. Fortified with Jewish scholarly training and with perceptions far beyond her years, she devoted her life—to use her own phrase—to the "noble dissatisfactions" of Jewish life: Zionism and Jewish education. As for Hadassah, the organization was originally designed by Henrietta Szold to engage in health work in Eretz Israel, with headquarters in Jerusalem. However, it rapidly became an extensive movement involved in many welfare, cultural, and educational programs, some named for distinguished American Jews such as the Alice Seligsberg High School and the Brandeis Center for training youth in fine mechanics and printing. The ramified activities of Hadassah in the *Yishuv* are meticulously depicted in several hundred file-cabinet drawers in the Hadassah archives.[7] The Hadassah–Hebrew University Medical Center continues to invite the best American talent to advance its life-supporting goals.[8]

CULTURE: ROCKEFELLER MUSEUM (1927)

On 13 October 1927, John D. Rockefeller, Jr., writing to High Commissioner Lord Herbert O. Plumer, pledged two million dollars to build an archaeological museum in Jerusalem. Eleven years later, the magnificent Rockefeller Museum was opened to the public. A fascinating collection within the archives of the Mandatory government includes reports, architectural plans, and additional material documenting the American role in the building and maintenance of the museum. Rockefeller corresponded with the High Commissioner, with James H. Breasted of the Oriental Institute of the University of Chicago, and the proposed staff and organization of the Department of Antiquities with special reference to Rockefeller's personal concerns. Of special interest in that collection is a four-page, handwritten proposal entitled "Proposed Palestine Museum" (7 November 1927) by E. J. Richmond, Director of Antiquities. The proposal was addressed to the High Commissioner, stating *inter alia* that procedures be adopted in which "the confidence of the authorities in America be retained" (Jacket 1). From this memorandum and other items, it was clear that Professor Breasted was the mastermind of the entire project—always keeping John Rockefeller informed of progress. Despite its difficult history, the museum leadership was proud that exciting archaeological projects were developed within its halls.[9]

HALUTZIUT/PIONEERING: **EIN HASHOFET (1937)**

By coincidence, the first North American *Hashomer Hatzair* (The Young Watchman) kibbutz in Eretz Israel, *Ein Hashofet*, meaning "The spring of the Judge," was settled on America's Independence Day, 4 July 1937. But not so incidentally, it was named in tribute to a giant figure in American jurisprudence, Louis D. Brandeis, popularly known as "the people's advocate." This appellation was not perfunctory. It sealed a profound personal and social relationship between the Justice and the American Socialist–Zionist youth movement. In Louis Brandeis, its members saw an American Zionist leader of uncompromising principle whose social philosophy brought him to the foreground of the progressive forces in American society, a spokesman who taught openly and clearly that his Zionism enhanced his Americanism.

The Justice Brandeis folders in the well-ordered archives at the kibbutz contain reports to him from the American *halutzim* about the vicissitudes of life at the kibbutz, especially during the first years of 1937–41. They were not easy years for the North American and Polish pioneers who tilled the land acquired from the village of Juara in the Samarian mountains overlooking the Jezreel Valley, as they suffered from rioters from neighboring Arab villages. Fortunately, the *halutzim* endured with a minimal loss of life. And they were grateful for their achievements as inscribed in the first year's "Scroll of the Harvesters."

> In number the fields we have cleared of stones and cultivated are small but we have been blessed with a crop that bears added witness to the everlasting covenant we have struck with this place. Death has ploughed here, too, but we will snatch the plough from his hands and build here a commonwealth of happy laborers.[10]

ECUMENISM: **TANTUR ECUMENICAL INSTITUTE (1972)**

"Tantur," the Arabic word for "hilltop," is situated on the main road from Jerusalem to Bethlehem. Its design as an international institute for theological research and pastoral studies sprang from discussions during the 1963 session of the Second Vatican Council between Pope Paul VI and delegated observers from other churches. Many of the participants urged the Pope that "someone somewhere" should establish an international, intercultural institute where Christian scholars and teachers could experience a life of prayer, study, and dialogue within a community. After his pilgrimage to Jerusalem in January 1964, the Pope purchased the Tantur site from the Knights of Malta. The rector since 1988, Thomas F. Stransky is an American Paulist

Father and an original staff member of the Vatican Secretariat for Christian Unity. He recalls the Pope's insistence: "The institute should be in Jerusalem, where today Christians of all Communions, one yet sadly divided, find the other two peoples of the Book—Jews and Muslims."[11]

From the start, the American input into Tantur was energizing and practical. The renowned Father T. M. Hesburgh, then president of the University of Notre Dame and of the International Federation of Catholic Universities, convoked and chaired all of the planning committees. After Tantur's opening in 1972, he headed its academic committee, which included several American Catholic and Protestant scholars. Father Hesburgh was also responsible for securing the funds for the construction and operational expenses of Tantur. The main donor for the building itself was the O'Shaughnessy family of St. Paul, Minnesota.

The University of Notre Dame continues to be the principal financial supporter of Tantur. A sizable number of American Catholics and Protestants are always among the international scholars, clergy, and religion teachers who participate in Tantur programs.

Under the learned guidance of Father Stransky, Tantur has explored new modes of interaction with the Jewish, Christian, and Muslim scholarly communities in the Holy Land and with worldwide religious leaders.

SUBURBAN SETTLEMENT: EFRAT (1981)

Residential suburbs around most large cities have become permanent features of modern city life.[12] With keen architectural insight, Frank Lloyd Wright described the character of this growth by a hyphen: sub-urbia. The economic, social, and geographic factors that stimulated such developments elsewhere are also rapidly changing the urban landscape of contemporary Israel.

The city of Efrat, in the Judean hills, south of Jerusalem, is "sub-urbia" with a difference. Oral testimony recounts that the dream of Efrat was inspired in 1976 when Moshe "Moshke" Moskowitz, a forceful Israeli B'nai Akiva leader also of Cyprus detention camps reputation, and Shlomo Riskin, then Rabbi of Lincoln Square Synagogue in New York City, joined their vision and talents to bring the dream to reality. Rabbi Riskin hoped to transplant a substantial section of his congregation to Efrat. Of the two hundred families who enlisted, eighty-five did come to Israel, but only ten settled in Efrat in 1983. Nevertheless, the American component assumed a secure place within the amalgam of Anglo-Saxon and Israeli residents in the rising community.

Efrat quickly emerged as a predominantly modern-Orthodox community of about one thousand families. Building on the special setting of commitment to learning and religious cohesiveness, a complex of Ohr Torah education institutions, co-directed by Rabbi Riskin and Rabbi Chaim Brovender, was established, from high schools to rabbinical seminary, with an extensive outreach program.

Whatever the future may hold for *sub-urban* Efrat on the four Judean hilltops, it has achieved its original design—what Lewis Mumford aptly described as "the sense of the neighborhood"—"a new consciousness of something that has been lost in the rapid growth of the city."[13]

These selected examples extending over a period of virtually one hundred and fifty years, reflect localized history of American presence in the Holy Land writ large. The most revealing comparative fact is the thread of continuity, from Clorinda Minor's Mt. Hope through Simon Goldman's Poriyyah until Moskowitz-Riskin's Efrat. While the reach of Americans in Holy Land settlement was greater than their grasp, their imagination was impressive, but their numbers faulted. The saving grace of these singular efforts was the staunchness of the remaining settlers who became an integral part of the Holy Land.

A second sustaining element was the support system that the American Zionist movement and pro-Holy Land Christian societies extended through their pilgrimages, institution-building, and personal commitment. A larger circumference of American involvement is delineated in the following, briefly annotated list of settlements with American connections spread throughout the map of the Holy Land.

SETTLEMENTS*

The numbers in parentheses refer to the position of the settlement on Figure 4.

Adams Colony: See page 148. (33)

Afulah: City founded by the American Zion Commonwealth in 1925, intended to be the urban center of the Jezreel Valley. (17)

American Colony: Founded in the 1890s, this was the third American Christian settlement established in the Holy Land. Under the leadership

---

*   An annotated study of American Place–Names in Zion is in preparation. Sponsored by the America–Holy Land Project, it is directed by Joseph B. Glass, with the assistance of Beverley Rubin and Ora Zimmer. The author will appreciate additions and corrections.

Figure 4:
America in Zion—Settlements

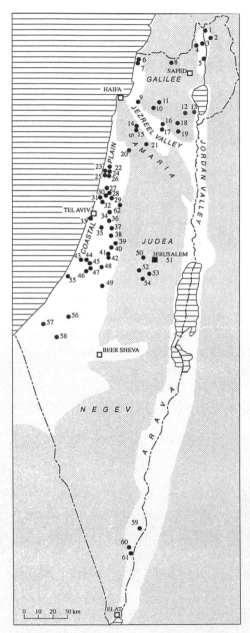

1. Ma'yan Barukh
2. Kefar Szold
3. Kefar Blum
4. Yiftah
5. Shoshannat haYarden
6. Liman
7. Gesher haZiv
8. Sasa
9. Ramot Yohanan
10. HaSolelim
11. Hanaton
12. Sharonah
13. Poriyyah
14. Ramat haShofet
15. Ein haShofet
16. Balfouriyyah
17. Afulah
18. Ein Dor
19. Ramat Zvi
20. Barkai
21. Mei Ammi
22. Bet Herut
23. Avihayil
24. Pardes haGedud
25. Netanyah
26. Kiryat Zanz
27. Benei Zion
28. Gan Hayyim
29. Zofit
30. Ra'anannah
31. Gan Rashel
32. Herzliyyah
33. Jaffa: Adams Colony; Mount Hope
34. Baptist Village
35. Kefar Habad
36. Neveh Efrayim
37. Kefar Truman
38. Kefar Daniel
39. Kefar Shmuel
40. Gezer
41. Mishmar David
42. Tal Shahar
43. Gan Yavneh
44. Hazor
45. Orot
46. Kefar Warburg
47. Kiryat Malakhi
48. Kefar Menahem
49. Galon
50. Neveh Ilan
51. Jerusalem: American Colony; Mishkenot Sha'ananim
52. Zur Hadassah
53. Artas
54. Efrat
55. Kefar Silver
56. Netivot-Morasha
57. Kissufim
58. Urim
59. Yahel
60. Ketura
61. Grofit

of the Chicago Spafford family, it was established in Jerusalem, near the Damascus Gate. It now serves as a privately managed hotel. (51)

Artas: See Mount Hope, page 148. (53)

Avihayil: The Jewish Legionnaires, including American volunteers, were granted land in Emek Hefer in 1932 by the Jewish National Fund. The Bet HaG'dudim Museum is situated in Avihayil, a *moshav*, and serves as a living memorial to the Jewish Legion. (23)

Balfouriyyah: First successful American Zion Commonwealth settlement in Eretz Israel. Named in honor of Lord Arthur James Balfour, this combination *moshav-moshava* founded in 1922 is situated in the Jezreel Valley. (16)

Baptist Village: In 1955, American Southern Baptists established a village located north of Petah Tikva. Originally started as an orphanage, it now serves as a conference center. (62)

Barkai: Meaning "morning star," Barkai became the sixth kibbutz of the American Hashomer Hatzair movement in 1949. It is located in the Sharon region. (20)

Bet Herut: This *moshav shitufi* (cooperative settlement) lies in the Sharon region, north of Netanya. It was founded in 1933 by thirty-five American immigrants, and today about one third of its population of 388 is of American origin. (22)

Benei Zion: *Moshav* organized in 1947 and named after the order "Benei Zion" (Sons of Zion) of America. It is situated in the coastal plain, north of Tel Aviv. (27)

Efrat: See page 152. (54)

Ein Dor: This kibbutz lies at the foot of Mount Tabor in the Lower Galilee and was the fourth settlement of the American Hashomer Hatzair movement. Founded in 1948, it was named after the biblical city (Joshua 17:11; 1 Samuel 28:7). (18)

Ein HaShofet: See page 151. (15)

Galon: In 1946, this kibbutz in the Judean coastal plain, was founded by the Hashomer Hatzair movement. The American pioneer group "Zion" joined the kibbutz in 1953. (49)

Gan Hayyim: This citrus plantation in the Sharon region was developed in 1928 through the initiative of American and Canadian investors and was managed by American agronomists. (28)

Gan Rashel: A settlement–plantation—now a neighborhood incorporated in the city of Herzliyyah—was developed by Dr. Meir Rosoff and a group of other investors from New York City in 1926. Its name is the Hebrew acronym for the biblical matriarchs, Rachel, Sarah, and Leah. (31)

Gan Yavneh: New York Ahouza Aleph, a society of American Zionists, bought the land for this *moshav* in 1931. The settlement, now a city, lies south of Tel Aviv in the Judean coastal plain. (43)

Gesher HaZiv: Kibbutz, meaning "Bridge of Splendor," is located north of Haifa. The American Habonim contingent joined the Israeli and Central European founding settlers in 1949. (7)

Gezer: A settlement in the Judean foothills to the east of Tel Aviv was founded in 1945. Disbanded in 1964, it was revitalized as a kibbutz by thirty-five American and Canadian Habonim members. (40)

Grofit: Kibbutz, whose name means a graft taken from an olive branch, was established in 1963 with the help of American Habonim. In 1977, twenty-five American Habonim made *aliyah* to this settlement in the Arava, reinforcing the founding American population. (61)

Hanaton: First kibbutz founded by the American Conservative Movement. In 1984, thirty-five American *olim* moved to the settlement located in the Lower Galilee. (11)

HaSolelim: Meaning "road pavers," this kibbutz was established in 1949. A year later, American youth from the *halutz* movement *"Plugat Ali-yah"*—the pioneer section of several American Zionist youth organizations—joined the kibbutz. (10)

Hazor: Founded in 1946 by the Hashomer Hatzair movement, American pioneers joined this kibbutz, situated south of Tel Aviv. (44)

Herzliyyah: An American Zion Commonwealth settlement created in 1924, north of Tel Aviv. The area on the Mediterranean coast was intended to be the "Atlantic City" in the Land of Israel. (32)

Kefar Blum: Named in honor of the Jewish French Prime Minister Leon Blum, this kibbutz in the Upper Galilee was developed in 1943. The founding group consisted of American Habonim pioneers. (3)

Kefar Daniel: Collective settlement named in honor of Daniel Frisch, a president of the Zionist Organization of America, was founded in 1949 by American *Mahal* (volunteers from abroad) and located southeast of Tel Aviv. (38)

Kefar Habad: Located in the Judean Plain, this Hasidic settlement was founded in 1949 by American devotees of the Lubavitcher Rebbe, Menahem Mendel Schneersohn. (35)

Kefar Menahem: Established in 1939, twenty-seven American pioneers, with Hashomer Hatzair training, joined this kibbutz in the Judean foothills. (48)

Kefar Shmuel: A *moshav* named for the prominent American Zionist leader Rabbi Stephen Samuel Wise. Founded in 1950, it is situated in the Judean foothills. (39)

Kefar Silver: This agricultural school and settlement in the Ashkelon region was established in 1957 and named for the American Zionist activist Rabbi Abba Hillel Silver. (55)

Kefar Szold: This kibbutz, founded in 1942, lies at the foot of the Golan Heights. It bears the name of Henrietta Szold, founder of "Hadassah." (2)

Kefar Truman: Located east of Tel Aviv, this *moshav*, formed in 1949, commemorates President Harry S Truman's recognition of the State of Israel. (37)

Kefar Warburg: Established in 1939, this *moshav* in the southern Coastal Plain is named in honor of the American philanthropist Felix Warburg. (46)

Ketura: Located north of Eilat, this kibbutz was founded in 1970. The pioneer group included the *HaShahar* (Dawn) contingent of the American Young Judea. (60)

Kiryat Malakhi: Development town in the Judean Plain founded in 1951. The name *"Malakhi"* refers to Los Angeles and the contribution made to the town's welfare by the American Jewish community. (47)

Kiryat Zanz: Holocaust survivor Rabbi Jekutiel Judah Halberstam, originally the Hungarian Klausenburg Rebbe, transplanted his court to the Williamsburg section of Brooklyn, with the vow to settle permanently in Eretz Israel. In 1956, fulfilling that vow, he led his American Hasidim and founded the suburb of Kiryat Zanz near Netanyah. (26)

Kissufim: American and Canadian members of the *HeHalutz Hatzair* movement augmented the South American and Israeli components of this kibbutz, which had been founded in the northwestern Negev desert in 1951. (57)

Liman: A *moshav*, located on the coast in the western Galilee region, was renamed in 1959 to honor Herbert H. Lehman, former New York State governor and later senator. (6)

Ma'yan Barukh: American Habonim *halutzim* joined the core group of South African and Rhodesian World War II veterans who had established this kibbutz in 1947. It is situated in the northern Galilee on the Lebanese border. (1)

Mei Ammi: Originally set up as a Nahal base in 1963 in the Samarian mountains, this *moshav shitufi* was converted into a civilian settlement in 1967. Its name means "my people's water." It was selected because of its similarity to the sound of "Miami," the American community that sponsored the settlement. (21)

Mishmar David: A kibbutz founded in 1948 in the Judean foothills. Its name honors the American army officer, Col. David Marcus, who served as commander of the Jerusalem front in the 1948 War of Independence. (41)

Mishkenot Sha'ananim: Meaning "tranquil dwellings," was the first settlement outside the walls of Jerusalem. It was built in 1860 with funds bequeathed by Judah Touro, the renowned American philanthropist. (51)

Mount Hope: See page 148. (34)

Netanyah: City on the coastal plain, between Tel Aviv and Haifa, founded in 1928 by B'nei Binyamin. It bears the first name of American philanthropist Nathan Straus. (25)

Netivot-Morasha: This was the first settlement of the American *Hashomer Hadati* (The Religious Watch Guard) movement. In 1949, they, together with the Israeli *Morasha* (Tradition) group, founded this kibbutz in southern Judea near the city of Yavneh. (56)

Neveh Efrayim: A rural community named for Fred Efrayim Monosson, a prominent Zionist activist in the United States. Located in the precincts of Ben Gurion International Airport, it was established in 1953 by El Al workers. (36)

Neveh Ilan: *Moshav shitufi* founded in 1970 by members of American Young Judea. It is situated in the Jerusalem mountains neighboring the historic Muslim village Abu Ghosh and a newly established American initiated suburb, Telshe Stone. (50)

Orot: Meaning "lights," it was founded in 1953 by members of the American *HaIkkar HaOved* ("The Working Farmer"). Some twenty families, offspring of the original *Am Olam* (Eternal People) settlers in Vineland, New Jersey, helped establish this *moshav* on the Judean coastal plain. It was originally known as *Be'er Tuvviyyah Bet*. (45)

Pardes haGedud: "Orchard of the Legion," was founded in 1926 by a group of Jewish Legionnaires led by American Sam Friedlander. It is situated just north of Netanyah. (24)

Poriyyah: See page 149. (13)

Ra'anannah: City in the Sharon region, neighboring Herzliyyah. It was established in 1922 as a *moshava* (private village) by members of the New York *Ahouza Aleph*. It continues to attract American immigrants. (30)

Ramat haShofet: Founded in 1941, this Hashomer Hatzair kibbutz is named in honor of Judge Julian W. Mack, American jurist and Zionist leader. Its name means "the Judge's Summit," and it is located in the Samarian mountains. (14)

Ramat Yohanan: Kibbutz situated east of Haifa, founded in 1932 by *halutzim* from Detroit together with agricultural students from Eretz Israel. It is named after Jan Christiaan Smuts, long-time Zionist advocate from South Africa. (9)

Ramat Zvi: *Moshav* in the Lower Galilee, named for Henry Zvi Monsky, Zionist supporter and unifying leader of American Jewry. This *moshav*, meaning the "heights of Zvi," was formed in 1942. (19)

Sasa: A pioneer kibbutz on the Lebanese border, founded in 1949 by the American Hashomer Hatzair. Some of the original members were veterans of World War II; others participated in *Aliyah Bet*, the illegal immigration to Eretz Israel. (8)

Sharonah: Like Poriyyah, this *moshava* was based on the *Ahouza* plan. In 1913, a Chicago group invested in this settlement in the Lower Galilee. Due to economic problems during World War I, it was disbanded and reestablished in 1938 by the Gordonia movement. (12)

Shoshannat haYarden: A farmstead, on the banks of the upper Jordan River, it was developed by Mordecai Lubovsky, an American merchant who immigrated to Eretz Israel in 1884. Its name means "lily of the Jordan." This short-lived effort was incorporated into an adjacent settlement fostered by Baron Edmond James de Rothschild. (5)

Tal Shahar: *Moshav* in the Jerusalem corridor, created in 1948, meaning "morning dew." It is named after Henry Morgenthau Jr., Secretary of the Treasury in the Franklin Delano Roosevelt administration. The War Refugee Board was formed on the basis of his report for the amelioration of refugees from Nazi persecution. (42)

Urim: One of eleven settlements erected on the same night of 6 October 1946. The name signifies "source of light" to symbolize the *Yishuv*'s response to the British Mandatory Government's restriction on land purchases. Its membership was reinforced by American Habonim pioneers in the 1950s. (58)

Yahel: This kibbutz is the American Reform Movement's first settlement in Israel, formed by the National Federation of Temple Youth. Established in 1976, it is located north of Eilat in the *Arava*. The name *Yahel* is derived from the book of Job 31:26, "If ever I saw the light shining. . . ." (59)

Yiftah: In 1950, the first aliyah group—*HaOleh*—of the Intercollegiate Zionist Federation of America (IZFA) founded this kibbutz in the Upper Galilee, together with members of the Yiftah (Jeptha) Brigade that fought in the War of Independence. (4)

Zofit: Meaning "Lookout Point," this *moshav* was modelled on the "Herut Plan," a program to settle Americans of limited means on Jewish National Fund land. Located in the citrus belt of the Sharon region, it was founded in 1933. (29)

Zur Hadassah: Located in the Judean Hills, this urban settlement was created in 1960. It is named in honor of its sponsor, the American Women's Zionist organization—Hadassah. (52)

In the context of America–Holy Land Studies, knowledge of place-names is more than a focus for cultural geography. Its details exemplify the manifold ways in which Americans integrated intrinsic elements of their native culture in the historical and evolving traditions of the Holy Land.

NOTES

1. Compare Alexander Bein, "American Settlement in Israel," *Israel: Its Role in Civilization*, ed. Moshe Davis (New York: Harper & Bros., 1956), 298–309.

2. Compare Ruth K. Kark, "Millenarism and Agricultural Settlement in the Holy Land in the Nineteenth Century," *Journal of Historical Geography* 9, no. 1 (1983): 47–62.

3. For relevant U.S. governmental sources, see *With Eyes Toward Zion: Scholars Colloquium on America–Holy Land Studies*, ed. Moshe Davis (New York: Arno Press, 1977), 228–32.

4. Compare Reed M. Holmes, *The Forerunners: The Tragic Story of 156 down-East Americans led to Jaffa in 1866 by charismatic G. J. Adams to plant the seeds of modern Israel* (Independence, Mo.: Herald Publishing House, 1981).

5. Bernard I. Sandler, "*Hoachoozo*—Zionism in America and the Colonization of Palestine," *AJHQ* 64, no. 2 (December 1974): 137–48.

6. Simon Goldman, "The Ahooza Movement and Poreah," *Maccabaean*, 25 September 1914: 101–108.

7. See *Guide to America–Holy Land Studies, 1620–1948: Economic Relations and Philanthropy* 3, ed. Nathan Kaganoff (New York: Praeger, 1983), 73–94.

8. Compare Marlin Levin, *Balm in Gilead, The Story of Hadassah* (New York: Schocken Books, 1973).

9. J. H. Iliffe, "The Palestine Archaeological Museum," *Museums Journal* 38 (1938): 1–22.

10. *First Fruits, Leaves from the Journal of Ein Hashofet* (Jerusalem: Keren Kayemeth & Keren Hayesod, 1938), 48. Compare Joshua Liebner, "Ein Hashofet," *Youth and Nation* 16, no. 8 (August 1948): 17–20.

11. *Catholic Near East* (October 1989): 18–21.

12. For a definitive analysis of the evolution of the suburb, see James H. Johnson, *Urban Geography*, 2nd ed. (Oxford: Pergamon Press, 1972), especially ch. 7, 129–54.

13. Lewis Mumford, *The City in History: Its Origins, Its Transformations, and Its Prospects* (New York: Harcourt, Brace & World, 1961), Ch. 16 "Suburbia— and Beyond," especially subsection 5, "The Suburb as Neighborhood Unit," 499–503.

PART IV
REDISCOVERY OF THE HOLY LAND

Chapter 9

Choice Readings: An Annotated Record

An ancient tradition concerning the origin of the cosmos teaches that the Holy Land was first in creation, after which the rest of the world was created. For centuries, this belief was visually demonstrated by the mapmakers who placed the Holy Land in the very center of the universe, the navel of the earth. With time, even as the scientific facts were established, the import of the tradition remained deeply impressed in the consciousness, learning, and creativity of Western civilization.

The purpose of this annotated choice of primary readings, as they were reprinted in the Arno Press Series in 1977, is to engage the contemporary reader in the wonder of the *rediscovery* of the Holy Land by the Western world. Out of many hundreds of books and pamphlets, I annotate a mosaic of writings by archaeologists, historians, scientists, biblical scholars, novelists, American consuls, missionaries, tourists, academics, students, clergymen of all Protestant churches, Catholics, Jews, Mormons, agnostics and atheists, settlers and builders of the land—all under Ottoman and then British caretaking.

Attracted by exotic places and the lure of antiquity, the authors convey customs, cultures, and conditions of the polyglot inhabitants in the Mediterranean region and the Near East. The comparative sections included in the selections offer a panorama of Mediterranean countries, of *Mare Nostrum*: the southern ports of France, Italy, Greece, and Turkey and the northern cities of Tangier and Cairo, all part of that historical entity called

Near Eastern civilization, as viewed by Americans of diverse backgrounds and interests. For all of them, to see was to believe; to believe was to see.

Babcock, Maltbie Davenport, *Letters from Egypt and Palestine* (New York, 1902)

Maltbie Davenport Babcock entered the Presbyterian ministry in 1882 and, after serving pastorates in Lockport, New York, and Baltimore, Maryland, he was called to succeed Dr. Henry Van Dyke at the Brick Presbyterian Church in New York City. In February 1901 he went on a trip to the Holy Land, sending back to the Men's Association of his church a series of well-written letters describing his journey. *Letters from Egypt and Palestine*, the collection of his travel narratives, was published by popular demand the next year. Written in simple, direct style in free moments during a hurried journey, the book lucidly describes the Holy Land of the turn of the century as seen by a devout minister with a keen eye for detail and a polished literary ability.

Barclay, J[ames] T[urner], *The City of the Great King: Or, Jerusalem As It Was, As It Is, And As It Is To Be* (Philadelphia, 1858)

James Turner Barclay, M.D., was a resident missionary in Jerusalem who made valuable discoveries in the Temple Enclosure and other sacred localities. When his book first appeared, a reviewer said of it:

> Dr. Barclay's volume, which is devoted chiefly to Jerusalem and the neighboring localities, is a very welcome help to this knowledge of Palestine. He enjoyed peculiar advantages for his task from his residence in that city for three years and a half, and access, through the favor of Turkish families, to places from which foreigners have heretofore been excluded. He clears up many difficulties, settles many controverted questions, and adds so large a sum to the stock of information, that his volume will be felt to be a most valuable and indispensable aid to a satisfactory knowledge of the subject.
>
> From *Theological and Literary Journal*, April 1858.

Bartlett, S[amuel] C[olcord], *From Egypt to Palestine: Through Sinai, the Wilderness and the South Country; Observations of a Journey Made With Special Reference to the History of the Israelites* (New York, 1879)

Samuel Colcord Bartlett (1817–98), a Congregational minister, alternated between teaching and preaching, first in New Hampshire, then in Chicago, where for nearly two decades he was a Professor of Biblical Literature and Sacred Theology at the Chicago Theological Seminary. It was during this period that he journeyed to Egypt and the Holy Land. His book, *From Egypt to Palestine*, and the journey that it records were undertaken with a distinctive purpose. Though a number of "judicious and learned travellers" had made many investigations of Egypt and the Sinaitic Peninsula, the results of their discoveries were at that point widely scattered. "Many persons," Bartlett wrote, "have desired to find them gathered up compactly, and passed in review by someone who should possess the requisite knowledge of these discoveries and theories, and sufficient personal cognizance of the scenes and facts to do it with some degree of intelligence and unity of view." To that task, the author devoted his own work. In addition, he wished to relate East to West by explaining the work of the American missionaries.

Bond, Alvan, *Memoir of the Rev. Pliny Fisk, A.M.: Late Missionary to Palestine* (Boston, 1828)

This *Memoir* is a companion volume to that devoted to the life of Levi Parsons by Daniel Morton and deals with the man who accompanied Parsons on the mission of the American Board of Commissioners for Foreign Missions (ABCFM) to the Holy Land. Alvan Bond was a Congregational minister in Sturbridge, Massachusetts. His subject, Pliny Fisk (1792–1825), outlived Parsons by more than three years, but, like him, contracted an illness that led to his death abroad. Typical of many memoirs of the time, the work is based extensively on the journal, letters, and other writings of its subject. The bulk of the work deals with Fisk's travels and labors in the Holy Land and vicinity. Written to honor Fisk, his faith, and his mission, the book also reveals a great deal about general conditions and the religious situation in the eastern Mediterranean region of that time.

Browne, J[ohn] Ross, *Yusef: Or the Journey of the Frangi; A Crusade in the East* (New York, 1853)

John Ross Browne was born near Dublin, the son of an Irish Protestant who was exiled in 1833, and he settled with his family in Louisville, Kentucky. In 1841, Browne became a reporter for the *Congressional Globe* in Washington, D.C., but soon tired of recording Senate debates. The next year he shipped out on a whaler. In 1851, his travels brought him to Beirut, where he employed Yusef Simon Badra as his interpreter for a trip to the Holy Land. Though he was to be disappointed by much of what he found in the Holy Land, he was enthusiastic about the Sea of Galilee. *Yusef* is a cheerful, entertaining book, salted with humorous tales, embellished with exaggerated episodes and colorful character sketches.

Burnet, D[avid] S[taats], compiler, *The Jerusalem Mission: Under the Direction of the American Christian Missionary Society* (Cincinnati, 1853)

The first foreign mission of the American Christian denomination, Churches or Disciples of Christ, was founded in Jerusalem in February 1851. The central figure in this effort was the physician Dr. James T. Barclay (1807–74), who later wrote *The City of the Great King* (1858). *The Jerusalem Mission* is primarily a collection of letters, reports, and journal entries by Dr. Barclay that describes the beginnings of the American Christian Missionary Society and its work in Jerusalem during the early years of that mission. Arriving with great hopes of winning converts among Jews and Mohammedans, and of reforming the Oriental Christian "sects" there, Barclay soon encountered difficulties. On 28 February 1851 he wrote, "We are all in good health, and highly delighted with the City of the Great King; but if I may credit what I am told on all hands, there is no worse missionary ground on all the earth than this same city;...." He did gather a few converts, but found himself in sharp controversy with the older Christian churches.

Cox, Samuel S[ullivan], *Orient Sunbeams: Or, From the Porte to the Pyramids, By Way of Palestine* (New York, 1882)

Samuel Sullivan Cox, better known as "Sunset" Cox, served in Congress for thirty-two years, from 1857 until his death in 1889. He was appointed American minister to Turkey in 1885 and remained for a year. *Orient Sunbeams* describes Cox's second visit, after thirty years, to Constantinople, and his journeys to Damascus, Palestine, and Egypt. David Lindsey remarks in *"Sunset Cox: Irrepressible Democrat"* that "his sensitivity to colors, sounds, smells, to the ordinary sights as well as to the spectacular, plus a feeling for thoughts that had popular appeal, undoubtedly contributed much to his success as a writer." Occasionally, Cox interspersed his travelogs with some scientific analysis of the region, country, city, or people he visited, but *Orient Sunbeams* is best in its descriptive passages, which offer a vivid picture of Cox's strictly personal view of the Holy Land.

De Hass, Frank S., *Buried Cities Recovered: Or, Explorations in Bible Lands* (Philadelphia, 1883)

During a residence as U.S. consul in Jerusalem, Frank De Hass sought to establish with accuracy the scenes recorded in biblical literature. The author traveled extensively throughout the Near East, visiting places that had never before been seen by Americans. He succeeded in recovering and identifying many sites that had been considered lost. In *Buried Cities Recovered*, De

Hass provides the results of his personal investigations, as well as those of other archaeologists in Egypt, Asia Minor, Western and Trans-Jordanic Palestine, and Syria.

Fosdick, Harry Emerson, *A Pilgrimage to Palestine* (New York, 1927)

Harry Emerson Fosdick (1878–1969) served New York's Riverside Church. His influence was extended by nearly four decades of teaching at Union Theological Seminary, the publication of more than twenty-five books, and years of national radio preaching. Fosdick's extensive knowledge of biblical history and geography contributed to making his *A Pilgrimage to Palestine* more significant than many other travel books about the Holy Land. When the book first appeared, a reviewer said of it: "Of many books dealing with the Holy Land, the writer has read not one which can surpass in interest and literary beauty, Dr. Fosdick's latest volume." Sixty-five years after its publication, the book remains outstanding among its kind in its lucidity, its illuminating movement from ancient to modern periods, and its dealing with locations sacred to three historical religions.

Fulton, John, *The Beautiful Land: Palestine; Historical, Geographical and Pictorial* (New York, 1891)

John Fulton (1834–1907), a native of Glasgow, was educated at Aberdeen and then migrated to the United States. He was ordained as a priest in the Episcopal Church at New Orleans in 1857 and later became Professor of Canon Law at the Philadelphia Divinity School. *The Beautiful Land* is a detailed account of travel in the Holy Land, with many illustrations and voluminous references to the Bible and history. "The author's aim," explained Bishop Henry C. Potter in his introduction, "has been to condense and to apply to his immediate purpose whatever he could find that was available in the works of nearly a hundred different authors and scattered through twice as many volumes, not many of which are at the command of the ordinary student."

Gilmore, Albert Field, *East and West of Jordan* (Boston, 1929)

Gilmore's sketches of his journeys in Palestine, Syria, and Egypt were published, for the most part, in the *Christian Science Monitor*. The author enlivens his travels by linking the places he visited with events in biblical history. This is an account of Palestine as it appeared in the 1920s, but his work also contains graphic descriptions of ancient religious monuments and

sacred shrines. Several chapters are devoted to political problems and the
Zionist movement.

Gordon, Benjamin L[ee], *New Judea: Jewish Life in Modern Palestine and
Egypt* (Philadelphia, 1919)

Three themes are developed by Benjamin Lee Gordon in *New Judea*: the
history of Jewish national revival in the nineteenth century; the emergence
of a new Jewish life in Palestine, exemplified in the rise of agricultural
colonies and educational institutions; and the basis for Israel's claim on the
Holy Land. What impressed Gordon most was the land's resurgence:
"Wherever I turned I saw a real new Judea transformed from an old land
by the will of young pioneers." The author details conditions in Palestine
and the efforts that contributed to the resettlement of the Holy Land.

Hyde, Orson, *A Voice from Jerusalem: Or a Sketch of the Travels and
Ministry of Elder Orson Hyde, Missionary of the Church of Jesus Christ of
Latter-Day Saints to Germany, Constantinople and Jerusalem* (Boston,
1842)

Elder Orson Hyde was privileged to enact the first formal resolution of the
Mormon Church when he prayed in Jerusalem on the Mount of Olives for
Jewish Restoration. *A Voice from Jerusalem* describes the dedicatory prayer
offered by Hyde on 24 October 1841 that "the land become abundantly
fruitful when possessed by its rightful heirs."

Israel, J[ohn], and H[enry] Lundt, *Journal of a Cruize in the U.S. Ship
Delaware 74 in the Mediterranean in the Years 1833 & 34: Together with
a Sketch of a Journey to Jerusalem* (n.p., 1835)

"One by-product of American Naval activity in the Eastern Mediterranean," David Finnie writes in his *Pioneers East*, "was literature. . . .
Service in the Mediterranean Squadron was much sought after by young
officers with a flair for the exotic and antique, and a good number of them
wrote books about what they saw during their trips ashore." The U.S.S.
Delaware was the first to visit the Syrian shore and a large party went up
to Jerusalem. Finnie cites a contemporary description of the Americans
before and after meeting the crew of the Delaware: "When I arrived on
board it appeared to me that I was dreaming, when I thought of the idea
we entertained here that the Americans were savage and an uncivilized
people—how grateful [sic] I was surprised to find them superior in every

respect to other nations that I saw, and particularly so, in politeness and kindness towards us strangers."

Johnson, Sarah Barclay, *Hadji in Syria: Or, Three Years in Jerusalem* (Philadelphia, 1858)

Sarah Barclay Johnson, daughter of Dr. James T. Barclay, was a native of Virginia. Her education was received under the tutelage of her father, a missionary, who was for a time stationed in Jerusalem, of which he wrote in the volume *The City of the Great King* (1858), for which she drew most of the illustrations. Sarah was married in 1856 to J. Augustus Johnson, American consul-general in Syria and lived with him for many years in that country, where she wrote her only published volume, *Hadji in Syria*. It became very popular, perhaps because of her manner of interweaving an American's attitudes with Oriental life.

Krimsky, Joseph, *Pilgrimage & Service* (n.p., 1918–1919)

Dr. Joseph Krimsky was a member of the American Zionist Medical Unit, which came to Eretz Israel in 1918 with forty-four physicians, nurses, sanitary engineers, dentists, and administrative staff. *Pilgrimage & Service*, Dr. Krimsky's diary of this tour of duty, contains descriptions of his work, individual portraits, sketches of places, and reports of events. Dr. Krimsky writes: "The greatest blessing that can be conferred upon this land, next to making it healthful, is to direct and assist its people toward useful and productive occupations, to become self-sustaining, self-supporting and self-respecting."

Kyle, Melvin Grove, *Excavating Kirjath-Sepher's Ten Cities: A Palestine Fortress from Abraham's Day to Nebuchadnezzar's* (Grand Rapids, Michigan, 1934)

Melvin Grove Kyle was lecturer at the American School of Oriental Research in Jerusalem in 1921; he returned in 1926, 1928, 1930 and 1932, to work with William F. Albright in excavating Tell Beit Mirsim. *Excavating Kirjath-Sepher's Ten Cities* is a lively narrative account written in the field, providing much basic information on biblical archaeology. Richly illustrated, it summarizes in a popular way many of the scholarly conclusions then current. Originally offered as the James Sprunt Lectures for 1932 at Union Theological Seminary in Richmond, the book gives what the author describes as archaeological testimony to the Bible.

Kyle, Melvin Grove, *Explorations at Sodom: The Story of Ancient Sodom in the Light of Modern Research* (New York, 1928)

Explorations at Sodom is the result of an expedition by the Xenia Theological Seminary in cooperation with the American School of Oriental Research. Kyle points out "that there was nothing sectarian in the expedition and that the strictly scientific character of the work may be assured." The book describes the fascinating story of Sodom and Gomorrah. "The Story of Ancient Sodom in the Light of Modern Science," Kyle concludes, "adds another instance to a long and ever growing list of evidences of the trustworthiness of ancient documents of Holy Writ."

Lee, Rosa C., *The Story of the Ram Allah Mission* (Manchester, New Hampshire, 1912)

Early in the twentieth century, Rosa C. Lee, originally from New England and a member of the Friends' Mission Board, served in Ram Allah, then a village north of Jerusalem. *The Story of the Ram Allah Mission* is a tribute to the earlier mission work of Eli Jones and his wife Sybil, who founded the mission.

Lynch, W[illiam] F[rancis], *Narrative of the United States' Expedition to the River Jordan and the Dead Sea* (Philadelphia, 1849)

During the mid-nineteenth century, a number of American naval officers, many having served in the Mediterranean Squadron, wrote books about what they saw on their trips ashore. Though many of these officers were essentially sightseers, some were more adventurous and genuinely sought to further scientific exploration. Among these was Lieutenant William Lynch, who for twenty years had wanted to visit the Holy Land. He wished to navigate the Jordan River and the Dead Sea, "the first teeming with sacred associations, and the last enveloped in a mystery, which had defied all previous attempts to penetrate it." This book is an account of his voyage, written in the form of a log and narrative. It details his experiences in Turkey, Syria, and Jerusalem, his arduous efforts to trace the source of the Jordan River, and his scientific analysis of the Dead Sea water and environs. Since Lynch was a pious Christian and a loyal American naval officer, his comments on Turkish customs, Moslems, and Jews have a special fascination.

Merrill, Selah, *Ancient Jerusalem* (New York, 1908)

Selah Merrill, a former American army chaplain, came to Jerusalem in 1882, where he occupied the post of consul for almost three decades. A graduate of a theological seminary, he preferred to be identified as a scientist, naturalist, and explorer. Merrill was the author of many travel books and antiquarian studies, including *Explorations East of the Jordan* and *Galilee in the Time of Christ*. A frequent lecturer on Oriental researches and discoveries at such institutions as the Lowell Institute in Boston and the Peabody Institute of Baltimore, his *Ancient Jerusalem* discloses an inquisitive and searching mind and his intimate acquaintance with the Jewish community in the Holy Land.

[Minor, Clorinda], *Meshullam! Or, Tidings from Jerusalem: From the Journal of a Believer Recently Returned from the Holy Land* ([Philadelphia], 1851)

In 1851 Clorinda Minor published her anonymous booklet subtitled *From the Journal of a Believer Recently Returned from the Holy Land*. According to the Reverend J. E. Hanauer in his "Notes on the History of Modern Colonization in Palestine" (*The Quarterly Statement of the Palestine Exploration Fund*, 1900, pp. 130–31), *Tidings from Jerusalem* "was the first report of the first Agricultural Manual Labour School in Palestine, written by Mrs. Minor under Mr. Meshullam's roof, in the midst of the unpacking of goods and the pitching of tents." *Tidings* describes Mrs. Minor's trip and work in the Holy Land in the form of a diary, which she kept from the day her ship entered the Mediterranean on 25 May 1849 until her return to America in April 1850.

Morris, Robert, *Freemasonry in the Holy Land: Or Handmarks of Hiram's Builders* (New York, 1872)

Robert Morris, founder of the Order of the Eastern Star, contributed greatly to the literature of Freemasonry. He published seventy-four volumes on the history and rituals of the Masons, including over three hundred lyric poems. In 1884, Morris was made Poet Laureate of the Order, a crowning event of his career. Yearning to visit Palestine, he undertook his first journey to the Holy Land. Morris remarked that "so many references to that country" were "contained in the Masonic rituals" that it was "a marvel that no one of us had made explorations there" prior to this time. In 1868 with the contributions of 3,782 members of the Order, he set forth on his venture, the results of which were embodied in his volume *Freemasonry in the Holy Land*. In this work, Morris sought to provide evidence of the Order's great antiquity by exploring the places named in Masonic lectures and by making "full collections of objects illustrating Masonic traditions and biblical customs." This book minutely describes Morris's voyage and places he visited, and includes poems composed, explorations of Jerusalem in 1868, as well as Damascus, the Jordan River, and the Sea of Galilee.

Morton, Daniel O[liver], *Memoir of Rev. Levi Parsons, Late Missionary to Palestine* (Poultney, Vermont, 1824)

Levi Parsons (1792–1822), a native of Massachusetts, was one of the first of the Protestant missionaries to labor in the Holy Land—but only briefly, because he was plagued by the illness that caused his early death in Alexandria. His letters back to family and friends in America had aroused considerable interest in him and his mission, and his devotion and determination became an inspiration to many. Following his death, a fellow Congregational minister, the Reverend Daniel O. Morton, pastor of a church in Shoreham, Vermont, undertook to compile Parsons's *Memoir*. In considerable detail, drawing extensively on letters written by Parsons and on his journal, Morton told the story of Parsons's education, his spiritual struggles, and growing piety. The way the missionary spirit captured the imagination of many devout youths of the time is well illustrated by this book. Its middle part deals with Parsons's service as an agent of the American Board of Commissioners for Foreign Missions traveling in the United States preparatory to his overseas service. In the last part of the book, the experiences of the young missionary in the Holy Land are described, with frequent selections from Parsons's own words.

Odenheimer, W[illiam] H., *Jerusalem and its Vicinity: A Series of Familiar Lectures on the Sacred Localities Connected With the Week Before the Resurrection* (Philadelphia, 1855)

William Henry Odenheimer (1817–79), born in Philadelphia, was ordained a priest in the Protestant Episcopal Church in 1841 and became rector of St. Peter's Church in his native city. During the winter of 1851–52 he toured the Holy Land. In 1859 he was consecrated Bishop of the Episcopal Diocese of New Jersey. *Jerusalem and Its Vicinity* originated as a series of seven lectures designed for church audiences. The lectures were organized around the movements of Jesus during Holy Week. Within this general framework, the author included accounts of his own pilgrimage and extensive descriptions of Jerusalem as it appeared to a devout minister. The book is presented as an aid to faith and to provide spiritual instruction.

Olin, Stephen, *Travels in Egypt, Arabia Petraea, and the Holy Land* (New York, 1843)

Stephen Olin, successively schoolteacher, Methodist preacher, and professor at the University of Georgia, was inaugurated in 1834 as first president of Randolph-Macon College in Virginia. Ill health, which troubled much of his later life, forced him to leave the college on indefinite furlough in 1837. After travels in Europe and the Mediterranean, he recovered sufficiently to enable him to travel extensively in the East, arriving in Egypt late in 1839 and in the Holy Land in 1840. He then wrote the journal that provided materials for his two-volume work, *Travels in Egypt, Arabia Petraea, and the Holy Land*. He regarded the book as a commentary on the Bible, as did so many devout Protestant travelers in the Holy Land. The book, by this eminent minister and educator, greatly influenced American Protestant understandings of the Holy Land.

Prime, William C[ooper], *Tent Life in the Holy Land* (New York, 1857)

William C. Prime traveled in Egypt and the Holy Land during 1855–56 and again in 1869–70. Mark Twain used Prime's book as a guide when he made his trip to the Holy Land a dozen years later, and in *The Innocents Abroad* he made Prime something of a romantic whipping boy as "Grimes." *Tent Life in the Holy Land* is the report of the journey by this very devout layman. "I visited the sacred soil, as a pilgrim, seeking mine own pleasure. I went where it pleased me. I acted as it pleased me, yielding with delicious license, to the whim of every passing hour. I prayed or I laughed; I knelt or I turned my back; I wept or I sang; and when I sang it was now a song of sinful humanity and now a grand old monkish hymn, to which my voice made the moonlit streets of Jerusalem ring as I strolled along them, or which I sent floating over the holy waves of Galilee. I have written my book even as I traveled."

Rix, Herbert, *Tent and Testament: A Camping Tour in Palestine With Some Notes on Scripture Sites* (London, 1907)

Herbert Rix toured the Holy Land in 1901 and published his account five years later. He wrote for the future tourist "who is confronted by two or more sites for most biblical scenes: Two Zions, two Temple areas . . . two or more Calvarys . . . several Bethesdas, put in their claim for veneration." *Tent and Testament* is a highly informative work with many photographs of places of interest and people. Throughout, the author refers to other works and includes an extensive bibliography. His appendices are particularly good, for he treats in a scholarly way such subjects as "The Nazareth Question," "The Bethlehem Question," "The Capernaum Question," including discussions on "The Fountain of Capernaum" and "The Town Capernaum," and, finally, "The Site of Herod's Temple."

Robinson, Edward, *Biblical Researches in Palestine, Mount Sinai and Arabia Petraea: A Journal of Travels in the Year 1838 by E. Robinson and E. Smith Undertaken in Reference to Biblical Geography* (Boston, 1841)

Edward Robinson was forced by ill health to resign an instructorship in Hebrew at Andover Seminary. As his health improved, he specialized in biblical study. He was puzzled by the contradictions and imperfections in the knowledge then available about the land of the Bible. Called to a professorship of Biblical Literature at New York's Union Theological Seminary, he set one condition—that he could explore the Holy Land before taking up his teaching duties. On April 12, 1838, Robinson, together with Eli Smith, a former pupil who had for many years been a missionary in Syria, entered Palestine through Beersheba.

His years of study had prepared Robinson for an unparalleled contribution to knowledge. After a day's exploration, the scholar would record in his journal in considerable detail what had been experienced and discovered. This provided the raw material for *Biblical Researches in Palestine*. The three-volume work was a massive landmark in biblical scholarship. Titus Tobler, Robinson's closest competitor, remarked that "the works of Robinson and Smith alone surpass the total of all previous contributions to Palestinian geography from the time of Eusebius and Jerome to the early nineteenth century." The work is enlivened by personal anecdotes.

Robinson, Edward, *Later Biblical Researches in Palestine and in Adjacent Regions: A Journal of Travels in the Year 1852 by E. Robinson, E. Smith, and Others (Boston, 1856)*

In 1852 Robinson again visited the Holy Land for another two-and-a-half-month period. This time he entered through the north, traveled through Galilee and Samaria to Jerusalem and then returned north to visit what he had missed. These journeys resulted in a volume of similar quality to the first three, called *Later Biblical Researches in Palestine*.

Schaff, Philip, *Through Bible Lands: Notes on Travel in Egypt, the Desert, and Palestine (New York, [1878])*

Swiss-born Philip Schaff taught at the Mercersburg, Pennsylvania, seminary of the German Reformed Church in the United States, and was installed as Professor of Church History and Biblical Literature in 1844. During the Civil War, he settled in New York and in 1869 began a long term of service at Union Theological Seminary. The death of his daughter in 1876 was the occasion for a trip to the Holy Land where he sought to gain relief and fresh inspiration from Bible studies. As had happened many times, the letters he wrote to friends at home became the material out of which grew a book, *Through Bible Lands*. His object in developing letters into chapters was "to give the general reader a clear idea of the actual condition and prospects of the East by a simple narrative of what I saw and heard and felt on the spot." Schaff also surveyed the religious conditions of the many places he visited, with particular but not exclusive attention to Christian institutions.

Silber, Mendel, *Palestine the Holy Land (Houston, Texas, 1927)*

Mendel Silber wrote *Palestine The Holy Land* for "the average tourist who visits Palestine." He wrote on the economic, political, and cultural condition of the Holy Land with authority and succinctness.

Smith, George Albert, et al., *Correspondence of Palestine Tourists: Comprising a Series of Letters by George A. Smith, Lorenzo Snow, Paul A. Schettler, and Eliza R. Snow of Utah* (Salt Lake City, 1875)

The four travelers were leading members of the Church of Jesus Christ of Latter-Day Saints: Smith, a founder of Salt Lake City; Eliza Snow, president of the Mormon Women's Relief Society, 1866–1887, and composer of several Mormon hymns; Lorenzo Snow, a founder of Brigham City, Utah, and elected president of the Church in 1898. The group spent several months in Europe and Egypt, arriving at Jaffa on 23 February 1873. Their letters to the *Deseret News*, the *Salt Lake Herald*, the *Women's Exponent,* and to individuals, including President Brigham Young, describe their experiences—both spiritual and physical—in the Holy Land. Young and Daniel H. Wells wrote in a farewell benediction to the tourists, "When you go to the Land of Palestine, we wish you to dedicate and consecrate that land to the Lord, that it may be blessed with fruitfulness, preparatory to the return of Jews in fulfillment of prophecy, and the accomplishment of the purposes of our Heavenly Father."

Sneersohn, H[aym] Z[vee], *Palestine and Roumania: A Description of the Holy Land and the Past and Present State of Roumania and the Roumanian Jews (New York, 1872)*

A rabbi from the Holy Land, Sneersohn traveled extensively throughout Europe, India, and Australia on behalf of the local Jewish communities in Eretz Israel. He came to the United States after the Civil War and was instrumental in effecting American consular changes in Jerusalem and Roumania. At an informal reception given by President Grant in 1869,

Sneersohn was given an opportunity to express his views on the immediate role of America in the Holy Land. As reported in the *National Intelligencer*, Sneersohn asked that the American consuls grant their protection to "the Israelites in Palestine [who] possess no political or civil rights whatever . . . which will enable my brethren in the Holy Land in the hour of need to seek refuge under the Stars and Stripes. . . ."

Szold, Henrietta, *Recent Jewish Progress in Palestine (American Jewish Yearbook 5676)* (Philadelphia, 1915)

Henrietta Szold had an extraordinary life and career in the United States and in Eretz Israel. Largely responsible for major public-health and welfare programs in the Holy Land, she assumed prominent leadership in American Zionism and stood in the front rank of the pioneer nation-builders of Israel.

As her biographer, Lotte Levinson, wrote: "All her life, Henrietta Szold lived by the light of her father's dictum that 'Judaism is not only a faith or a creed, but a way of life.' 'You cannot have Judaism in full flower,' he explained, 'unless you have a normal human life in which you illustrate your Jewish principles.' Under the impact of the Jewish problem, Szold held that 'Judaism in full flower' was possible only in a national home in the Land of Israel." Henrietta Szold's realism, sense of humor, human insight, as well as her uncanny ability to transcend "her daily crisis" are amply evident in her thorough "progress report."

Talmage, T[homas] de Witt, *Talmage on Palestine: A Series of Sermons* (Springfield, Ohio, 1890)

Leading a group of pilgrims to the Holy Land, Talmage, a Presbyterian clergyman and lecturer, relived history within himself as he visited the sites holy to Christendom. With a journalist's eye—Talmage was an editor of several magazines—he did not confine his interests to spiritual history and included, among other matters, a chapter on "Horticulture and Hydraulics in Palestine." Talmage looked forward to increasing pilgrimages by Americans and deplored the fact that in all of American history only five thousand pilgrims had visited the Holy Land. "Thousands," he preached, "will go where now there are scores."

Taylor, Bayard, *The Lands of the Saracen: Or, Pictures of Palestine, Asia Minor, Sicily, and Spain* (New York, 1855)

Bayard Taylor began to write while in his teens, and after a brief apprenticeship as a printer, he traveled abroad sending "foreign letters" to newspapers. In 1851 Taylor set out on extensive travels as a correspondent, visiting Egypt, Syria, Palestine, and Asia Minor. He then journeyed to the Orient and at Hong Kong, joined Commodore Perry's expedition to Japan, sending back to the *New York Tribune* graphic accounts of his experiences. In 1878 he became U.S. minister to Berlin and died there later that year. *The Lands of the Saracen* is a travel book written by a master of effective description. His accounts have a literary quality missing in other such journals. A sincere Christian layman, he tells of meeting Edward Robinson and Eli Smith in Jerusalem and mentions an "American Colony" at Artos, near Bethlehem, "a little community of religious enthusiasts, whose experiments in cultivation have met with remarkable success, and are much spoken of at present."

Thompson, George, et al., *A View of the Holy Land: Its Present Inhabitants, Their Manners and Customs, Polity and Religion* (Wheeling, [West] Virginia, 1850)

The principal author of this book was not George, but Charles, Thompson, a well-known eighteenth-century English traveler and scholar. Though it was published in the United States in 1850, this work was based on extensive journeys in Turkey, the Holy Land, and Egypt, undertaken from September 1733 to February 1735. The first half of the volume deals with "Turkey in Asia"; the third quarter with "Palestine: or The Holy Land," and the last quarter with "Egypt and Arabia." At the time of his visit, Thompson found many pilgrims in the Holy Land, among them a number of "Franks." Combining lucid descriptions with considerable historical information from biblical to modern times, Thompson gives a picture of the Holy Land as it appeared to a devout and learned Christian observer from the West at a much earlier period than that described in the usual nineteenth-century travel book.

Van Dyke, Henry, *Out-of-Doors in the Holy Land: Impressions of Travel in Body and Spirit* (New York, 1908)

Henry Van Dyke (1852–1933) served in several Presbyterian pulpits before becoming Professor of English Literature at Princeton. He was the author of many fiction and nonfiction books. Invited by a friend to journey through the Holy Land in exchange for his impressions for a magazine, Van Dyke accepted the offer and produced *Out-of-Doors in the Holy Land*. When it appeared, a reviewer in the *Dial* wrote: "The record of a journey thru Palestine was a religious revelation to the author. Dr. Van Dyke has discovered that 'Christianity is an out-of-doors religion,' and journeys in the faith that 'the shut-in shrines and altered memorials are less significant than what we find in the open, among the streets and on the surrounding hill-sides.' His 'impressions of travel in body and spirit' are therefore not heavy with human creeds and contentions, but breathe the spirit of the land itself. His writing always combines poetry, religion, and the love of nature, and the threefold felicity could not be more appropriately displayed than in celebrating the birthplace of Christianity."

Vester, Bertha [Hedges] Spafford, *Our Jerusalem: An American Family in the Holy City, 1881–1949. With an Introduction by Lowell Thomas* (Garden City, N.Y., 1950)

Our Jerusalem is the story of the American Colony of Jerusalem from its founding in 1881 to the middle of the twentieth century. Horatio and Anna Spafford, devout Presbyterian lay persons, lost four daughters in an accident at sea in 1873; seven years later their only son died of scarlet fever. The religious pilgrimage that grew out of these tragic experiences led the Spaffords to found the Colony, to which they brought two surviving daughters, Bertha, the author of *Our Jerusalem*, and Grace. The Colony grew to include about one hundred and fifty persons, and carried out ministries of welfare, teaching, and nursing. The older missionaries did not trust this group of autonomous lay persons, and neither did the Reverend Selah Merrill, American Consul in Jerusalem for a total of some eighteen years. Yet the Colony prospered; during World War I it was feeding up to six thousand persons daily.

Wallace, Edwin Sherman, *Jerusalem the Holy: A Brief History of Ancient Jerusalem with an Account of the Modern City and Its Conditions Political, Religious and Social* (New York, 1898)

This book presents a history of Jerusalem from a Christian point of view. Wallace's work, based on a five-year residence as U.S. Consul in Jerusalem and on diligent personal investigation, had a twofold purpose: to awaken an interest in the city's sacred memories and holy sites; and "to prepare visitors for an intelligent comprehension of what they shall see when they arrive in the Holy City." His narration was intended to explain "the experiences through which it had reached its present condition." Writing at the turn of the twentieth century, Wallace describes Jerusalem as it existed in 1898: its walls and gates; its hills and valleys; and its places of special interest. Despite the sorry spectacle he beheld, Wallace predicted that the Holy Land would be restored by the Jewish people to its former condition of productiveness.

Yehoash [Bloomgarden, Solomon], *The Feet of the Messenger. Translated from the Yiddish by Isaac Goldberg (Philadelphia, 1923)*

Yehoash revived many forms of literature in Yiddish: biblical and postbiblical legends, tales from medieval Jewish chronicles and hasidic lore, versified fables from the Talmud, Aesop, La Fontaine, and Lessing, and created new fables of his own. He also translated Longfellow's *Hiawatha* into Yiddish. In January 1914, Yehoash left for Eretz Israel and settled in Rehovot. He mastered classical Arabic and translated portions of the Koran and Arabian tales into Yiddish. Upon his return to New York, he published the story of his experiences, which were translated into English by Isaac Goldberg as *The Feet of the Messenger.*

Index

About the Author

MOSHE DAVIS is Founding Head of the Institute of Contemporary Jewry at the Hebrew University of Jerusalem, and Stephen S. Wise Professor Emeritus in American Jewish History and Institutions, as well as Academic Chairman of the International Center for University Teaching of Jewish Civilization under the aegis of the Israeli Presidency. An authority on contemporary Jewish life, Professor Davis specializes in the field of American Judaism. He is Project Director and General Editor of American-Holy Land Studies. His publications include: *The Emergence of Conservative Judaism; Jewish Religious Life and Institutions in America; The Shaping of American Judaism* (Hebrew). He is the author of numerous articles and editor of several series of publications, among these 13 volumes of *World Jewry and the State of Israel.*

ISBN 0-275-94621-5

HARDCOVER BAR CODE